Full Time & Sub-Nine

ISBN: 0-9765498-0-8

⊗ Printed on Acid-Free Paper
Automated Graphic Systems - White Plains, Maryland, USA
Front Cover Photo: © 2004/2005 Bird's Eye View, Inc.

Rainmaker Publishing LLC
Oakton, Virginia
info@rainmakerpublishing.com
www.rainmakerpublishing.com

Full Time & Sub-Nine

Fitting Iron Distance Training into Everyday Life

David Glover

Acknowledgements

Thank you to all the folks at the Blue Devil Triathlon, especially Dorrys, Bill and Brad, for your support and for putting together such a special triathlon for a great cause.

Thank you to my family for understanding my commitment to this sport and for being there to cheer me on all over the country and the world. Thank you also to Clare and Jen, for putting up with my lifestyle and choices as long as you did. I hope you are both happier now.

To my friends and training partners, thank you for teaching me about the sport of triathlon, balance in life and most importantly, friendship. And thank you to Laura for becoming part of my life and for accepting my lifestyle as an endurance athlete.

Finally, a special thanks to Michaela and Renee from Rainmaker Publishing for making my book a reality.

Introduction

"You cannot teach a man anything; you can only help him find it within himself."
- *Galileo Galilei, Italian astronomer and physicist*

I am a triathlete.

With the exception of my triathlon training and racing, I live a normal life. I work full time as a business analyst for a financial services company, where I travel frequently and spend the bulk of my day sitting in front of a computer screen or engaged in meetings with colleagues. I am divorced and currently live with my girlfriend and two dogs in a townhouse in the congested suburbs of Washington, D.C.

I live a common life with normal demands on my time. Yet, I am fortunate to achieve uncommon results as an amateur triathlete. The Iron distance triathlon (2.4-mile swim, 112-mile bike and 26.2-mile run) is both my passion and my proving ground. I have four overall Iron distance wins, a personal best time of under nine hours and dozens of podium finishes at all triathlon distances.

This is not a training book, although I hope you find useful tips in it for your own endurance training. The purpose of this book is to address the question I'm asked the most about my triathlon career. How do I find time to train for long distance races while meeting the demands of everyday life?

I have one advantage over most endurance athletes. Like American cyclist Lance Armstrong, I am also a cancer survivor. My experience with cancer has helped me push myself harder and dig deeper than I ever did before. Triathlon has become my vehicle to prove to myself that even though I had cancer, cancer does not have me. This outlook on life has forced me to be creative with choices I make on a daily basis. Triathlon training is a priority for me, but not a career.

I write from the perspective of having raced as a top age-group athlete for more than 10 seasons in over 50 triathlons including 19 Iron distance races. Each race is a chance to excel against myself in spite of the suffering and discomfort. Like life, each race presents its own unique and often unexpected challenges. I don't always achieve my goals, but the ultimate destination is always the same, the finish line.

Living an active life has become my lifestyle. To me, working out is not a chore, but simply something I do and more importantly, something I enjoy.

Although each of us is motivated by something different, my hope is that by sharing what I've experienced, you will find some value, or more importantly, inspiration in your own training by lessons I've learned and the choices I've made along the way.

Table of Contents

"When you are at the pinnacle and there is no place to go, the absolute best that you can hope for is to stay there just a little longer."

Prologue: A Tough Pill to Swallow

Race: Blue Devil Triathlon
Distance: 2.4-mile swim, 112-mile bike, 26.2-mile run
Date: Saturday, October 8, 2005

When I lined up at the start of the Blue Devil Triathlon, I had a single line inscribed on my arms and legs in permanent black marker—the number "1." The number "1" signified that I was the returning champion and the race favorite. I had won the race each year for all three years of the race's existence.

When you are at the pinnacle and there is no place to go, the absolute best that you can hope for is to stay there just a little longer. The question is, "How long can I stay at the top?" as it is so much easier to fall down. The question then becomes, "How far down?"

Cold rain was forecasted and when the starting horn went off shortly after sunrise, the sky was dark and gray. I dashed into the water next to my 6' 5" Clydesdale friend, Mike Guzek, who is ideal to draft off since he virtually creates his own wake with his long frame. Unfortunately, I immediately lost sight of him in the pandemonium. Strobe lights were placed on the nearest buoys, so we wouldn't swim blindly in the dark. Until I passed the second buoy, I was in the middle of a thrashing pack of arms and legs. Given the small field, I was surprised how aggressive the group was. I swam with people all around me and over me. The gap in front of me would close as swimmers converged, and I would either force my way through the gap or be forced to swim around them. After five minutes, the group splintered, and I was soon alone.

I focused on my stroke and my body position. Reach, stroke and roll. Reach, stroke and roll. My mind frequently drifted to random thoughts, and I would consciously force myself to re-focus on my swim. "Stay relaxed." I told myself. "Swim efficiently."

I felt comfortable and in control—not too fast, not too slow. My swim split after the first lap was 29 minutes, so I knew that I would likely finish in around an hour which was not a fast time, but not a bad time for me either. No sign of Mike. I guessed that he was somewhere ahead of me. After a quick dash up the beach with my heart rate spiking, I dove back into the water for my second loop. I latched onto a woman's feet for 100 meters or so before she slowly pulled away. I was alone again for the rest of the swim.

I exited in just under an hour. Volunteers made quick work of my wetsuit, and I dashed through the changing tent to don my biking gear before grabbing my bike and heading out on the bike course.

I started the bike in 9th place with an unknown mix of relays and individuals ahead of me.

For the past two years, my strategy for this race was to move aggressively to the front on the bike leg by the end of the first loop. I wanted the lead coming off of the bike so that I could set, then control the pace of the run. I would set a reasonably fast run pace which would force any chaser to work harder to catch me. This strategy had worked in the past, but not today.

The bike course was moderately hilly, but not with lung-busting climbs. I think it's a good course for me because I like the variety of terrain without excessive climbing. I quickly passed two riders by the time I left the park for the open roads. The next couple of riders that I passed came more slowly. When I finally caught Mike about an hour and twenty minutes into the ride, he was in 2nd place. Mike and I exchanged some quick chitchat in passing.

Flying through one of the police-controlled intersections, I glanced up to see my dad standing in the intersection wearing an orange reflective vest and waving a bright orange flag. He had been recruited to help on the bike course. "You're about four minutes back." he yelled. I didn't have a chance to say anything before I blew past him.

I kept throwing glances back to see if Mike was there. Mike wasn't, but after a while someone else was. He was slowly and systematically overtaking me and there was nothing that I could do about it. This startled me as no one had ever overtaken me in this race before.

As he passed, we exchanged greetings. Mike was carrying quite a bit of muscle on his frame, so I figured that even if he led off of the bike, I would take him on the run. No worries for now.

I kept him in sight for 20 to 30 minutes before relinquishing and settling back into a more comfortable pace.

The weather during the bike alternated between wet and dry. The sun came out for a brief moment and then it poured. The only constant was the high humidity.

Again, I flew through the intersection where my dad was volunteering. "You're four and a half minutes back on the lead," he said. I was shocked that I had given up so much time so quickly. I tried to re-engage my legs and pick up the pace but my legs didn't respond.

By the time I finished the bike, I was in second place and eight minutes down on the leader with someone else close in tow behind me.

The previous year in this race, I started the run in the lead with a margin of at least three minutes. Today, I had to play catch-up.

"No worries." I said to myself. "Just settle into a groove and slowly tick off the time and the miles."

The Blue Devil run is a challenging five-loop course that is hilly. Even without the hills, a marathon is a challenge, especially after swimming 2.4 miles and biking 112 miles. But after all, isn't it the challenge that we want?

I typically start out at a fast pace on the run as I generally feel good getting off the bike. Today, I didn't feel strong, and I started off feeling "bad" which is my nebulously-defined term meaning that I was not running fast and there was absolutely nothing that I could do about it except hope that I would eventually feel better and run faster.

After the first lap, I realized that I was not making up time on the race leader. The gap remained the same.

I could not race with my facial emotions hidden behind my dark sunglasses. I expected a rainy, cloudy day so my sunglasses had clear lenses. I had to surrender my expressions of discomfort and suffering to the world.

Eventually the sun peeked out again from behind the clouds then fully emerged to dramatically heat the wet air. I wilted. Ten minutes later, the sun disappeared behind the clouds and the skies dumped rain, cooling the hot pavement. I felt better again and picked up my pace until the sun came out again. The cycle repeated itself several times.

My mettle was fading, and I badly wanted to stop and walk to reduce my discomfort. I rationalized that it would not be so bad to just walk and maybe wait for Mike or Chris Coby or any number of other folks out on the run who would like someone to talk to.

Chris, like me, is a cancer survivor. We met at the second Blue Devil Triathlon when Chris raced on the third anniversary of his last chemo treatment. The race was not only Chris' first Iron distance race, it was his first triathlon. Chris was now racing in his third triathlon—all Iron distance races.

The real battle was fought in my mind. True, my body was not as prepared for the run as usual due to some nagging injuries that had kept me from building up much of a running base, but I knew I could gut out a reasonably fast marathon as I had done before.

My gap to the leader stayed within eight to eleven minutes for almost the entire run. He was running consistently and strongly. I dominated the run the previous year with a 3:17 marathon split. Today, I would be lucky to go in under four hours.

My legs ached from the hills and the effort jacked up my heart rate as I engaged my muscles to move my body against gravity. Running downhill jammed my body weight on weak and trembling muscles.

By the end of the third loop, I resigned myself to second place and possibly further down as I closely monitored the chasers behind me. My strategy for letting the leader break away from me on the bike then catching him on the run had backfired. I was not up to the challenge today.

I crossed the line in 10:07, 30 minutes slower than last year, 50 minutes slower than two years ago and 70 minutes slower than three years ago—not a promising trend. The winner was waiting for me at the finish line. We shook hands and congratulated each other. I could read the emotion in his face. I could tell that winning this race meant so, so much to him. I was happy for him.

Back in the office the Monday after the race, a co-worker inquired via email: "How did your race go?"

I replied, "I finished in 2nd place overall in a time of 10:07, about eight minutes behind the winner." trying to sound happy.

He emailed back, "Were you satisfied with your race?"

I replied, trying to not sound as glum as I felt at the time, "No, not really. I finished 30 minutes slower than last year. Plus, I just didn't have a good race. The winner had a great race."

"You should be proud of 10:07," he said. "I can't imagine doing that time or that distance."

I thought about what he said, and I thought about how I felt during the race. I thought about why I did the race and about all the people that I impacted in some way. I thought about the $3,000 I raised for The Leukemia & Lymphoma Society in order to help find a cure for cancer. I thought about the feedback I received from other cancer survivors or friends and relatives of survivors on how I inspired them. I thought about how life itself is a gift, especially to a cancer survivor like me. Being able to compete in an Iron distance race is icing on the cake.

Maybe I did win a more important race after all.

"...I could not comprehend how anyone could physically complete the grueling event in a single day."

Chapter 1: The Path I Traveled

"In the beginning is my end."
- *T.S. Eliot, Anglo-American poet*

When I first saw the Ironman World Championship® in Hawaii on television in the early 1980s, I could not comprehend how anyone could physically complete the grueling event in a single day. At the time, I had no concept of the distances of the swim, bike or run, except that they seemed impossibly long alone, and unimaginable when combined for a total of over 140 miles.

In my mind, the athletes in the race were superheroes, not ordinary mortals like me. I remember watching an interview with the last triathlete to make the swim cut off time. She was ecstatic. I was in awe that someone could swim that far. The thought never crossed my mind that 20 years later, I would race in that very triathlon and others the same distance. The seed was planted.

Finding Myself

"The child is the father of the man."
- *William Wordsworth, English poet*

I was an active child and participated in numerous sports, but I was never a gifted athlete.

I was born in Lafayette, Indiana in 1971. My mother was an elementary school teacher who placed a strong emphasis on education and the importance of attending college. She grew up in Illinois and played tennis like I would later "play" triathlon. Although I inherited some of her physical features, I don't have my mother's extroverted personality, nor do I have the hand-eye coordination that runs on her side of the family.

My father was a submariner who began his 31-year Navy career as an enlisted sailor. The Navy sent him back to school for a Bachelor's degree in Electrical Engineering and awarded him a commission as a Naval officer. I inherited my father's build and his desire to stay fit.

My brother Chris is three years younger than me, and we fought as typical siblings. He would torment and hit me, but I ultimately won our fights because I was larger.

When I was four, we moved to Idaho Falls in southeastern Idaho where it was not uncommon for snow to remain on the ground for months at a time. In elementary school, I loved to climb on the monkey bars at recess. My friends and I dueled in pairs while hanging from our hands until one of us pulled the other to the frozen ground with just our legs. I don't remember ever losing a monkey bar battle, but not surprisingly, I have a scar on my forehead and another on my chin from falling.

When I was five, I learned to downhill ski and ride a bicycle. My parents bought me a Raleigh dirt bike that I rode around the neighborhood with my friends. We had no fear as kids and made jumps out of dirt on the trails and open fields that surrounded our community. Electronic games were not yet on the market, so I didn't have those distractions, and I played outside all the time.

In the summer I rode my bike and in the winter I skied at two small ski areas about 30 minutes from Idaho Falls. Things were simple.

When I was five my parents divorced, and my brother and I stayed with my mother. My father maintained visitation rights so we could spend a month every summer with him. He was soon remarried to a woman named Charlotte, who he is still with today after more than 25 years. The marriage brought me two new stepsisters who are the same ages as Chris and me.

As far back as I can remember I always wanted to be active and fit. I read comic books and saw ads for Charles Atlas® that showed how a skinny, wimpy boy like me at the time, could build big muscles. I didn't see how something in the mail could turn a skinny kid into a muscle-bound hunk, so I never bothered to send away for the information. Over time, I did build a picture in my mind of what my body should look like in the future.

My first athletic competition was a third grade track meet. I was never one of the fastest kids so I ran the longest distance, which was 200 meters. This seemed like a really long run to me at the time, and I remember being winded halfway through the event. I finished in the middle of the pack. The fastest sprint runner was a girl. At that age, girls tended to be stronger and faster than boys.

In fourth grade physical fitness class, my teacher timed us to see how many push-ups and sit-ups we could complete in one minute. I remember a petite girl who did over 80 sit-ups, beating the second place student by a huge margin. This was my first realization that you don't have to be big and muscular to be athletic. Although ripped muscles are typically portrayed in the media as being desirable, athletes come in all shapes and sizes and some body types may favor one form of exercise over another. Football, which was the most popular sport amongst boys my age, did not favor my small size and slow sprint-distance speed. It wouldn't be until much later in life that I found a sport that complemented my strengths and maximized my desire to excel at sports.

Several years later, my mother also remarried, and I gained two more stepsisters. My stepfather's job as a nuclear power plant operator moved us from Idaho Falls to Southern California about 40 miles north of San Diego near the coast in Carlsbad.

Moving from a relatively rural town to the trend setting, surfing culture of the California coast was a shock. When I look back at my adolescent years in California, they are not something I remember fondly. I was a small kid without much self-confidence, and I never really fit into the new environment. Even now when I visit my mom there, I still feel out of place.

My shy personality made it difficult for me to try new things, but my mom encouraged me to sign up for sports. I'm thankful for that, because I probably would not have taken the initiative to sign up on my own. I can now appreciate the benefits of the exposure to a variety of activities.

In sixth grade I doubled my long distance running and raced the 400 meter distance (one full loop around the school track). I was relatively slow and usually finished near the back of my heat. Although I had never been on the podium at track meets before, my competitive nature began to emerge, and I felt I needed to prove myself. I began to search for a sport that I could excel in.

When my junior high class tested for the President's Challenge in Physical Fitness, I finally scored at the top of my class. I enjoyed doing push-ups and sit-ups and improved my upper body strength through gymnastics routines. This type of exercise suited me.

As a smaller kid with an introverted, non-confrontational personality, I was intimidated by larger kids and somewhat hesitant to play contact sports like football, basketball and baseball. I also lacked the self-confidence and aggression needed to be successful at team sports. After playing soccer for several years, I became a decent player, but never a great player because I wasn't driven enough to improve my ball handling skills by practicing on my own. By junior high it was clear that I was gravitating toward individual sports like running and enjoyed doing exercises like push-ups rather than team sports.

My other challenge with fitting in with the cool California crowd was that I was a nerd. I was one of the smart kids who took all the honors classes and scored at the top of my class. I even dressed like a nerd, but had no one to tell me otherwise. I excelled in all areas academically, but especially in math. This subject made sense to me because it was logical.

My idea of what I wanted to look like continued to form. I wanted to be lean and muscular, but without the unnecessary excesses of a body builder or the gauntness of a pure, gazelle-like runner. I wanted something in between, the best of both worlds. I had not yet found the path or my niche.

The Young Boys' Leadership Laboratory

"To keep myself physically strong, mentally awake, and morally straight."
- *From the Boy Scout Oath*

When I think of all the activities I did growing up, the one thing that influenced my life more than any other was the Boy Scouts of America. From scouting, I learned about leadership and built my self-confidence.

I started out as a Cub Scout when I lived in Idaho, but didn't take away many memories from the experience until we moved to Carlsbad. One day when I was 12, my mom came home from the grocery store and told me she met the 16-year-old Senior Patrol Leader from a local scout troop. I spoke with the Patrol Leader over the telephone, and he invited me to visit the troop. His maturity and self-confidence impressed me, and I joined Troop 784 a few weeks later.

Troop 784 was the "poster troop" for San Diego County. Whenever the county council needed Boy Scouts to act as a color guard by marching in uniform with the American flag, we were the troop they called. We ran the troop by the book. When I say "we," I mean that the scouts basically ran the troop. The adult leaders were hands-off and mostly managed the administrative side of scouting. I learned about wilderness survival, first aid, camping, campfire cooking, the environment, canoeing and many other practical skills that I still carry with me.

There are six ranks in Boy Scouts: Scout, Tenderfoot, Second Class, First Class, Start, Life and Eagle. According to the Boy Scouts of America, only about four percent of all Boy Scouts achieve the Eagle rank. I advanced quickly, reaching each level after spending only the minimal amount of time at the previous rank.

I liked the structure of scouting, the organization and the clear expectations of what I needed to do in order to advance. This was very much like the Naval Academy and the Navy, which came later in my life. Scouting dovetailed nicely with my competitive nature.

The final task before becoming an Eagle Scout is the Eagle Scout Project. I was 14 at the time and my Eagle Scout project was my first experience with project management. I approached the local Carlsbad Historical Society and they steered me toward a project to restore a water cistern at historic McGhee Park near downtown Carlsbad.

A water cistern is a concrete tank built into the ground for the purpose of catching and storing rainwater. The water cistern at McGhee Park was built in the late 1800s and was in poor shape. The cement walls were cracked, the top had disappeared and the cistern itself was full of dirt and weeds. Working with the historical society, I developed a plan to repair the concrete wall, build a new wooden platform for the cistern and a wooden gutter for an adjacent barn, paint the cover and gutters to match the barn and affix a hand pump to the cover.

After a formal Eagle Board of Review that made sure I met the high standards for the Eagle Scout award and had satisfactorily completed my Eagle Scout project, I was approved to receive the Eagle Scout award.

The preparation and planning that went into my Eagle Scout project taught me a valuable lesson, that a difficult task can be accomplished with adequate preparation and by breaking down the task into smaller, more manageable sub tasks. As my Scoutmaster used to say, "The seven Ps: Proper Prior Planning Prevents Piss Poor Performance."

I gained confidence as I progressed through the scouting ranks and this self-confidence ultimately spilled over into other areas of my life. The last lines of the Scout Motto are "…to keep myself physically strong, mentally awake and morally straight." I took all three to heart. Even though I was doing very well in school, I realized that education was only one piece of a whole person. Strong morale values and a healthy body were equally important.

Southern Hospitality

As a small teenager, I spent much of my time trying to avoid getting picked on by the larger kids. When I played soccer in grade school, size didn't matter much, and I could handle the fitness with no problem. However, I lacked the aggressiveness and confidence to play soccer at a high school level. After being cut from the team, I decided I needed a new sport and signed up for water polo.

I had never really seen water polo played before, but the coach was looking for players for a newly formed team, so I told her I would play. Water polo was a challenging sport for me because I didn't have a competitive swimming background. I learned to swim when I was young, but I never raced. When I walked onto the junior varsity water polo team, the only thing I knew about the game was that it was played in the water with a ball the size of a volleyball.

The learning curve was steep, and I was dunked many times by teammates in practice and by opposing teams in games as I fought for the ball to either defend or score. Practices were typically two and a half hours after school at a community pool. We spent the first part of the workout swimming laps before moving into drills and then scrimmage games. Although I didn't know it at the time, the routine swimming workouts built a healthy swimming base that I could build upon later in life.

My water polo teammates called me "Scrappy" after Scooby Doo's little sidekick, "Scrappy Doo." Although not a nickname that I would have willing chosen for myself, it gave me an identity, and I felt like I was a part of a team.

By the time I earned my Eagle Scout, I was the Senior Patrol Leader of Troop 784. I enjoyed being in charge, although it was difficult as I don't believe I'm a natural leader. I had good Scouts and Scout Leaders to help me out though.

Our Scoutmaster had led the troop for many years. He was very charismatic, an excellent leader and the primary reason Troop 784 was as successful as it was. He was also my friend and advisor, especially in my role as Senior Patrol Leader.

One day I had a somewhat mysterious conversation with my mother who said our Scoutmaster was no longer with our troop. I was surprised and a little confused, so I called him. After telling him what I heard, I asked him if something was wrong.

"Listen David." he said, "I'm in trouble for some things I've done. I won't be the Scoutmaster anymore."

"I don't understand." I told him, but I didn't get a response. I found out later from my mother that he was arrested for child pornography and child molestation.

Reflecting back, the signs were visible. We had a number of Scouts who suddenly left the troop to join other troops and then made comments that the Scoutmaster was a pervert. He also invited me over to his house several times to watch movies, which I thought nothing of, but my mom, thankfully, never let me go.

After my Scoutmaster left, my world fell apart. I no longer wanted to be Senior Patrol Leader, and I felt I needed a break from the Scouts. I lost self-confidence, and I lost faith in people since someone I looked up to and thought was my friend had betrayed me.

In the middle of my sophomore year, I moved to Hanahan, South Carolina (near Charleston) to live with my father after being raised by my mother most of my life. I was comfortable with the thought of moving in with him, my stepmother Charlotte, and my younger stepsister Michele, since I spent time each summer with them.

When I first showed up at Hanahan High School, I was the "new kid from California." My social life went from zero to suddenly having several girls calling me every day. I didn't know how to manage the attention and likely gave up several opportunities to date some of them. Some of these girls became my best friends.

My dad ran regularly and the summer before I moved in with him, we began running together. When I moved to Hanahan, I ran my first foot race. It was the Hanahan Fun Run, a local one-mile race through the neighborhoods near my high school. I finished in 2nd place overall just ahead of my dad. It was the first time I ran faster than him. I was recruited on the spot by the high school track coach and my events became the one and two-mile distances, which pushed the boundaries of what I thought was long distance running.

Although I was on the track team, I was never formally coached for running. I learned what I could from my dad, but my coach simply said, "Go do what you need to do." Our team only had 15 members (14 boys and 1 girl). We competed one day a week, but never had meets at our school since our track had a poorly maintained, unmarked dirt track that was full of ruts. My teammates and I did our best to self coach ourselves and each other. Training usually consisted of running two or three miles four times a week with some occasional speed work and hill repeats thrown in randomly. We thought the best training approach was to run fast all the time. Training at longer, slower distances was a foreign concept at the time.

Racing at near maximum effort each time I competed shocked my body. In the first few races of the season, I hacked, coughed and dry heaved immediately after the race as my body rebelled against the sudden stress. My legs were sore and my lungs ached for a few days after each meet.

My race was always against the clock. I either hit my times or I didn't. I could leverage faster people to push me harder, but ultimately I had myself to answer to. For me it was a solitary sport, and I liked it.

Unlike high school football, track meets weren't popular for spectators. Typically, we had more athletes on the field than people in the stands. When my dad was at sea, Charlotte would come watch me and occasionally some of my girlfriends (friends who were girls) would come watch, which they did, I think, to humor me. I liked to run and mostly, I liked the anonymity that the track allowed me.

Despite my lack of formal coaching, I typically finished on the podium within our small conference of schools. Unfortunately, both times I competed in an AA Lower States meet (the prequel to the South Carolina State Championships) I finished near the back of the pack, even with my personal best time of 4:55 for the mile. I realized then that I had no chance of getting a track scholarship.

Every spring, my dad ran in the local Cooper River Bridge Run®, the largest running event in the area. I decided to do the race with him my first year in Hanahan. The Bridge Run was 10 kilometers and seemed like a really long distance at the time.

My dad and I slowly worked our way up from three to four, to five, then eventually six miles as we ran through our subdivision and tried to come up with creative loops to minimize repetition.

The area surrounding Charleston is appropriately named the "Low Country" because the terrain is absolutely flat. The hilliest points in Charleston are the two spans of the Cooper River Bridge that we had to run over. In order to prepare for the "hills," we ran on the narrow sidewalk of the newer bridge one early Sunday morning. Running on the bridge with traffic, especially large diesel truck traffic, created anxiety for me as I'm afraid of heights. The sidewalk was half the width of a normal sidewalk and, at places, more than 100 feet above the water. Every three or four minutes, a large diesel truck rumbled by, and I cringed between the fears of being hit and falling. Needless to say, I only did the practice bridge run once.

When it came time to do the run, we drove to Mount Pleasant early in the morning to take our place at the starting line. In 1986 when I first ran the bridge, there were approximately 5,000 runners. In contrast, there are more than 42,000 runners and walkers in the race today. I was intimidated by the crowd and uncertain where to place myself at the start. My dad encouraged me to start with him close to the front and said to not wait for him if we became separated.

Boom! The pack around me surged slowly at first then more quickly as the runners thinned out and space to run opened up. I had no real concept of how to pace myself, so I started fast although there were others around me going faster. At the first mile, I began passing the runners who had gone out too fast.

The first two miles were flat, but then we hit the first span of the old bridge. I was near the front of the race, but there was still a small sea of bodies before me. My dad had warned me that the bridge shakes with all the runners pounding over it. He was right. The bridge shook and swayed as thousands of sneakers pounded its concrete surface. The swaying in conjunction with my fear of heights steered me toward the center of the road.

Each span of the bridge is roughly a mile long. As I exited the second span to make a hairpin turn down to the city level, a passing runner clipped my trailing foot and down I went. I rolled to a stop, stood up, checked for anything broken or bleeding and started running again.

"Are you okay?" inquired a concerned runner.

"Yeah, I'm fine." I said. I had a few scrapes on my knees and palms, but was discouraged more than anything because the fall cost me time and pride.

After the bridge, the rest of the route was flat. I had solid results, finishing in a little over 37 minutes for 5th place in my age group of 15-19 year old males. I won a Bridge Run coffee cup that I still use today.

***

The important muscles to the male adolescent are abdominals, pectorals and biceps. The corresponding exercises for each are crunches, bench presses and arm curls. All of these muscles are muscles that you see in the mirror so the results are rewarding—I call them cosmetic muscles. It was not until college that I learned about the need to balance muscle development across the body.

With the image of the Charles Atlas ad still in the back of my head and the perception that girls liked guys with muscle, I asked my dad to show me how to lift weights. I also wanted to build mass so I wouldn't be the small kid anymore. My dad had a weight set at home that he showed me how to use. I started lifting weights, intent on building up my upper body.

I had heard somewhere that ideally I should be able to bench press twice my weight, so 300 pounds became my goal. I built strength and mass quickly as I worked through massive pyramid sets of bench press exercises.

By the middle of my senior year, I weighed 155 pounds and could bench press 290 pounds (one repetition); not quite my goal, but very close. I worked out in the gym with weights three or four times a week. I wanted strength and size. By the end of my senior year I had put on 10 pounds of muscle.

At the time, lifting weights for my upper body muscles and running for my lower body muscles plus cardiovascular benefits seemed to me to be a balanced approach to fitness. I figured that the running would keep my legs and lungs fit and strong while keeping my body fat low.

By focusing on muscles that I could see, I neglected the muscles that I couldn't see like those in my back and the back of my arms. The potential consequences of unbalanced development are poor posture, increased risk of injury and an unbalanced look. You can typically walk into any gym and see examples of unbalanced weightlifters. These are the guys with the massive chests, undeveloped backs and the skinny legs who look disproportionate and unhealthy. I think a lot of them wear baggy pants to hide their skinny legs.

"We held ourselves in an upright push-up position with our arms extended to support our stiff bodies as we shouted '...We're waiting for our classmates, Sir!' until our classmates finally arrived in formation. The goal was never to be the one who everyone else was waiting on."

Chapter 2: Four Years Together by the Bay

"Stand Navy down the field,
Sails set to the sky,
We'll never change our course
So Army you steer shy-y-y-y
Roll up the score, Navy,
Anchor's A-Weigh,
Sail Navy down the field
And sink the Army,
Sink the Army grey."

- Navy Anchor's Aweigh song

Throughout his 31-year naval career, my dad spent a significant portion of time at sea or on his vessel. It was not uncommon for his submarine to be gone for more than two months at a time as they patrolled vast regions of the ocean. During my first year in South Carolina, he was out to sea most of the time, which was somewhat ironic since I moved there to spend more time with him.

Although my dad talked about retiring from the Navy at various times in his career, he never did. This created some stress at home for Charlotte, but my dad loved his job and the Navy. He never took the easy tasks at work. In fact, he took the harder job whenever given the option.

My father never encouraged me one way or the other to join the Navy. By living with him, I saw the toll the Navy took on families and the amount of work required of him to do his job. In spite of the negatives, I think my dad's respect for the Navy, his sailors' respect for him and his love of his job served as a catalyst for me to apply to the Naval Academy in Annapolis, Maryland.

I had never even heard of the Naval Academy until high school. I was familiar with West Point after visiting the campus as a Boy Scout, but I didn't know much about Annapolis other than it was the Navy's equivalent of the Army's West Point. I liked the idea of going into the Navy versus the other services because there were so many career options that the other services didn't offer. In the Army, I could have been on the ground as infantry or driving a tank. In the Air Force, it was either planes or missile silos. In the Navy, I could captain a ship or submarine, fly a jet plane or helicopter or salvage sunken ships among numerous other options.

Analogous to being in an elite Scout Troop, I wanted to get into an elite college. In my mind, I was at the top of my class and well rounded in much more than academics. When I applied for colleges, the Naval Academy was accepting less than 10 percent of all applicants and, I believe, was the toughest school in the U.S. to gain acceptance. Applying to the Naval Academy went way beyond just filling out application forms, writing essays and mailing a check. Applicants had to qualify with superior grades, high SAT scores, exceptional health demonstrated via a full-day medical exam and excellent physical fitness.

Even after making the physical and academic cut, applicants had to be nominated by either their member of congress or senator or apply through a special program. The special programs included nominations for a limited number of young active duty enlisted sailors and Marines, nominations for children of Medal of Honor winners and nominations for children of active duty military personnel.

I had no clearly defined career goals at the time so going into the Navy for a minimum of five years after graduation to re-pay my schooling seemed like a good option until I could figure out what I really wanted to do with my life. Maybe I would make the Navy a career like my dad did.

"Congratulations, David, you have been granted an appointment to the United States Naval Academy in Annapolis, Maryland." said Captain Terry O'Brien, a friend of my father's, who presented me with my Presidential appointment. My dad and Charlotte were on hand to witness the presentation during our high school's senior year awards ceremony.

I mention Captain O'Brien by name because he died a few years later of cancer. I didn't know him well, but I will always remember him for having given me my Academy appointment and for not surviving cancer.

Plebe Year

I arrived in Annapolis on July 3, 1989.

Plebe Summer, or the Naval Academy's equivalent of military boot camp for the incoming freshman class, felt like the sudden shock of jumping into freezing cold water. On Induction Day, the first day that I arrived, the Academy shaved my head, took away my civvies (civilian clothes) and clothed me in a "white works" sailor's uniform with a Dixie cup (blue rimmed white sailors cap). My vocabulary for Plebe summer quickly and simply became:

"Sir, yes, sir!"
"Sir, no, sir!"
"Sir, no excuse, sir!"
"Sir, I'll find out, sir!"
"Sir, aye, aye, sir!"

These phrases are the Plebe's five basic responses to an upperclassman's commands or questions. My life became a flurry of activity and elevated stress levels as my classmates and I sweated our way through six weeks of Plebe Summer in hot, humid Annapolis.

For six weeks:

We "chopped" up and down the hallways, which meant we tucked our arms against our sides, held our forearms parallel to the "deck" (floor), and looked straight ahead as we jogged with high knees.

We yelled, "Go Navy" or "Beat Army" every time we squared a corner while "chopping." Squaring a corner meant planting a foot with the outside leg then sharply turning 90 degrees before planting the inside leg.

We held ourselves in an upright push-up position with our arms extended to support our stiff bodies as we shouted, "We're waiting for our classmates, Sir! We're waiting for our classmates, Sir! We're waiting for our classmates, Sir!" until our classmates finally arrived in formation. The goal was never to be the one that everyone else was waiting on.

For hours at a time, we stripped and waxed the floors in our small dorm rooms; neatly folded hospital corners into our taut bedspreads; scrubbed our showers until they sparkled; crisply folded our clothes which were lined up by color; and dusted all horizontal and vertical surfaces in our dorm rooms in preparation for white glove room inspections which we inevitably failed. There was always something that we missed.

We learned to drill with M-1 rifles and that a "trucker's meal" meant to eat everything on the table including the bottle of catsup. I faked trying to drink the ketchup bottle, as I couldn't stomach the thought of throwing it up later. I still became sick as we drilled with our rifles immediately after the meal.

We woke up every morning before dawn for PT (physical training) on the athletic fields with Dr. Heinz Lenz. "Good morning, 93!" yelled Dr. Lenz in his heavy Austrian accent as he led us through push-ups, crunches, flutter kicks and a medley of other exercises to hone our young bodies into athletic shape.

We suffered through heat rash, dehydration and fatigue as we were slowly molded into Midshipmen. My clothes reeked of stale perspiration, and I lost 10 pounds during those six weeks. Ironically, we all were fitted for our uniforms during Plebe Summer. Not surprisingly, many shirts and pants were too snug come Christmas time as we slowly returned to our normal weights.

At the end of six weeks, we were still Plebes, but we also became students and went to 15 plus hours of classes per semester. Fifteen was the minimum number of class hours at the academy, on top of the other challenges and stresses in our new lives. We still had to chop, square our corners and yell, "Go Navy, sir! Beat Army, sir!" as well as be subject to upperclassmen harassment.

Many times, the stress and exhaustion became almost unbearable. Plebes lived for the weekends when the upperclassmen went away and we had some quiet time for ourselves. As Plebes, we had a sponsor family nearby who offered a place to go on the weekends. My sponsor family lived about a 15-minute drive from the Academy. Their house became my home away from home. During visits, I had the opportunity to become a civilian again, if only for a few hours. My visits the first year were mostly spent eating and sleeping or just plain relaxing. I needed an escape from the Academy and they offered it to me.

All midshipmen at the Naval Academy had to do some type of sport whether it was a varsity sport, club sport or intramural. As a Plebe, I spent a few months with the Plebe lightweight crew team after realizing in a single water polo practice that I didn't have the talent or the experience to play water polo at a collegiate level with only two years of high school junior varsity experience.

At the end of our Plebe year, my entire freshman class climbed up an obelisk greased with 200 pounds of lard to pull down a Plebe's "Dixie cup" hat and replace it with a Midshipman's cover (hat). We were no longer Plebes, but fourth class midshipmen. Mr. Smith became Stuart and Mr. White became Kyle as we dropped the "Sirs" to other midshipmen.

Upperclassman Years

Even without all the stress of being a Plebe, academics at the Academy were demanding as an upperclassman. I took between 15 and 21 hours of class each semester in addition to required PE classes like swimming and boxing. When I initially selected my major, I thought I wanted to be an electrical engineer like my dad. After nearly failing physics as a freshman (I worked my way up from a "D" to a "C"), I turned toward a subject that I felt much more comfortable with—computer science.

Days at the Academy typically went something like this[1]:

0530	Arise for personal fitness workout (optional)
0630	Reveille (all hands out of bed)
0630-0700	Special instruction period for plebes (i.e., come-a-rounds)
0700	Morning meal formation
0710	Breakfast
0755-1145	Four class periods, one hour each
1205	Noon meal formation
1215	Noon meal for all midshipmen
1240-1320	Company training time
1330-1530	Fifth and sixth class periods
1530-1800	Varsity and intramural athletics, extracurricular and personal activities; drill and parades twice weekly in the fall and spring
1700-1900	Supper
1930-2300	Study period for all midshipmen
2300	Lights out for plebes
0000	Taps for upper class

The Academy ran by the bell. There was a bell for every event during the day starting at 0630 for reveille. The bells stopped finally at 1930 for study time only to ring a final time at 2300 for Plebe bedtime.

When we sat down for meals, everyone sat at once—all 4,500 midshipmen.

Within two minutes of sitting down after announcements and blessing, the dining room staff served the food family style on our tables. We passed around big platters of a variety of foodstuffs from burgers to spaghetti to steamed vegetables to trays of Jell-O. The Academy had its own dairy farm, which provided milk and ice cream for each table.

Plebes were responsible for knowing their rates, or trivia, about the Academy, famous and not so famous quotes, lines from Navy songs and facts about the Navy and other services. The penalty for not knowing one's rates would often mean a "come-around" at the upperclassman's door later in the day. Come-arounds frequently turned into push-up sessions for other classmates who happened to be in the area as the Academy preached teamwork and the willingness to step up to help your shipmate in time of need. Reflecting back, some of the customs and ritual seemed silly, but I believe they were grounded on important behaviors needed to successfully navigate the life and death situations of combat—which is ultimately what we were all training for in the first place.

During my Youngster (sophomore) year, I met Clare who would one day become my wife. We met through mutual friends at her college, Hood College, in Frederick, Maryland. After a night of drunken festivities that included jumping into a pool and passing out on top of her bunk bed, we began dating.

Because I was only a Youngster, I was relatively constrained in what I could do outside of the Academy. As a Plebe, I couldn't even date so being a Youngster was a step up.

I had a lot of good times with Clare and spent many weekends at her college and at her parents' house in nearby Silver Spring, Maryland. I now had a place to go and someone to see away from the Academy. Plus, she was a senior that year and working part time so she had disposable income, which I did not.

My running background and relatively high level of pre-Academy fitness benefited me tremendously during all four years at the Academy. I excelled in everything physical that the Academy threw my way and could do push-ups and pull-ups better than most of the upperclassmen when I was a Plebe. I maxed out all of the fitness tests all four years—1.5-mile run, pull-ups, sit-ups, push-ups and the obstacle course. Because I was in excellent shape, I was never the weakest link in Plebe "team building exercises." I could outlast most everyone in anything physical except for activities that required pure strength that favored my larger and stronger classmates.

As an upperclassman instructing Plebes, I wanted to set an example (i.e., leadership by example) for them by performing every push-up that I asked them to do and more. I would never ask anyone to do anything physically that I was not willing or able to do myself. I felt that this was the right thing to do.

The Naval Academy was an athlete's dream although I didn't fully appreciate it for that benefit as a midshipman. There were three swimming pools, multiple weight rooms, an ice rink during the winter months, many athletic fields, roads to run on and my favorite venue—the pull-up bars on Farragut Field. All of the facilities were within a five-minute walk from my dorm room. At least one of the gyms was always open and there was dedicated time each afternoon for sports and intramurals. It seemed like there was almost always someone to work out with whether it was 5:00 a.m. in the dark or 10:00 p.m. in the dark.

More than any other exercise or sport at the Academy, I loved the physical training exercises known as "PT," which consisted of pull-ups, push-ups, sit-ups and other calisthenics for strength and flexibility. I would often do the workouts led by the Navy SEALs on staff and the midshipmen who were planning to become Navy SEALs after graduation. It was the PT workouts that showed me that I could do almost anything if I put my mind to it, and I became quite good at it.

The Navy SEALs (SEAL stands for SEa, Air and Land) are the Navy's elite special operations commandos known for their superb fitness conditioning and mental toughness. They're the "go anywhere, do anything to get the job done" units in the sea, in the air and on land. Even though I could never be a SEAL because I had poor eyesight, I wanted to think that I had the fitness and the mental toughness to be one. I will never know. I believe this desire to prove myself led me to Iron distance triathlons later in life.

As an upperclassman, I would coax my classmates out to the pull-up bars where we would PT for two or three hours at a time sometimes in the dark of the early morning or late night. We would do a set of pull-ups, push-ups and dips using the bars and concrete support blocks which we then repeated across all 300 pull-up bars, sometimes doing more than 200 pull-ups, 600 push-ups and 300 dips in a single workout. I wanted to be the best at PT although there always seemed to be someone better than me.

The Academy was my first indirect exposure to triathlon. The Navy Triathlon team was created as a club sport. I didn't know much about triathlon other than there were three events—swim, bike and run. I remember seeing some of the Navy triathletes leaving the campus for bike rides for roads surrounding the Academy, but I didn't know where they went or what they were training for specifically. I was comfortable in my world of PT, running and occasional swimming, but lacked the impetus to make the jump to triathlon.

I did make one significant running breakthrough while at the Academy. Until 1991, my longest race was a 10-kilometer run. At the Academy, I trained with several friends to run the 26.2-mile Marine Corps Marathon during my second class (junior) year. Like before, I was self-coached.

The Marine Corps Marathon is a big event. Called the "People's Marathon," the course takes runners all around Washington, D.C., passing by many of the major monuments. There were thousands of runners and the start was crowded, so it took me a few minutes after the gun went off to reach the starting line. When I did get there, I couldn't run effectively because the people around me were all bunched up. I made a mental note to start closer to the front the next time.

For the first dozen miles, I felt good and ran hard at just above a three-hour pace. I held my pace steady until the 13-mile marker when my stomach suddenly seized with a stabbing pain in my gut. I felt like slowing down to a crawl, but I realized that it might only prolong the suffering so I kept plodding along. My will to continue was driven not so much by tolerance, but more by the fear of prolonged pain. This attitude toward pushing through the discomfort to finish sooner would ultimately carry over to my triathlon competition years later.

The Marine Corps Marathon was a good experience for me and I did many things during that race that I later learned not to do:

1. I started the run with a long sleeve cotton shirt. By the 10-mile marker, my shirt was soaked with perspiration, so I carried it for the

next 16 miles. Cotton leads to chafing and bloody nipples. I now wear synthetic fibers that wick away moisture and don't chafe the skin.

2. My legs were beginning to ache so I grabbed a handful of Bengay® from a volunteer Marine and slapped it on my skin. The Bengay felt warm for a minute then rapidly cooled my legs down so much that I became cold.

3. I slammed a couple of aspirin down as well, which did not help my stomach situation.

As I slowed down later in the race, I struggled against the desire to stop and walk. I finally lost the battle at mile 22 and walked for a few minutes. I eventually pulled myself together and started running again to ultimately cross the line in 3 hours and 21 minutes. I was a marathon finisher!

In my Firstie (senior) year at the Academy, I won the "Iron Mid" contest which was my first experience in "multi-sport" racing. Iron Mid consisted of a 1,000-meter swim in the morning then a 10-kilometer run immediately followed by as many pull-ups, push-ups and sit-ups that I could do in two minutes for each. I had a respectable swim, the second fastest run overall, and I cleanly dominated the PT portion with 37 pull-ups, more than 170 push-ups and over 150 sit-ups each within two minutes.

I learned to love and appreciate fitness at the Naval Academy. I became psychologically dependent on exercise as part of my daily routine and often gave up adequate sleep in order to get to the pull-up bars for an early morning PT session. Incredibly fit people surrounded me, and I always had someone to work out with. With help from others, I also learned to push myself beyond what I thought was previously possible.

I did well academically and graduated with distinction in the top 10 percent of my class. Following my dad's footsteps, I selected submarine service and graduated from Annapolis as an Ensign in May of 1993.

In the Navy

"I wish to have no connection with any ship that does not sail fast—for I intend to go in harm's way."
-John Paul Jones, Scottish-born American naval hero

After graduating from the Academy, I needed to have some fun. Three friends and I caught a "MAC" flight to Frankfurt, Germany. MAC, which stands for Military Airlift Command, was the Air Force's fleet of cargo planes responsible for moving military "stuff" around the world. The planes ran the gamut from small C-141 Starlifters to the larger C5 Galaxies. Frequently, there were available seats for active duty and retired military to travel for practically free, there was only a nominal charge for a meal. The catch was that there was no guarantee that there were any flights let alone seats. The seats were first come, first serve depending on when you put your name on the list for travel. We waited a full day in Dover, Delaware, before we finally caught a flight to Frankfurt, Germany. Traveling on the planes was different than a commercial flight. Upon entering the plane, the uniformed flight attendants handed everyone earplugs to block out the engine noise, and there were no windows. On the plus side, it was cheap.

We declared the trip an international beer tour and proceeded to sample beer in Germany, Austria, Switzerland and Italy. Even on vacation, I had to exercise. I couldn't go more than a day without exercise without feeling out of shape. Not working out created stress for me. My friends, although active, did not seem to feel the same need for exercise as I did while we were traveling.

Following my trip to Europe, I spent the next year and a half attending three more Navy schools specific to submarine officers. Suddenly, the weight rooms, pools and running routes that were no more than a five minute walk on the Academy's campus were miles away. I now had to allocate time for driving to the pool and weight room and to make time for my workouts. For the first time, exercising became something I had to fit into my schedule rather than something that was part of my schedule.

Nuclear Power School

Nuclear Power School in Orlando, Florida, was extremely demanding of my time. At Power School, we sat through a full eight hours of class five days a week and were required to put in a mandatory amount of study hours on top of that. Because the class work was confidential, we couldn't take it home with us. As such, we had to be in the classroom in order to study. The instructors highly encouraged us not to put in extra time over the weekend, so the weeks were extremely busy with some time off to relax on the weekends.

During the week, I normally arrived one to two hours before class to study, attended class all day, studied for an hour or two after classes, ran to the gym for a quick workout then returned again to the classroom at night for two more hours of studying. The cycle repeated itself every weekday for six months.

Power School was tough. My classmates were all in the top third of my graduating class at the Academy. We had all been rigorously screened and interviewed by Naval Reactors, the governing body for the Navy's nuclear power program, in order to be accepted into nuclear power. A quarter of my classmates at Power School failed during the six months. My goal was to finish in the top half of my classes at both Power School and my next stop, Nuclear Prototype School as this would open up more career options down the road.

All Navy bases have fitness centers to various degrees. The center at Orlando was a typical Navy gym with a plethora of weights, cardio equipment and a mix of Nautilus® machines that fit my lifting and running routine perfectly. There were lightly traveled roads and trails around the school and near my apartment to run on or I could, as an alternative at night or during excessive heat, run inside. I averaged about an hour of exercise a day during the week with maybe another hour on the weekend.

On the weekends, I raced in several 5-kilometer and 10-kilometer runs, achieving a 10-kilometer personal best time of less than 35 minutes, which is still my personal best today. I placed well in my age group in all my races, but never placed top three on the podium. I was not a pure, lean runner like the race winners.

I was happy with my fitness level although I was drinking a lot of alcohol on the weekends. I, like many of my classmates, felt the need to make up for our shortage of partying at the Academy by partying after we graduated. We frequently chased the "free beer" or "10 cent wing" nights at the local bars.

I was still dating Clare when I left for school in Orlando, but decided to take a hiatus with my newfound freedom. I began dating my apartment neighbor, who wanted more of my time than I could reasonably handle given my course load, yet I struggled to give her the time. I was still on mandatory study hours, but added the task of spending a few hours with her after I finished studying in the evenings. My average sleep went from a needed eight hours to a paltry four hours, and I really needed the full eight hours to be effective in class. My grades started slipping so I had to make a choice, the girlfriend or my career.

I decided that my fitness, my grades and my health were more important than trying to maintain the relationship. I chose wisely and dropped her, or maybe she dropped me. I can't remember.

After six months and an eight-hour written exam, I graduated in the top 50 percent of my class with the 75 percent of my classmates who survived Power School. We were split into three groups for the three separate Nuclear Prototype Schools in Idaho, South Carolina and New York. I went to Idaho Falls, where I grew up.

Nuclear Prototype School

Nuclear Prototype School demanded even more of my time. My roommates and I had a 60-minute bus ride from the bus stop near our house to the power plant. All students were required to take the bus to the site. Once we arrived, armed guards in fatigues greeted us and walked us through metal detectors before allowing us into the power plant areas. We worked on eight-hour shifts—eight hours on, 16 hours off. As a student, we had to stay an extra four hours. Eight hours on shift plus an additional four hours for studying plus another two hours roundtrip on the bus equaled 14-hour days. We then had 10 hours to do everything else we needed to do like sleep, eat, run errands, do laundry and work out. Time became precious, especially for someone like me who needs eight hours of sleep each night and wanted to exercise every day.

As I did in Nuclear Power School and have had to do many more times since then, I made the time to workout. Depending on my shift, I would either run before or after the bus ride. I occasionally made the trip across town to the local swimming pool because I liked the feeling of upper body exhaustion that swimming gave me. Plus, it seemed like a good complementary exercise to running which was lower body focused. There was also a paved trail along the Snake River that ran through the middle of town that I would frequently run on.

One of my roommates was an avid triathlete who raced triathlons for several years at that point and was quite successful. On a pure running and pool swim basis, he and I were similar in speed and ability, and we sometimes worked out together. I had my bike with me from high school (a 10-speed that was too big for me and even with the seat and handlebars lowered flush against the frame, left me stretched out like Superman when I rode), but I was not riding consistently so he definitely had more bike fitness than I did. I wish I had taken the time to learn more about triathlon from him. If only I had simply asked for his help. I was interested in the sport, but was intimidated by it and chose to put off actually trying one. I told myself it would be something I would do when I had more time. I think time is one of the most widely used excuses for not doing something. My answer now, "Make the time."

A few weeks into Prototype, my competitive drive kicked in, and I decided that I wanted to be the first among my classmates to qualify for the distinction of Engineering Officer of the Watch (EOOW). Qualifying to stand watch as EOOW is the goal of nuclear power training for an officer who will serve on a nuclear-powered ship or submarine. EOOWs run the engine room in order to provide propulsion and power to the vessel.

I stopped going home on the bus at the end of my 12 hours. I spent the night in the bunkroom at the site so that I had an extra four hours to spend learning and qualifying on site. This schedule change actually worked to the benefit of my exercise schedule. When I stayed over, I had the time to run outside the facility in the desert or workout in the small weight room. Literally, there was nothing in the environment other than dirt, sand and dry brush, but I was happy to be able to run.

Ironically, the extra time and nights that I spent trying to qualify didn't pay off. Because I rushed myself through the learning, things didn't sink in as much as they should have and I failed my Final Oral Board. After six months of Power School and six months of Prototype, I was on the verge of being kicked out of the submarine service before I had even arrived at my submarine.

After two intense weeks of one-on-one instruction with the senior enlisted sailors and civilian power plant staff, I re-took the oral test and passed. My next stop was Submarine School in Groton, Connecticut for three months.

Submarine School

Between Power School and Submarine School, I asked Clare to marry me. I had my fun in Orlando, but when I went to Idaho Falls, the girls my age were few and far between. I realized that Clare was a lucky catch and that I either had to fish or cut bait. If I did not plan to marry her, I needed to break it off so that we could both move on with our lives. Looking back, I was probably somewhat influenced by the fact that several of my classmates had recently gotten married and my stepsister, Kristy, was to be married the following spring. I chose to marry Clare, and she said, "Yes."

Submarine School seemed like a vacation. We still had eight hours of classes a day, but there were no mandatory study hours nor did the tests require us to study much on our own time. I enjoyed the extra time and once again became an active visitor of bars for happy hours and cheap food.

We all live....

Following Submarine School I transferred to a submarine, the USS Memphis. The USS Memphis did not go out to sea as it was up on blocks like a car in a junkyard with holes cut in the hull for maintenance and equipment upgrades. Because of the long hours and shipyard working conditions, the morale on the boat was low. The boat also had a bad reputation for having run aground a few years prior.

My only time at sea as a naval officer was on the USS Atlanta in January of 1995. Talk about a culture shock. Imagine living with over 100 other guys in a cylindrical tube that is only 30 feet in diameter and a little over the length of a football field. The reactor and engine rooms take up the majority of the space within the hull with the remaining one third of the space for the control room, torpedo room, dining rooms and living quarters.

Besides standing watch, daily activities included training, paperwork, studying, and drills simulating events like fires, broken equipment or high-pressure steam leaks. A submariner might stand watch all night, eat breakfast then spend the rest of the day in training and fighting simulated fires before going back on watch in the evening. Sleep became a luxury.

During my ride on the Atlanta, I shared a bunkroom called a "Nine-man" with eight other sailors and junior officers. The bunks were stacked three high along three sides of an L-shaped room, and each bunk was roughly the size of a coffin. The commanding officer and the executive officers were the only ones on board who had their own private quarters. My only privacy on the boat was in my bunk behind a small curtain that I could open and close once I was inside. The only two things that I had the space to do in my bunk were read and sleep.

When I feel crunched for time now and listen to my friends talk about how hard it is to fit their triathlon training into their hectic work schedules, I think back to the time I spent on the sub. Submarine days were 18 hours, which repeated themselves. Since I was underwater, I had no real sense of night and day other than the time on my watch. I often gave up sleep just to be able to get in 30 to 40 minutes of exercise on the Lifecycle® or Stairmaster® we had on board, plus a few sets of pull-ups and push-ups on whatever available floor and hanging space I could find. This typically meant wearing ear plugs in the heat and noise of the engine room.

Like sleep, exercise became a luxury. There is a cartoon I remember seeing that was a "before and after" shot of a submariner and his wife. Before the submarine goes to sea for a couple of months, the husband is shown as thin and fit while his wife is fat. When he comes back, he's fat while his wife has trimmed down from having to take care of the kids and the house by herself. There's actually some truth in that.

After 10 days at sea, I wanted to be outside and running again. My worst fear was to go to sea for several months and come back being overweight and severely out of shape. As fate would have it, I never faced that situation. After riding the submarine USS Atlanta only once, I never went out to sea again.

"As I saw it, I had three options: I could be a cancer victim, I could be a cancer survivor or I could be something else altogether. I chose to go beyond being a victim or just a survivor to be something else."

Chapter 3: Dramatic Changes

I have cancer.

"It's a dangerous business going out your front door."
- *J.R.R. Tolkien, author of* The Lord of the Rings

"Ensign Glover, please take a seat. I'm sorry, but your tumor is malignant. You have cancer."

With those few words, I instantly joined the club that members don't choose to join, but are selected for randomly. This is an elite club with membership growing all the time. Membership is permanent and joining the club changes your life forever because you come face to face with your own mortality. The club is open to everyone and does not discriminate by age, race, gender or lifestyle although it may favor some lifestyles over others.

Nineteen ninety-five was a life changing year for me across multiple dimensions. Cancer was just one.

I was 23 years old. I had only been attached to the submarine USS Memphis for approximately one month when I first noticed a small lump just under the surface of the skin on the right side of my groin at the crease between my right leg and my abdomen. I noticed it while lifting weights at a fitness center over the Thanksgiving holiday in 1994. My first thought was that I had somehow given myself a hernia. I didn't know much about hernias other than they occur when part of the small intestine pokes through the abdomen wall. The lump felt a little tender to the touch, but wasn't painful. I shrugged it off initially, but decided I should get it checked out when I got back to the boat.

When I returned to the submarine the following week, I went to see the sub's Corpsman, the boat's equivalent of a nurse. The Corpsman examined the lump then sent me to the shipyard medical clinic for testing for possible infection. This began a two-month ordeal of discovery to determine what exactly the lump was. As a new Ensign onboard the submarine, I was working diligently to qualify for supervisor of the nuclear power plant in the engine room so I didn't have much time to think or worry about what was physically wrong with me. Diagnosing the lump was simply another thing to do in a long list of things.

The initial clinical tests came back negative for any type of infection and the clinic doctor decided that I needed to see some specialists. I first went to a urologist who then sent me for a sonogram to visually identify the mass. The doctor said the mass contained fluid and might just be a swollen lymph node. "You will need to have it removed," he told me.

The following week, a surgeon removed the mass for a biopsy. Two days later, I returned for a follow-up appointment after receiving a phone call from the surgeon, "I need you to come back in to see me on Thursday as a follow-up." I didn't give much thought to the call at the time.

When I arrived for my follow-up appointment, the surgeon brought me into his office, shut the door, sat me down and simply said, "The results show that the mass is some type of tumor, but it is most likely benign." The surgeon had already informed my commanding officer who decided I should go to the National Naval Medical Center in Bethesda, Maryland, the premier Navy hospital. Bethesda is where the U.S. President typically goes for medical treatment.

As a precautionary measure, the doctor gave me a sample of the biopsy tissue on slides to hand carry with me to Bethesda. In parallel, the surgeon sent another tissue sample on slides to Massachusetts General Hospital (Harvard Medical School) for their pathology department to diagnose as well.

The Memphis arranged for transportation to Bethesda. The ship's van drove me to nearby Hickham Air Force Base in Massachusetts. From there, I boarded a plane with other "sick" active duty military personnel and flew down the East Coast in an Air Force MEDEVAC plane, stopping at several military bases for other sick passengers along the way until we finally reached Andrews Air Force Base in Maryland where I rode another bus to the Naval hospital.

The next day I met with an oncologist, who became my primary cancer doctor at Bethesda. While waiting for the pathology results from Bethesda and Massachusetts General, my oncologist arranged for me to meet with several cancer specialists from Bethesda, nearby Walter Reed Army Medical Center and the National Institutes of Health across the street from Bethesda. "Just in case." the oncologist said. In parallel, I underwent a chest CT scan and pelvic MRI to determine if the tumor, if it was cancerous, had metastasized (spread) to other areas of my body.

My mom flew into Maryland from California to be with me at the time of the initial testing and diagnosis. She kept me company as we traveled between hospitals visiting doctors. The week after my mom left, my dad and Charlotte came to Washington, D.C. to be with me. The day before I received the cancer diagnosis, Charlotte and I solemnly visited the museums at the Smithsonian. Reflecting back, Charlotte said that the day we spent in the museums was a very sad day for her.

During this week of uncertainty and doubt, I felt like I had lost control over my life and was passively "just along for the ride." trusting and depending on a group of strangers to make a diagnosis which could affect my career, my long-term health and possibly my life or mobility. Everything seemed to be happening so fast, and I couldn't react to it other than just accept what others told me.

My life changed forever in a single moment: "I'm sorry, but your tumor is malignant. You have cancer."

The doctor went on to say, "You have a Grade IIA schwannoma which is a type of cancer that originates from a Schwann cell, a nerve sheath cell."

I have cancer.

I can't believe this.

I have cancer.

"No, this can't be." I thought.

"Why me?" I said to myself, as my life seemed to flash before my eyes. "What had I done to get cancer?"

I was blindsided by a locomotive. Up until the declaration of the diagnosis, I was somewhere in limbo between denial and acceptance that I might have cancer. I could not respond directly to the doctor's statement other than to mumble something like, "Yeah, I sort of figured that."

Until this point, the conversations with the different doctors had allowed me to hold out some hope that there was nothing to worry about:

Corpsman:	"It's more than likely an infection. We'll get some tests done just to make sure."
Clinic Doctor:	"Don't worry about it. It's probably just a cyst or a hernia. We'll do a sonogram just to make sure."
Urologist:	"I wouldn't worry about it. It's probably just a swollen lymph node. We'll biopsy it just to make sure."
Surgeon:	"Well, it looks like a tumor, but it's probably benign. Just in case, I sent a tissue sample to pathology at Mass General and we are sending a tissue sample with you to take to the medical center in Bethesda, Maryland."
Oncologist:	"I'm sorry, but the tumor is malignant. You have cancer. The good news is that is does not appear to have metastasized."

Fortunately, that is as far as the conversations went regarding my diagnosis. The cancer had not spread to other parts of my body. That was the good news.

According to the National Institutes of Health, a schwannoma is a type of soft tissue sarcoma:[2]

"A soft tissue sarcoma is a disease in which cancer (malignant) cells are found in the soft tissue of part of the body. The soft tissues of the body include the muscles, connective tissues (tendons), vessels that carry blood or lymph, joints and fat."

A schwannoma is named as such because it originates in the cells covering the nerves, called the nerve sheath or schwann cells. Most schwannomas are benign or non-cancerous. Because my tumor was cancerous, it was called a malignant schwannoma.

Grade, according to my research, was a term used to describe how closely a tumor resembled normal tissue of its same type. As a general rule, the grade of a tumor corresponds to its rate of growth or aggressiveness. Referencing the

American Joint Commission on Cancer, my Grade II cancer was "moderately well differentiated" on a grade of one to four.

According to my doctor's diagnosis, I had "approximately a 60-70 percent disease-free five year survival." The odds were in my favor, but there was still a 30-40 percent chance that the cancer would recur after my treatment. The critical time period was the first year. If the cancer came back, it would likely show up within a year. First one year, then five years disease-free became the goals that I needed to achieve.

I think in order to make me feel better about the cancer, my oncologist casually remarked, "Medicine has come a long way in the last 20 years. Twenty years ago, we would have had to remove your right leg."

His comment didn't do much to lighten my mood. I remember thinking to myself; "There is no way in hell that anyone is removing my leg." I would take my chances with the cancer if that were an option. Luckily, I never had to make that choice. In hindsight, I am somewhat curious if that was really the case as the tumor was in the middle of my pelvis, not my leg.

This Shouldn't Be Happening to Me

I was somewhat in denial. I couldn't comprehend how I, a young, physically fit, healthy person could have cancer. I exercised regularly, maintained a healthy body composition, ate healthily, drank socially and never smoked. I had no family history of cancer that I was aware of, nor did I have any risk factors like obesity or working with asbestos. Cancer was something that happened to smokers and old people. To this day, I still wonder if there is anything that I could have done to avoid the cancer.

I received the news about the cancer two weeks before I was to be deployed on the USS Atlanta somewhere in the northern Atlantic Ocean for three months. If I had gone out to sea on deployment, I wouldn't have had access to medical specialists or specialized treatments and might possibly have been in a location where evacuation would have been impossible. The cancer likely would have metastasized throughout my body, and I probably would have been seriously ill or dead by the time I could get to a medical facility. Fate had intervened.

My cancer case was reviewed before a panel of doctors called the Tumor Board, which was made up of doctors from the Naval hospital and the nearby

National Institutes of Health. I felt more confident in that there was a panel of doctors reviewing my situation from institutions that were (and still are) highly thought of by the medical community. Luckily for me, based on the chest CT scan and pelvic MRI results, the tumor did not appear to have metastasized to other parts of my body.

The Tumor Board recommended treatment for me consisting of:

1. Six weeks of x-ray radiation treatments at Bethesda starting the following week. I would receive one treatment of radiation a day, five days a week for six weeks for 30 treatments in all.

2. Two weeks of recovery to allow my skin to heal from the radiation prior to surgery so that it would heal better after the surgery.

3. A second surgery called a "wide area excision" performed by an Army Orthopedic surgeon at nearby Walter Reed Army Medical Center to remove tissue surrounding the tumor bed to ensure that any cancerous cells that escaped the radiation were removed.

4. At the time of surgery, hollow catheters (long narrow tubes roughly the diameter of a cooked spaghetti noodle) would be implanted perpendicular to the tumor incision such that each catheter entered the skin on one side of the incision and exited on the other side.

5. I required one week of bed rest in Walter Reed to allow the incision to heal before more radiation in order to minimize movement of the catheters from the tumor bed.

6. Back at Bethesda, I would undergo a relatively rare procedure called brachytherapy whereby radioactive seeds attached to long, thin wires are implanted near the tumor bed through the catheters to provide a high dose of localized radiation at the tumor site.

Reflecting back now, I have a difficult time trying to remember exactly what I thought or felt at the time because everything happened so quickly. There were definitely some feelings of shock and denial. At some point, I just accepted the cancer, feeling resigned to my fate. In a sense, I was dealt a bad hand of cards in the game of life. My choice became how I would play that hand.

The Cure that Might One Day Kill Me

Radiation causes cancer. I knew that from reading about and seeing the pictures from the atomic bomb sites of Hiroshima and Nagasaki at the end of World War II. Navy nuclear power training had also taught me specifically what dosages of radiation cause different levels of damage to the human body. Not much radiation at all causes minor changes to the blood. As part of my treatment, I would receive a radiation dosage hundreds of thousands of times the radiation limit the Navy allowed me to receive while serving on a submarine. I was scared.

The best way to describe x-ray radiation therapy is that it is almost identical to receiving an x-ray for a broken bone except that the radiation technician leaves the x-ray machine on a long time—perhaps 30 seconds. The treatment works because cancer cells divide more frequently than normal cells, and cells that are dividing are more sensitive to radiation. By exposing both cancerous cells and non-cancerous cells to high doses of radiation over a six-week period, the radiation kills the more radiation-sensitive cancerous cells without doing as much damage to the normal cells. However, as a side effect, there was also some damage to my healthy cells.

During my treatment, I stayed with Clare's family in Maryland. I went to the hospital every morning at 7:00 a.m. so I would avoid the traffic on the Capital Beltway as much as possible. When I arrived, I removed all my clothes and put on a plain, blue hospital robe. The radiation technician escorted me into the x-ray treatment room where I lay down on the table. For every treatment, my legs were positioned in the "spread eagle" position to expose the critical areas of the tumor area to the radiation. The radiation technician placed lead shielding on surrounding areas outside the approximately 8" x 8" "cancer zone" then left the room. About a minute after being zapped by the x-ray machine, I was off the table and headed to the changing room to put on my own clothes before leaving for home.

I believe that many people typically associate cancer treatment with chemotherapy and its side effects, which include nausea, vomiting, loss of appetite, loss of all body hair and loss of energy. Unlike chemotherapy, which affects the entire body, x-ray or beam radiation side effects are local to the site that is radiated, which for me was the right side of my groin area. I experienced none of the chemo side effects like nausea or sickness with my radiation treatment except for the loss of hair from the radiated area, which has never grown back even after more than 10 years.

During the first week of x-ray radiation treatment, I felt absolutely no different and my irradiated skin at the tumor site looked the same. "This isn't so bad," I thought.

I continued to exercise as usual. My workouts at this time consisted of running, physical training on a nearby trail and swimming at the local aquatics center. I needed my workouts more than before, as I had to prove to myself that I was not getting sicker.

At the same time I began my treatments, I decided I wanted a dog. I convinced Clare's family that it would help me through the ordeal plus provide me company when everyone else was at work during the day. After visiting the county animal shelter, I found a four-month-old puppy named Toby that was a mix of Staffordshire Terrier and Pointer. She became my best friend.

During the second week of radiation, my irradiated skin became red, looking like slight sunburn before becoming bad sunburn. I still exercised as normal, and my body felt the same.

After three weeks, my skin became super sensitive and anytime my radiated area rubbed against clothing or other skin, it became raw. I soon noticed that I had to urinate more frequently, and when I did have to go, I couldn't hold my bladder for more than a few minutes before it became unbearable. Frequent diarrhea was next followed by loss of hair in my groin area. I easily pulled out tufts of hair with my fingers.

Eventually, my groin began to look like raw hamburger meat, and I was forced to wear loose fitting clothing over my sensitive, oozing skin. Until that point, I was still active and felt no real loss of energy. Now, it hurt to walk since anything that brushed against the skin created sharp pain. When I did walk, I walked bow-legged to alleviate the potential for rubbing as much as possible. With advice from the radiation clinic nurse, I treated the raw skin as best I could with soaks and steroid foam, but soon had to take the painkiller Percocet to alleviate the pain. After taking Percocet for several weeks and doubling my dose from one to two pills at a time to combat increasing discomfort and pain, I worried about possible addiction. My doctor simply smiled and said, "Don't worry."

The radiation treatments lasted for six weeks. The last few weeks were tough because I was forced to give up the one thing I could cling to that proved to me that I was healthy—exercise. I longed to feel the burn in my arms from push-ups and the sweet exhaustion of running effortlessly for miles. Psychologically, I was afraid of losing years of my fitness after years of exercising. Before the cancer, I worried when I missed a day or two of working out. These feelings of loss and being out of shape intensified as I knew that I was missing more than a month of exercise.

Following the radiation, I had two weeks off to give my skin time to heal as much as possible prior to the surgery. Without this recovery, there would be a greater risk that the radiation damaged skin would not heal properly from the surgery. At this stage in the treatment, I was fairly certain that I wasn't going to be a submarine officer much longer, but was still waiting for the official word from the Navy.

When I checked into Walter Reed in Washington, D.C. for surgery, I shared a room with a bed-ridden, Army Colonel who was on "standby" for surgery to remove a large tumor from his right femur (thigh bone). The Colonel woke up early each morning to wait for a surgery slot to open. He could not eat any food all day while waiting. He had been doing this for about a week when I moved into the shared hospital room. When the Colonel finally underwent surgery, he went under the anesthesia not knowing whether or not he would wake up with his leg. Luckily, the doctors were able to save his life and his leg. By pure chance, I saw him several months later at an amusement park with his kids. He was still in a wheel chair but he had both of his legs and he was happy to be alive.

The night before my scheduled surgery, the nurse had me shave my pubic area, well, at least the half of my groin that still had pubic hair left. I woke up early the morning of surgery, and a technician brought me on a gurney to the surgery staging area for an IV drip. I opted for an epidural to numb only the lower half of my body, as there was less risk than with general anesthesia. As the doctor was administering the epidural into the base of my spine, I discovered rather painfully that the epidural did not work properly as one nurse poked my leg and another tried to feed a hollow tube into the urethra of my penis. "Oww! That hurts!" I exclaimed. The attending staff quickly switched me over to a general anesthesia via the IV, and I was almost immediately unconscious.

I half woke up, groggy and incoherent as I dozed in and out of consciousness. I tried to talk to the doctors who were talking about me, but they ignored me. At one point, I asked for morphine for pain although I'm not sure if I really felt that much pain at the time or, in my drug-induced state, it seemed like I should ask for the morphine since I had just come out of surgery. That is all I remember.

My tumor scar was eight inches long and ran diagonally up the crease in my pelvis. The irradiated skin on either side of the incision was held together with staples to support the stitches under the skin.

The surgeon informed me afterward that the surgery was successful. I was now waiting on pathology of the surrounding tissue to see if there were any live cancer cells. A few days later, the pathology report, thankfully, came back negative.

During the surgery, the radiation oncologists from Bethesda had also inserted five catheters into one side of the incision, down across the tumor bed and back out of the skin on the other side of the incision in preparation for the brachytherapy. The catheters were placed so that they passed near the tumor bed. Radioactive "seeds" on long thin wires could then be lowered down to the tumor bed to give a large localized dose of radiation to the tumor site. I had to spend the next week in a hospital bed so that I didn't disturb the precise placement of the catheters. I was not allowed to walk except to hobble over to use the bathroom in my room. The week in bed was to give my skin time to heal before radiating it again.

A week after the surgery, I rode in an ambulance from Walter Reed back to Bethesda for the brachytherapy. My radiation oncologist wheeled in a cart with a lead container called a "pig" which contained the radioactive seeds attached to thin wires. He then lowered the wires with seeds down into the catheters to place them near the tumor site. There were half a dozen medical interns and residents on hand to witness the relatively rare procedure.

With the radioactive seeds implanted within the catheters, my hospital room became a restricted radiation area with radiation warning signs posted everywhere. I had the end of the hospital wing all to myself with no one else in my room or the room next to me. The radiation technicians placed lead panels for shielding around my bed to protect others from radiation, relying on the floors and ceiling to shield those above and below me. A radiation technician measured the level of radiation in the room several times each day with a type of Geiger counter. Anyone who entered the room had to wear a small device to monitor the dose of radiation exposure received while in the room.

Once the seeds were in place, the doctor told me I could not get out of bed for any reason for 40 hours. I was forced to lie on my back and use a bedpan. My dad, who as a nuclear submariner was familiar with radiation and its effects on the human body, questioned the radiation physicists about the radiation exposure to the rest of my body from the seeds. The doctors explained how they had carefully calculated the dosages that each of my vital organs would receive from the implanted seeds. The radiation exposure received by each organ based on the organ's proximity to the seeds and any shielding (i.e., body parts) in the way. All dosages to my organs were calculated to be within safe limits.

My dad and Charlotte stayed nearby while my dad participated in training for his job. During the day while he was working, Charlotte practically lived in my rooms at both Walter Reed and Bethesda. She kept me company as I impatiently sat through 10 days of immobility. We talked, played cards and cribbage, and watched television as we tried to kill time. Time crawled by at a snail's pace, and I was very thankful for her company.

In the early morning of the 10th day after surgery, I swallowed a Quaalude to settle my nerves. After 40 hours of localized radiation from the seeds, my doctor removed the radioactive seeds placing them back in the "pig" then quickly yanked out each individual catheter. I felt nothing but a slight tug on my skin. I slowly and awkwardly climbed out of bed, exchanged my hospital gown for my civilian clothes and walked out of the hospital, a little stiff from having laid on my back for the past week and a half.

...But Cancer Doesn't Have Me

"Before cancer I just lived. Now I live strong."
- *Lance Armstrong, seven time winner of the Tour de France*

When I found out I had cancer, I had to make a choice about how I would deal with it. As I saw it, I had three options: I could be a cancer victim, I could be a cancer survivor, or I could be something else altogether. I chose to go beyond being a victim or just a survivor to be something else.

I fundamentally believe that attitude influences outcomes—a positive attitude drives positive outcomes. My attitude shifted

I believe that attitude influences outcomes - a positive attitude drives positive outcomes.

from being helpless during the treatment to proving that the cancer didn't have me. I would beat my cancer and go on with my life, yet with the real perspective that it could be taken away from me at any time. I did not see a positive attitude as a compromise in my competition with cancer. I had to win.

When I walked out of the Naval hospital following the brachytherapy, I hadn't exercised in more than a month, and I had been lying down for the last 10 days. I felt frustrated and wanted my fitness back.

I needed a goal. I needed something that dangled in front of me like a carrot to motivate me back to the fitness level I had before the radiation and the surgery. I wanted to prove to myself that I had beaten the cancer.

Ever since I had won the Iron Mid multi-sport contest as a Firstie at the Academy, I had toyed with the idea of competing in a multi-sport event like triathlon, but with my schedule and demands from Navy training and the sub, I didn't pursue it. When I walked out of the hospital, I suddenly had the time and the motivation. Cancer became the catalyst for me to try a triathlon. Finishing a triathlon became the goal to bring myself back to and beyond my prior fitness level.

I decided that triathlon epitomized the ultimate physical and mental challenge. I would compete not only against others but against myself, which is who I wanted to test, as it was my body that had the cancer. I was somewhat intimidated by the event. Previously, I lacked the courage and motivation to move beyond running races, which is where I felt most comfortable and in control. I was a decent runner and could finish well in most races. Triathlon was a big unknown.

The future, as the cancer pointedly showed me, is never guaranteed for any of us at any age. There may not be a tomorrow. I needed something that I could cling to, something that proved I was still alive and healthy. Triathlon became that something.

The radiation which was supposed to kill the cancer also damaged my healthy cells, slowing the healing of the incision site and increasing the risk of infection. For a few weeks after the surgery with dozens of staples and stitches holding my incision together, I couldn't risk any activity that might pull open the incision, cause infection or slow the healing. So I walked. Walking was the only exercise that I could do until the doctors removed my staples. I walked with Charlotte and Toby on the trails near my dad and Charlotte's apartment. We walked and talked for hours.

I initially visited Walter Reed three times a week for follow-up on the surgery. The surgery resident first removed one or two staples then a few more and then asked me to come back a few days later. He then removed one or two more and said to come back again.

Finally, the attending doctor, realizing my frustration caused by the resident's follow-ups every other day, said, "Just remove half of them," to the resident.

The doctor turned to me, "Come back in two weeks."

Once all of the staples were out, I could begin running again—slowly, very slowly.

My initial pace was forced, and my movements felt awkward. I had lost the fluid feel of running I had acquired over the years, and my breathing rate seemed too high at first. I was working too hard for the slow speed my legs generated. I felt frustrated, but I needed to get back into shape.

Once the incision site healed and I was no longer in danger of infection from pool water, I began to swim again. Attempting a breaststroke kick for the first time stabbed sharply as my groin muscles were tight and sore. This was caused by the surgical removal of the surrounding tissue from the tumor site. I still wonder what specific tissue the surgeons removed. I suspect that they removed some of the muscle tissue, which explains why my right hip and leg are less flexible than the left side.

My first few weeks of swimming, like running, felt slow and awkward. I had lost my "feel" for the water. I had never been an effortless, natural swimmer, but I had clearly taken a step backward.

I was determined and driven. I had my goal in front of me. I wanted to compete and, perhaps more importantly, finish a triathlon as a symbol of beating my cancer. I didn't know where or when I would race, but I needed to do one for my own peace of mind and proof of health. I swallowed my not so distant memories of past fitness levels and kept swimming and running.

While working out at the Bethesda gym, I saw a flyer on the wall advertising a free triathlon clinic. The clinic consisted of four sessions each covering four different aspects of training with different speakers. A nearby Performance Bicycle® shop in Maryland hosted the clinic. I went to three of the four sessions and sat there in awe as I listened to the coaches and experienced triathletes share training advice. What impressed me the most was that several of the speakers and attendees had competed in the Ironman World Championship in Hawaii, which I had watched on television years before. I took meticulous notes on the handouts. Even now, I occasionally reference those handouts.

The last exercise that I focused on was cycling. While in the sixth grade, I once biked 17 miles with my stepfather. Seventeen miles seemed like forever at the time. The ride lasted about three hours because we stopped several times, and I was very uncomfortable riding on the open road with traffic. Reflecting back, we must have been biking painfully slow, and my stepfather must have been extremely patient. I don't, however, remember him taking me out for any more rides after that initial one.

After being diagnosed with cancer, I gave away my too large 10-speed to charity and bought a brand new road bike with 14 speeds—two gears on the front chain ring (where the pedals are attached) and seven on the rear wheel. I had no clue what bike to buy or even if I would like triathlons, so I stayed away from a triathlon-specific bike in favor of a more general road bike. My former Navy roommate who did triathlons owned a Cannondale® bicycle, so I also bought a Cannondale bike. With the advice garnered from the triathlon clinic sessions and the bike shop, I added clipless pedals and clip-on aero bars to convert the bike more into a triathlon-like bike. Clipless pedals allowed me to clip my bike shoes to the pedals giving my foot a firm surface of contact and enabling more direct energy transfer from my legs to the rear wheel. The aero bars enabled me to lean forward with my elbows resting on the bar pads and hands on the extensions in order to flatten out my profile facing the wind and thereby reduce aerodynamic drag.

Once the soreness in my groin dissipated, and I could sit comfortably on a bike saddle without fear of tearing the incision wide open, I began cycling. I didn't have the fitness base that I had from running, so I didn't feel like I had lost as much. Besides, I had not found anyone to bike with, so I had no basis of comparison as to how strong (or weak) I was as a cyclist relative to others.

I received official word that I would "retire" from the Navy in July. While waiting to be processed out, I continued to live with Clare's family in the congested Maryland suburbs north of Washington, D.C. I rode my bike tentatively around the neighborhood, staying primarily on residential streets or streets with marked bike lanes confining myself to a limited riding area. I was reluctant to ride with traffic and not confident enough of my bike handling skills to ride with others. I didn't know anyone else who competed in triathlons, so I learned by reading books and posts from triathletes in online chat groups and through my own trial and error.

Every cyclist that I know who has ridden with clipless pedals has a story to tell about them. The story typically goes something like this:

> I just got clipless pedals, so I went out for a bike ride to test them out. I came up to a traffic light and slowed down, but forgot to unclip one leg. As I came to a stop, I lost my balance and started leaning to the left, but could not get my left foot out in time to stop the fall. I fell right in the middle of the road. I think all of the people in their cars were laughing at me.

This happened to me several times in the first few weeks of riding with clipless pedals. Even now, with more than 10 years of experience under my belt, I still occasionally fall down when I'm not paying attention.

While reading about triathlons at an online chat group, I came across a term for a workout called a "brick" and wondered what it meant. Whatever it was, it sounded hard on the legs. After reading a few more posts, I realized that a brick was simply a bike ride followed quickly by a short run to simulate the race transition from biking to running in racing.

So I started adding bricks to my workouts. At first, my legs felt unsteady and rubbery when I tried to run after a bike ride. I ran slowly and awkwardly at a forced pace not like my normal feeling of fluidity and natural stride. After one brick workout a week over several months, then several years, running after biking became more and more natural and eventually seamless.

During the summer after my surgery, I spent a week with my dad and Charlotte in Kings Bay, Georgia, where my dad was stationed in the Navy. While browsing the local newspaper, my dad discovered a Sprint distance race in nearby Atlantic Beach, Florida.

According to USA Triathlon (the governing body for triathlons in the United States), the proper terminology for the four common triathlon distances are: Short, Intermediate, Long and Ultra. These correspond with other commonly used terms and usually have distances as follows:

1. Short/Sprint: 750-meter swim, 20-kilometer bike, 5 kilometer-run

2. Intermediate/International: 1,500-meter swim, 40-kilometer bike, 10-kilometer run

3. Long/Half-Iron: 1.2-mile swim, 56-mile bike, 13.1-mile run

4. Ultra/Iron distance: 2.4-mile swim, 112-mile bike, 26.2-mile run

Looking at the distances, most people new to triathlon would pick the Sprint distance as their first race, which is what I did. I have had friends, however, who amazingly went straight to the Iron distance in their first season of racing or even as their first race.

"Am I ready?" I asked myself. "It's only been three months since the surgery." I was doubtful and reluctant.

After talking myself through my self doubt and feelings of intimidation, I decided I needed to do the Sprint race if only to experience it. Besides, the race was nearby, and I could wait to sign up until race morning in case I decided to chicken out at the last minute. The course consisted of a short ocean swim; a flat, but windy, beachfront bike; and a flat run through the local neighborhood streets. My dad and I drove to Atlantic Beach the morning of the race for me to register and race.

I was nervous as I carefully watched the other athletes prepping before the race. I wasn't quite sure what to do, so I mimicked them as I set up my own space within the transition area. I readied my bike which meant checking the tires and making sure the brakes worked properly and then I warmed-up with an easy jog along the beachfront road.

As the starting time approached, I felt nervous and unsure of myself. I had no idea what to expect. The athletes were segmented into swim waves by gender and age group, and I was assigned to one of the earlier waves. The water was calm and it was a beach start for the point-to-point swim course, which lay parallel to the shore.

Bang! The starting gun went off. I dashed into the water and quickly forgot my apprehension. My arms churned like windmills, and I quickly winded myself to near exhaustion in the first hundred meters. I had no concept of pace other than to keep moving my arms without stopping. My transition from the swim to the bike was slow as I never thought to practice beforehand. Quite a few triathletes who didn't look like they were in shape blew past me on the bike. Given my running background, I made up some of my lost time from the bike as I overtook the slower runners.

I sprinted across the finish line in a little over an hour, finishing in the middle of my age group. My race was nothing special and gave no indication of future talent, but I was ecstatic and felt a tremendous sense of accomplishment. I was now a triathlete, and I had the t-shirt to prove it! I instantly caught the triathlon bug. I knew that I had found my sport.

I was sore for a few days after, but I wanted to do another race. I wanted to try something longer since the Sprint race was over much too quickly. Plus, I didn't enjoy the feeling of having to race "all out" over such a short distance. It seemed like longer races would necessitate a slightly slower, more comfortable pace.

While waiting to be processed out of the Navy, I began looking for a job in the Washington, D.C. area, so I could be close to the Naval Hospital in Bethesda. When I first began to look, I had no idea where to start, nor did I know what I wanted to do. Before being diagnosed with cancer, my plan was to serve in the Navy for five years and then worry about a career choice. Now, I had to make a choice immediately. Because I attended the Academy, I had no experience with corporate recruiters or job hunting.

I spoke with a military headhunter, but he didn't point me to any jobs that appealed to me or fit my background. My dad passed my resume to a few of his friends who had left the Navy for the corporate world. I interviewed at several locations in the D.C. area and finally settled on Lockheed Martin, the U.S. government's largest defense contractor. Lockheed seemed to be a good place to transition from the military to civilian life. I was intrigued by the opportunity to work on top secret projects for government customers. Plus, the people who interviewed me were all ex-military, so I felt comfortable that I made a good choice.

Clare and I were married in August, and we purchased a townhouse in Reston, Virginia. My criteria for finding the right place to live was that it needed to be close to work to minimize my commute. Lockheed was located in Reston, and I was impressed with the area and its planned community assets. There were trees, pools and running and biking trails everywhere, so it seemed like an ideal location for an active person. One of the best features was the W&OD Trail, which is the old Washington and Old Dominion railroad line in Northern Virginia that was converted to a paved biking and running trail. The W&OD runs from Arlington, Virginia, through Reston and on to Purcellville, Virginia for a total distance of 45 miles. I would spend many hours on the trail in the coming years as a means to get to less congested communities where I could safely ride my bike on the roads.

Although I was busy with wedding plans, moving and my new job responsibilities, I managed to find the time to exercise and train for my new sport. What I didn't realize yet was that Reston was a regional triathlon mecca and supported dozens of amateur triathletes and training groups. I was hooked on triathlon and this was just the beginning.

Within a week of moving to Reston, I joined the Fitness Equation, a fitness center located halfway between my home and office. I have found that *If my gym is easy to get to, I'm more likely to go.* the location of an available fitness center is key to my training. It's simple: If my gym is easy to get to, I am more likely to go. I never had to pay for a gym membership before, so the $34 a month fee was a big commitment for me. I planned to workout at least three times a week though, so it seemed like a worthwhile investment in my personal well-being.

I was still in the mindset that I needed to lift weights several times a week to maintain muscle tone and strength. I didn't want to give up being able to bench 200+ pounds for multiple sets. Perhaps it was a bit of vanity.

I learned that it was better for me to go to the gym in the morning before work because my job sometimes required me to work late. By working out in the morning, I could get my workout out of the way, plus exercise made me feel relaxed and ready for work. I was never a late night person growing up and both the Navy and the Naval Academy had required many early mornings so I was used to getting up early. Of course, it also meant that I was in bed by 10:00 p.m. as my body craved eight hours of sleep. This was something I aspired to but didn't always achieve.

During this period of time, my typical workout schedule for a week looked something like:

- Sunday: Off day
- Monday: Lift weights (upper body); swim for 50 minutes
- Tuesday: Bike for 90 minutes; run for 30 minutes
- Wednesday: Swim 2,000 meters
- Thursday: Lift weights (upper body)
- Friday: Run 35 minutes; swim 25 minutes
- Saturday: Bike 115 minutes; swim 2,600 meters

I usually ended up only lifting upper body weights on a regular basis because otherwise my legs would be too tired to run and bike. I also found that lifting weights, not surprisingly, caused my arms to fatigue if I swam later in the day. I did all of my workouts by myself because I hadn't met anyone else who was a triathlete. This was partly my own fault though, since I didn't take the time to meet people at the gym. When I went to the gym, I went there to work out and usually didn't socialize because that took away from time spent exercising. I didn't understand how people could go to the gym and chat for 20 minutes before they started to work out, then again after they were through. I had a full-time job, a wife to spend time with, and other responsibilities—it just didn't make sense to me.

I still didn't have much structure to my training schedule other than I tried to fit in two or three sessions of each event per week: three swim, three bike and three run workouts. I picked this schedule based on information I took away from the triathlon training seminar earlier in the year. In reality, my day-to-day schedule jumped around from week to week, and I didn't have a long-term focus or plan.

In September, I completed another triathlon. It was the Make-A-Wish® triathlon, an International distance race (1.5 kilometer swim, 40 kilometer bike and 10 kilometer run) in Delaware, about a three-hour drive away.

The ocean was rough during the race with waves breaking heavily on the shore. I borrowed a sleeveless, long john-style wetsuit from a co-worker who was an open-water swimmer. The race director instructed all the athletes to walk north for almost a mile so that we could swim back to the transition area with the current. The strong current made the swim times incredibly fast. The top swimmer covered the 1,500 meters in a little over 10 minutes. The bike course took us out and back along the highway starting into a strong headwind, but likewise we returned with a strong tailwind. I had not yet built up a strong cycling base, so I quickly lost momentum and position during the bike. Like my first race, I again made up some time on the run to finish in the top third of my age group.

In my mind, I had bumped up in the triathlon world. I was now an International/ Intermediate distance triathlete and had the race t-shirt to prove it.

When I returned home after the race and was in the process of unloading my bike and gear, I met my next door neighbor. He came over, introduced himself as Phil, and asked if I did triathlons. I smugly replied, "Yep, I'm a triathlete."

He turned out to be a long-time resident of the area, and he lived with his wife and their Greyhound. Phil taught at the local high school and coached the school's basketball team. He was eight years older than me and had raced triathlons for a decade. I later learned that his racing career included a brief stint as a professional triathlete in the Bud Light Triathlon Series®. Phil had also completed an Iron distance triathlon in New Hampshire. I was in awe.

In spite of cancer, I ended my year on a high note with a feeling of accomplishment. I eagerly looked forward to racing again the following year and without knowing it, I had found an open window into the local triathlon community through Phil.

Chapter 4: More Triathlon

My transition to civilian life was going well. My job at Lockheed was fine, but turned out to be fairly mundane. Although working in "black operations" sounded exotic and exciting, in reality, as the systems integrator for a large program, my team spent much time managing the communications and paperwork between the government and other contractors. It was clear that my job wasn't going to provide the excitement and challenge I felt I needed in life, so triathlon started to become an important outlet for me.

When the Fitness Equation introduced Spinning®, a high-intensity, 40-minute stationary bike class to music, I was one of the first students to sign up. Instantly, I found a challenging activity that closely simulated riding outside. I had tried riding a wind trainer, where the back of my bike was locked into the trainer with the wheel rubbing against a flywheel to simulate road resistance, but I was extremely uncomfortable sitting in a static position for any length of time. The music, the instructor and the other students motivated me to push myself during the Spinning classes. In addition, the pedals had attachments for cycling shoes, which gave a much firmer and more comfortable attachment than tennis shoes.

When I walked into a class, I felt a desire to demonstrate that I was the strongest cyclist there. During the climbs, I added more resistance. During the sprints, I spun my legs faster. I caught the attention of the instructors who said to me, "You're strong. Why don't you teach?"

"Why not?" I thought. I attended a one-day certification class and received my certification after a six-month probationary period. I initially taught two or three classes a week. The biggest challenge for me was not the fitness or the instruction, but preparing my music tapes for class. Many of the instructors taught aerobics, so they had experience creating music workout tapes with the type of music that seemed to motivate people. My first Spinning tape had the Police and Ozzy Osbourne on it since that was music I had at home. I tried to mix up the music as much as possible to appeal to different preferences, and the feedback I received was mostly positive perhaps because it was atypical. I eventually bought a dozen CDs to expand my music selection for class.

I enjoyed teaching Spinning because it gave me the opportunity to work out and be paid for it. I even got a free gym membership. Spinning also provided a good biking workout indoors when the weather was bad and it fit nicely into my training.

Until I met Phil, I trained alone. I had no source of triathlon information other than the Internet; three sets of handouts from the triathlon seminar I had attended and a beginner's triathlon book that I picked up from a local bookstore.

Phil quickly became my training partner, my mentor and my friend. I estimate that I learned 75 percent of what I know today about endurance sports training from Phil. He had a common sense approach built on years of experience. I valued his opinions and his advice, plus he was a top-performing athlete who had normal life commitments like me.

Not only was Phil my training partner, but he became my first triathlon coach. I called him "coach" like his students on the high school basketball team. I learned from him through observation, questions and informal conversations during our workouts. Even now, when I learn or experience new things, I realize that most of the time these are things that he told me that didn't register at the time or I had since forgotten.

One of the most important things I learned while training with Phil during my second year of triathlon competition, was how to pace during training and, perhaps more importantly, during a race. I discovered that I didn't need to run fast all the time in order to be a fast runner. My early philosophy for run training that I developed in high school was to run hard for as long as I could while training and racing. That philosophy worked for the mile-distance races, but not so well when I did the Marine Corps Marathon. I began to enjoy the more moderately paced runs that Phil prescribed which enabled me to recover faster. I wouldn't understand why running at a more moderate pace worked well until years later, so I was initially running on blind trust and faith in Phil.

I also learned that it's a waste of time to run in place at an intersection while waiting for a traffic light to change. There's nothing gained from jogging in place other than entertaining drivers in nearby vehicles. I also think it helps to train the body to stop and start up again which simulates slowing at an aid station during a race. Now, I just chuckle whenever I see a runner jogging in place at a traffic light and think, "That used to be me."

Phil also taught me about endurance exercise nutrition. He introduced me to PowerBars®, Cytomax® energy drink mix and energy gels. These were all foreign to me, but 10 years later, I still use Cytomax for training and racing.

I learned how to improve efficiency by drafting off of other swimmers, staying aero on the bike as much as possible and pacing myself during the run. This allowed me to maintain a more consistent pace and ultimately a faster time than when I started out too fast and ended up fading.

I also learned how important hydration is before, during and after training and racing. In later years when Phil and I trained for longer distance races, I discovered, as Phil had hinted, that a single water bottle cage on my bike was inadequate to meet hydration needs during long, hot training days.

I learned to ride flats and climb hills more quickly and more efficiently. I was what cyclists call a "masher," which means that I put my gearing into the hardest gear I could maintain while pedaling at a powerful but relatively low cadence (60-70 rpm). "Mashing" my big chain ring generated substantial power but my legs fatigued quickly as compared to Phil's faster, more efficient cadence (80-90 rpm).

Perhaps the single biggest impact of my friendship with Phil was that I now had a training partner who was similar in ability to me, although of much greater experience, such that we could constantly challenge each other. Through Phil, I also connected with the local running and swim clubs and suddenly found myself surrounded by like-minded triathletes. This brought back memories from the Academy where there always seemed to be someone to work out with. Through these local clubs, I made many friends of all different experiences and abilities.

I soon settled into a routine of swimming two or three days a week, biking long on Saturdays and running long on Sundays with my new running club. During the week I often met Phil early in the morning or after work to run or bike. As a schoolteacher, he had to be at work by 7:15 a.m., so we had to finish up by 6:45 a.m. in order to give him enough time to shower and drive to work. It was much easier to get out of bed early on dark mornings knowing that someone was waiting on me to show up for a workout.

Even though I was newly married and working at a new job, I always made the time to train. I typically exercised six days a week, and sometimes fit a second workout into my day.

As a government contractor, I was on a time card for work. As such, I had to bill 40 hours per week, no more and no less, which essentially meant an eight-hour day plus another 30 minutes for lunch. My work team's core hours were from 10:00 a.m. to 3:00 p.m., so I had the flexibility to either leave early by coming in early or arrive to work late and stay late.

This opened up blocks of time on either end of the workday for exercise. I found that it was easier and more time efficient to sometimes work in back-to-back workouts (e.g., swim then bike) as opposed to workouts at different times during the day. One reason for the efficiency was the reduction in travel time to the exercise location, if any, and preparation time. Plus, I only had to shower once rather than twice.

For work, I traveled to Boulder, Colorado every month for three or four days. While I was there, I found a local community center that had a fitness center and indoor pool. For a daily fee, I could lift weights, ride a Lifecycle

Take advantage of opportunities to work out while traveling. Find a local gym, pool or running trails. Consider joining a gym or YMCA with locations around the country that you can use as a guest member.

or swim. For running, I took advantage of the city's trail system, sometimes running up into the mountains. I always made time to exercise on travel, which typically meant working out early or eating dinner late.

Clare was traveling during the week for her job, so I was on my own a lot. When she was around, I kept my workout routine. "I'm off to Master's Swim practice." or "I'm running with Phil in the morning." My mindset back then was that I felt that I could only lose a day or two of exercise before I began losing fitness. Spending time with her took time away from my fitness and hindered my ability to be a better triathlete, so at times, I resisted.

My preference toward exercise over our relationship foreshadowed future conflict and troubles. I was very selfish with my time and did not make Clare a larger priority.

Since the completion of my cancer treatment, I continued to follow up with the Navy for medical exams. My typical routine was to visit my Hematologist/ Oncologist for an exam. He would order a chest x-ray that day and would then write me a referral for a chest CT scan and pelvic MRI. If the tumor reappeared, it was likely to metastasize in my lungs, which are rich in oxygen and therefore a breeding ground for the cancerous cells. The pelvic MRI gave the doctors cross-sectionals view of the tumor bed and surrounding organs and tissues, which would show local recurrence.

As I passed through the one-year mark of finishing my cancer treatment, I breathed a sigh of relief. I had accomplished my first important cancer goal.

My follow-up visits to the Naval Hospital became less frequent after the first year. Although it would be four more years before the Navy could declare me "cured," the first year was the most critical year. If the cancer were going to recur, it would likely happen during the first twelve months because of its aggressive nature. My next cancer goal was to reach the five-year point disease free.

My least favorite activity was lying in the MRI machine. I am slightly claustrophobic in tight spaces, and the MRI was even tighter than my bunk on the submarine. At least in the bunk, I could roll over on my side and move the curtain to see out into the aisle. With the MRI, even though I was fed in feet first and my head was just inside the lip of the cylinder, the only thing I could see was the white wall of the cylinder a few inches from my face. I fought through panic attacks on several occasions and often left the session in a cold sweat vowing to never go through the scan without taking a Valium to reduce the anxiety.

Cancer still weighed heavily in the back of my mind that first year. I needed to be able —and still do today—to prove to myself every day that even though I once had cancer, cancer did not have me. Triathlon became the physical proof that I had beaten the cancer and that it had not come back. If I could continue to improve in fitness as evidenced by improved performance in triathlon, I rationalized that I could not be sick with cancer.

During my second year of triathlons, I raced in seven local races including the Columbia, Hawk and Spud Triathlons in Maryland, and the Reston Triathlon in Virginia. Most of them were International distance races. With Phil's sage guidance, which provided me with more structure, and focus on training, my race results improved. Success created more success and more desire as I craved faster times and a podium finish. I achieved several top-10 overall finishes in smaller, local Sprint and International distance races, but did not make the podium.

I came close to not finishing the Spud Triathlon about 30 seconds into the swim. In the chaos of the first few minutes, I inadvertently swallowed a gulp of water while turning to breathe. I started choking then hyperventilating as I panicked. I treaded water for a few seconds trying to calm my gasping breath and fighting the urge to get out of the water. I slowly put my head down and kept swimming. It would take me a few more races before I finally became totally confident in the water.

One of the things I learned early on was race etiquette. My simple definition of race etiquette is respect for the sport (i.e., the rules), the athletes and the volunteers. At the end of a race, I want to know that I reached the finish line fairly without adversely impacting others in any way.

The swim in a triathlon, especially at the start, is a chaotic swirling of stroking arms and kicking feet. I have been kicked and elbowed in the face numerous times. For the most part, I believe it is accidental. I try to keep my distance from others as much as possible during the swim and lessen my kick to avoid hitting others. It still frustrates me when someone intentionally swims over me, grabs onto my leg to pull themselves forward or constantly bumps my feet from drafting too close. Sometimes, I'll give a gentle kick to remind them that it's not nice to play that way.

One of my most vivid memories in my second year of racing was at the Reston Triathlon. The Reston Triathlon is an International distance event held annually in Reston, Virginia, on the second Sunday in September. The race attracts more than 400 local participants each year and has been in existence since 1994. During this particular race, I was in the top 10 overall coming off the bike and was about to start my strongest event, the run. As I ran toward the exit of the transition area, another athlete rudely yelled, "Watch out!" as he came barreling by at a much faster pace. His yelling startled me, and I almost fell. He just kept moving and was soon out of sight, never looking back. To this day, I have no idea who he was other than he finished somewhere ahead of me. From that experience and others, I took away a desire to respect other athletes, rather than push them aside or kick someone's face when they bump me in the swim.

Triathlons have rules established by USA Triathlon. Two of the most widely abused rules are drafting and blocking on the bike. Drafting occurs when an athlete rides too closely behind another athlete to take advantage of the reduced wind resistance. The rules clearly dictate how far back an athlete must be in order to be considered outside of the drafting zone as well as the rules for overtaking and passing.

During a race athletes are supposed to ride to the right and pass on the left. Blocking occurs when an athlete rides to the left thereby "blocking" an overtaking athlete's path. To me, blocking and drafting show a total lack of respect for the sport and the other riders. Triathlon should be a test of oneself against the clock.

Okay, I admit that I drafted during the bike leg intentionally in a race once. When my friend rode by me, I jumped on his wheel. We traded places off and on for the rest of the bike leg then went on to place near the top of our respective age groups. Afterward, as we sat waiting for the awards to be given out, I overheard other athletes complaining about the cheating (drafting) that took place during the race. I felt embarrassed and uncomfortable as I was one of the cheaters. I threw away the plaque I received that day and never intentionally drafted again.

As my second racing season finished in the fall, I began graduate school at the Catholic University of America to pursue a Master's of Science in Engineering Management. Lockheed covered the cost of the tuition assuming that I received at least a "B" in each class. The program only required 10 classes and no thesis. I also received two class credits for my six months of Nuclear Power School which meant I only had to take eight classes. If I took two classes a semester in the evenings, I could finish the program in 15 months.

Classes were two and a half hours each twice a week from either 5:00 p.m. to 7:30 p.m. or 7:30 p.m. to 10:00 p.m. in the evening. I chose a class schedule that allowed me to take back-to-back classes on the same night. Essentially, I would leave work a little early on either Tuesday/Thursday or Monday/Wednesday, and sit in class until 10:00 p.m. that night which made for a very long day. Because I was at the end of the training season, it didn't impact my training that much. I could usually squeeze in a short workout in the morning before work or just use one of those days as off days. I didn't give much thought to the following spring and summer when training and racing would pick up.

Partly a coping mechanism and partly just a desire to excel in something, triathlon had now become an integral part of my life and my routine. Training and racing were my lifestyle and a form of identity. I called myself a triathlete and associated with other triathletes. My improving results were feeding my desire to spend more time training and less time with other aspects of my life.

Chapter 5: Going Longer

"Men go back to the mountains, as they go back to sailing ships at sea, because in the mountains and on the sea they must face up, as did men of another age, to the challenge of nature. Modern man lives in a highly synthetic kind of existence. He specializes in this and that. Rarely does he test all his powers or find himself whole. But in the hills and on the water the character of a man comes out."
- Abram T. Collier

Cancer is a permanent fixture in a survivor's life even for those of us lucky enough to be "cured"—a term that I use loosely. Thinking about my cancer sometimes makes me sad because the reality is that it could happen again. Every time I feel sick or run down, I wonder if the cancer has invaded my lymphatic system or is sitting in my lungs slowly taking over my body like an alien invader. Every time I find a cyst or some other lump on my body—I have had four lumps removed since the cancer—I go directly to my doctor for a check up and potential biopsy. I am again reminded that I had cancer and that if I get it again, I may not be as lucky: I could lose a limb, an organ or my life.

Not long after I was retired from the Navy for cancer, my Uncle Walter, who had served in the Navy in World War II, suddenly became sick. In a matter of a week, he went from healthy to bed-ridden due to a very aggressive stomach cancer. When I saw him, he was already in a coffin. Since the Naval Academy, I had stayed in touch with Uncle Walter and his wife (Aunt Jenny). When I was in Submarine School and on the USS Memphis, their house was a short drive away, so I spent quite a few weekends there. We had become very close.

Until my Uncle Walter's death, I never had anyone close to me die. I vividly remember the wake where hundreds of friends and family gathered. Everyone was crying and sad. When I saw Uncle Walter lying there, I started crying, too. At the funeral the next day, my dad and I dressed up in our white Navy dress uniforms. For the final act at the burial ceremony, my dad and I took an American flag that had been draped over the coffin and folded it into a small triangle. My dad presented the flag to my Aunt Jenny with the words, "From a grateful nation." Even now, I choke up in tears thinking about this incident.

Years later, Uncle Walter's son-in-law brought up that scene in the graveyard and said how that simple act had made all the difference in the world to Aunt Jenny and the grieving family. I also remember that day as the last day I ever wore a Navy uniform.

One of my biggest fears is that I will have to go through the cancer experience again. Knowing that I have received as much radiation as I have, radiation is not likely to be a treatment option for me any longer. I also fear the potential future side effects from all the radiation I received during my first treatment. These fears are a burden that I will always carry. I may not be as lucky the next time.

Because of my cancer, I am also stronger. I can best explain this by sharing an article about cancer survivor and cyclist Lance Armstrong. Shortly following Lance's 5th consecutive win of the Tour de France in 2003, Sally Jenkins wrote an editorial,[3] that appeared in the *Washington Post*. Ms. Jenkins is the co-author of Lance Armstrong's two autobiographies, *It's Not About the Bike* and *Every Second Counts*. In the editorial, Sally wrote:

> "Why do you do it?" I asked him once. "What's the pleasure in riding a bike up a mountain for six hours?"
>
> "I don't understand the question." he said.
>
> "Well, there has to be some pleasure in it." I said. "I mean, your back hurts, your neck hurts, your butt hurts. What's the payoff?"
>
> "I still don't understand the question."
>
> I went away baffled — and convinced that unless I could get him to talk to me on that subject, I'd never understand him. After a couple of days of thought, I realized I'd been asking the entirely wrong question.
>
> "You don't do it for the pleasure." I said. "You do it for the pain."
>
> "That's exactly right." he said.
>
> So instead we began to talk about suffering. Gradually, I understood that suffering was as important to Lance as happiness. The pain on the bike is so intense, the suffering so complete, that there is no room for anything else. The effort becomes all, absolute. And in that absoluteness is a kind of peace. "It's not a good day if I haven't suffered a little." he says.

I can relate to what Lance says. I also train for the suffering and the relief that the suffering provides.

Completing an Iron distance race was still beyond my comprehension. I elevated ultra athletes to a pedestal for having done something that I could only dream about.

When Phil and I swam at the 50-meter outdoor pool in Reston, we occasionally ran into a triathlete who had completed Ironman Lanzarote®. Lanzarote is part of the Canary Islands off the coast of Spain. The race, which takes place annually in May, is known for a challenging, hilly course in hot and windy conditions. As such, it is often referred to as the Ironman Hawaii of Europe. I remember listening in awe as the triathlete talked about his race experiences. He was an Iron distance triathlete. I was not.

As Phil talked more and more about his Iron distance experiences in New Hampshire in the late 1980s, he slowly planted a seed in my mind that I could do one too. I began to crave a bigger challenge than the Sprint and International distance races that I had been competing in. At the end of my second year of racing, Phil and I eventually talked each other into doing Ironman Canada® in Penticton, British Columbia the following August.

When I first seriously considered Ironman Canada, the distance intimidated me. In total, it was roughly four times the distance of any triathlon that I had done to date. I had not biked more than 40 miles at a time or swum more than the 1,500-kilometer distance in an International distance race. I had completed two stand-alone marathons (I raced the Marine Corps Marathon again in the fall of 1996), but I had walked part of the first race and both left me exhausted and sore for a week. I could not comprehend combining all three events over 140.6 miles. Until I could experience the race, I needed something to help me build the confidence and the fitness to take me to the finish line.

My other consideration for not doing the race was time or potentially lack thereof as I was recently married, worked full time, attended graduate school in the evenings and had responsibilities at home. I knew from talking to Phil that training for an Iron distance race was a much bigger time commitment than training for an International distance race. For example, my long rides on the weekend were typically only two hours in preparation for the one-hour bike leg of an International distance triathlon. The 112-mile bike leg of an Iron distance race would take me anywhere from five to seven hours. Consequently, I would need to bump my training distance to four to five and ultimately a six-hour ride. Because I worked during the week, I would need to do my long distance training on the weekends.

I was still on a time card at Lockheed Martin so I knew my time bounds at work and that I would not have to worry too much about work conflicts. My manager was ex-military and was active so he partially understood my passion for exercise. My co-workers already knew I was a fitness freak and a triathlete. I had begun giving fitness tips via PowerPoint® slides at weekly team meetings.

Thankfully, I had the common sense to only take one graduate school class during the summer semester when our schedule dictated the longest bike rides and longest runs.

What would ultimately suffer the most from my training was my marriage, but I was in my own little selfish world of infatuation with triathlon and didn't give much thought to my relationship. I was married, so the hard part was over, or so I thought. I honestly and stupidly did not realize that I would have to continuously work on the relationship. I took it for granted that Clare always came to my races and was willing to bend her own vacation desires to my race schedule.

Training for an Iron distance race opened up a whole new world of experiences. I had to learn a new skill set and training philosophy to make the step from a two-hour International distance race to a 10-hour plus Iron distance race. A linear jump in race distance didn't correspond to a linear jump in race time. I couldn't swim, bike or run at the same intensity as I could at the shorter distances. No longer could I rely just on my fitness and determination to gut through a two-hour race, I had to plan and think more about things like pacing, nutrition and hydration.

Being neighbors of similar abilities and training for the same races made Phil and me ideal training partners, especially training for something as difficult and time-consuming as an Iron distance race. Living next to each other also made it extremely convenient to meet for workouts. We used to joke that during Ironman Canada training we saw more of each other than we did of our spouses. From the perspective of our spouses, this was probably true.

At Phil's suggestion, I purchased and read *SERIOUS Training for Endurance Athletes*[4] by Rob Sleamaker and Ray Browning. This book was my introduction to training with a heart rate monitor and structuring specific workouts geared toward specific purposes at specific times. The SERIOUS methodology dictated different types of workouts dependent on factors such as the distance of the race, how many weeks before the race and the current fitness level and goals of the individual training for the race. SERIOUS was an acronym for the different varieties of workout types: Speed, Endurance, Race-pace, Intervals, Overdistance, Up-hill Intervals, and Strength.

Phil also bought a customized six-month training schedule designed by the SERIOUS authors. The Iron-specific plan provided structured workouts targeted to specific heart rate zones and structured for specific purposes. Phil and I were in similar shape, so we shared his training plan although I made age adjusted modifications to his heart rate zones by adding five beats to his designated ranges. In general, there were three to four sessions of each exercise discipline (swim, bike and run) per week with one of each being a long workout, one a speed session and one a higher intensity tempo workout. In addition, there were key long workouts designated at specific weeks.

Beginning in March, Phil and I slowly increased our exercise frequency, duration and intensity leading up to the race at the end of August.

Having a structured Iron distance-specific training plan created by knowledgeable and established triathlon coaches plus training with an experienced athlete like Phil, greatly reduced my pre-race anxiety and apprehension toward Canada. Phil and I both felt that if we stuck to the training plan, we would have successful races. Perhaps due to our anxiety and dependency on the training plan, Phil and I were religious about our adherence to the plan.

One of us at the end of a run: "We're three minutes shy of sixty minutes for our run."

The other one: "Let's run around the neighborhood for three more minutes."

So, we ran around the neighborhood three more minutes.

In reality, the extra three minutes probably didn't make any difference, but we ingrained in our minds a need to follow the schedule to the minute.
Training for Ironman Canada created many "firsts" for me:

1. It was the first time that I biked from Reston to the end of the W&OD trail in Purcellville.

2. It was the first time that I raced in a Half-Iron distance race.

3. It was the first time that I swam in open water for more than an hour.

4. It was the first time that I followed a structured and detailed training plan.

It was also the first time that I bonked.

When Phil and I exchanged emails years later, he mentioned my first "bonking" episode during one of our key long brick workouts leading up to Ironman Canada.

The workout was a 60-mile bike ride followed by a 12-mile run. Unfortunately for me, I didn't listen to Phil's advice about hydration and pacing that day:

On a hot early summer day, Phil and I left for our 60-mile bike ride from the nearby Herndon Community Center. We left from the community center because it was adjacent to the W&OD Trail. We rode strong since we were well conditioned from four months of training. I only had two water bottle cages attached to my bike frame so I carried two bottles. With only two cages for a three-plus-hour ride on a hot day, I had to ration my water; consequently, I was dehydrated at the start of the run.

In order to ensure that we met the "letter" rather than just the "intent" of the SERIOUS plan workout, we also ran on the W&OD trail, which is clearly marked in one-mile increments. It was hot out and the trail was crowded with cyclists, runners and walkers.

At the start of the run, I felt light on my feet and went out fast, averaging six and a half minutes per mile which is a hard effort for me but not quite race pace. I quickly learned that running a sub-six minute mile with fresh legs in a 10-kilometer road race early in the cool morning is much easier than trying to run sub-six minute miles after biking for three plus hours during the dog days of summer.

At the start of the run, Phil softly suggested that I slow down and pace myself, but I felt good, and I was stubborn so I ignored him and ran ahead.

During the bike ride, I had ingested two energy gel packets and now carried only one additional gel on the run plus a bottle of water. I quickly sucked my water bottle empty in the first few miles. There was no place to refill my bottle. I held my pace.

After four or five miles, my pace began to slow and become uneven, as my legs felt heavier and my body overheated. At the six-mile turn around point, Phil caught me then passed me. He was maintaining his steady, even pace, looking relaxed and effortless as he glided along.

I tried to keep pace with Phil, but he slowly pulled away still running his steady pace as I slowed down even more. As much as I wanted to will my body forward more quickly, it wouldn't respond. My perception slowly became fuzzy and uncertain as I transitioned into what I now call "survival mode." If I were ever to have a near out-of-body experience, this was the feeling I think I would have. My goal became simply to keep moving forward in order to finish. Pace no longer mattered.

Phil patiently waited for me at a street crossing and then filled my water bottle for me at a convenience store while I stood there dumbly. I thanked him then turned back to the task at hand: getting back to the car.

A few minutes later, Phil was out of sight ahead of me again. A friend on a bike passed me going the opposite direction, calling out, "Hi, David!" I struggled to connect a name with the face and could only weakly wave back. My sole focus was to make my feet keep moving as I stared down at the broken line dividing the trail in half.

I withdrew into myself, oblivious to everything and everyone else. I stopped to walk a few times especially on the hillier sections. When I arrived back at the car, I realized that I had nothing left to eat or drink post workout. Phil shared some of his energy drink, but it was not enough to make up for the calories and fluids my body needed. Somehow I managed to drive home safely although I hesitate to think what a police officer would have thought if he pulled me over. I imagined that my drive was what a drunk driver experiences behind the wheel. I would have failed a "walk a straight line" test.

After my experience that day, I mounted two more water bottle cages on the back of my saddle.

From my simple, non-scientific perspective, bonking means that my body, which uses primarily glycogen (carbohydrates) as fuel for endurance exercise, ran out of fuel.

In hindsight, I should have paced myself better from the start, backing off the pace as needed and taken in more fluid and calories. These *Pacing, nutrition and hydration are critical factors in longer distance races.* were all things that were suggested to me ahead of time. I thought lightly of Phil's recommendation to carry more water and wrongly assumed that two bottles would be enough. Having never experienced bonking, I needed to learn its early signs and consequences. I also learned that pacing, nutrition and hydration are critical factors in longer distance races.

I think the lesson I learned from the experience was well worth the distress that I caused my body in the short term. Unfortunately, the pacing part of the lesson during the run did not sink in when I raced a few months later in Canada.

***

Iron distance training takes time. From March through August, it pretty much consumed my life outside of my job. My weekends were spent training as they provided the only time to get in large workout blocks. Clare and I didn't go on any vacations during this period, nor did I do anything with my family. I didn't feel I had, nor did I make the time.

The upside of all the exercise was that I slept like a baby at night. I was usually out by 9:00 p.m. or 10:00 p.m. at the latest. My mornings typically started before 6:00 a.m. I would wake up and walk then feed Toby before heading out to meet Phil for a run or a swim. I liked working out in the mornings because I felt I had accomplished something before work, plus I didn't have to stress about unforeseen events like last minute meetings getting in the way of my workouts.

Time became a luxury. I nearly stopped watching television altogether in the evening because I just didn't have time. When co-workers congregated at the water cooler to talk about the previous night's "Friends" episode, I could only listen. Consequently, I felt like an outsider to many of my co-workers unless they also happened to be the one or two percent like me who were engaged in a very active lifestyle.

***

The Ironman Canada bike course was known for two long, steep climbs: Richter Pass and Yellow Lake. In my first two years of triathlon training, I did most of my bike riding on the relatively flat W&OD trail and Reston roads. We needed to find a place to ride that would mimic the climbs in Canada.

Phil and I drove west to Marshall, Virginia to start a 56-mile ride that we called the "Marshall Loop." The official name for the ride is the "Blue Ridger" as described in a book called *Chuck & Gail's Favorite Bike Rides*. After an hour of rolling flats, we started together at the base of the first big climb from the tiny town of Bluemont to the top of Mount Weather. A few minutes later, I could only watch as Phil slowly rode away, and I struggled to keep him in sight. Sometimes, I wouldn't see him until a half hour later on the other side of a mountain where he was patiently waiting for me. In spite of all my effort and willpower, I just couldn't keep up with him on long climbs. Being dropped was a humbling lesson and a clear indicator of an opportunity for me to improve my cycling fitness. Phil had a tremendous advantage because he had been riding consistently for years. This was a muscular adaptation advantage that I would realize years later as well.

Unlike biking where Phil clearly dominated over me on the hills, we were much more evenly matched in running and swimming ability, although I usually managed to sneak a few seconds on him during a 10-mile running race. Neither of us loved swimming, but we swam because we had to. It was a good upper body exercise to complement the fitness and strength that running and cycling provided our legs.

I swam with the local master's swim team (Reston Masters) on Tuesdays, Thursdays and Saturdays then ran with the local running club (Reston Runners) on Sunday mornings. Meeting a group for a specific workout helped motivate me to get to the pool or to the run. I knew that I would have friends there to push me as well as to socialize with (which I discovered that I enjoyed, despite my earlier distaste for socializing at the gym). Peer pressure is a good motivator to finish a workout.

Phil introduced me to many of the other long-time triathletes in the area, many who would train with me at different times and different distances over the years as we pursued similar goals. As I began swimming and running with other athletes, we became friends and training partners. Having a support group helped me. Like the Academy, I found myself surrounded by like-minded athletes with similar interests and abilities. Even though I was doing much of my training with Phil, I now had other friends to train with if needed.

According to Phil's training schedule, we needed to do a Half-Iron distance race about 12 weeks before Canada. The timing of the Eagleman Half-Iron distance triathlon in Cambridge, Maryland, in early June (now called the Eagleman Ironman 70.3®), mapped to our prescribed training plan perfectly. This was my first Half-Iron distance race. I was nervous since it meant doubling the International distance that I had been racing. I expected to finish in around four and a half hours versus two plus hours in an International distance race.

At the time, Eagleman hosted about 600 athletes, as compared to today when the race signs up more than 1,800. To date, this was my longest race and largest field of competitors. The course preview slideshow on Saturday showed a choppy swim in the appropriately named Choptank River, a completely flat bike course through the Blackwater Wildlife Refuge and a flat out and back run through neighborhoods and on lightly traveled, rural roads.

Racing at Eagleman, I had a decent swim, decent bike and a strong run, as I maintained a surprisingly strong average pace of 6:30 minutes per mile over the 13.1 miles of flat, hot asphalt.

In preparation for the distance and long climbs of the 112-mile bike course at Canada, Phil and I rode a century (100 miles) on Skyline Drive riding south from the northern entrance to Shenandoah National Park. Skyline Drive starts in the valley and runs along the ridgeline of the Shenandoah Mountains. The first section of road climbs up from the park entrance for six miles of pure climbing; the remainder of the Drive is either up or down with few flat sections. The climbs are not exceptionally steep, but they are exceptionally long. As a general rule of thumb for an out and back ride on Skyline Drive, we climbed 1,000 feet of vertical for every 10 miles of riding.

After six hours and 10,000 feet of vertical climbing, we had biked 100 miles. I rewarded myself by stopping at a nearby convenience store for a soda and a bag of salt & vinegar potato chips. I craved the fat and salt from the chips, which became my post long-ride staple, especially after long, difficult rides. Training and racing are the only times I drank soda. The caffeine and sugar provide quick energy during and after races and training rides. Later at home, I dozed off from exhaustion while soaking in the tub.

Ironman Canada

After six months of strict training and preparation, Phil and I were as prepared for Canada as we could expect to be. Phil had backed off of running prior to the race, so his running fitness was in question. Otherwise, we both felt ready but nervous.

Clare and I flew to Seattle where we met my mom before driving across Washington state and up to Penticton, British Columbia.

I was very much on edge in the few days leading up to the race. Having my mom along created some extra stress, as she was one more thing I had to worry about. When we met at the airport, she had brought along a bike rack for the back of the car. We couldn't figure out how to make it work, so we ended up throwing away the rack and upgrading the car to an SUV into which we could fit the bike case and the three of us.

When we arrived in Penticton a few days before the race, the entire town seemed to be taken over by the race. Athletes and their families were everywhere and the athletes were easily recognizable by their race t-shirts, fit physiques, shaved legs and race wristbands. I didn't yet have an Iron distance race t-shirt to wear, so I wore my Eagleman t-shirt. Signs at local restaurants and stores welcomed participants with pasta dinners and official Ironman merchandise. The surrounding community provided more than 4,000 volunteers, almost three times the number of race participants. Phil and I had signed up for the race almost a year in advance because of the high demand for race slots in a race known for the beauty of its course and its friendly, small town appeal. Ironman Canada was also one of the few Iron distance races in North America.

Clare, my mom and I stayed in the southern side of the town several miles from the swim start. The three of us shared a single hotel room, which was a mistake, since I desperately needed more privacy and quiet time.

The day before the race, Phil and I swam in the lake in our sleeveless long john wetsuits. After 15 minutes of swimming, we were still shivering and unable to generate and retain enough heat to stay warm. We immediately marched over to the expo where we each spent $300 for brand new full sleeve wetsuits to the chagrin of our spouses. I didn't really care what Clare thought at the time, I was about to do an Iron distance race and I needed the wetsuit. Back in the lake, I swam in comfort. I now owned two wetsuits—a long sleeve and a sleeveless.

This was my big race. I had prepared six months for the day, but my head was full of questions, worries and self-doubts:

Have I trained enough?

What if I have a flat tire?

Where should I seed myself in the swim?

How often and how much should I eat on the bike?

What kind of pace should I try to hold on the run?

Racing at this distance was new to me so I had no basis of comparison. I only had my training experience, my book knowledge and Phil's advice to guide me. In some ways, though, being new to this distance removed some of the pressure I normally felt while racing. My ultimate goal was simply to finish, but in the back of my mind I wanted to finish in less than 10 hours, which seemed achievable on paper when I looked at each of the three events individually.

The first decision I made that morning was what to wear during the race. I opted to change outfits between events. I would wear a Speedo® during the swim under my wetsuit; change into bike shorts and a short sleeve bike jersey for the bike leg; then switch to running shorts and a tank top for the run. Although I was dressing for maximum comfort, I would waste an extra five or six minutes in the transition area.

The swim had a mass start of 1,600 swimmers in mostly black neoprene wetsuits. There were a few who braved the cold water and raced without a wetsuit. I seeded myself about a third of the way back from the front, not quite sure where to place myself and feeling extremely nervous with the massive number of bodies surrounding me. I engaged in small talk with a number of people as we frequently glanced down at our watches trying to anticipate the start.

"Athletes, you have one minute." said the announcer.

"Athletes, you now have 30 seconds."

"Ten." This time many of the athletes joined in.

"Nine."

"Eight."

"Seven."

"Six."

"Five."

"Four."

"Three."

"Two."

"One."

Boom! Complete pandemonium! Arms and legs were thrashing against me at every angle. I swam over others and was swum over by others. After a few minutes, I managed to find my own space within a small pack of swimmers, but we frequently bumped against each other and swam over each other as we fought for forward progress toward the next buoy.

My worries and fears were soon forgotten. I was in motion and there was no turning back.

After what seemed like forever, I climbed out of the water with help from volunteers. I was a little dizzy when I stood up, and I jogged to the transition tent to change into dry clothes before beginning the bike leg. I came out of the water at a peak exit time and was surrounded by many other people in the changing tent as I jockeyed for an empty chair to sit in. I dumped my transition bag in front of me as I dried off then exchanged swim gear for bike gear as volunteers stuffed my wet swim gear into my transition bag for me.

The start of the bike leg was congested with riders in front of and behind me. I didn't use a bike computer, so I didn't know my exact speed. I felt like I was working reasonably hard but maintained control of my pace.

The roads were narrow in the first 10 miles with quite a few turns. A woman yelled at me to move over as she screamed by on her bike and was soon out of sight. "A little rude." I thought.

At one point, I glanced down to see a nice pair of Oakley sunglasses lying on the road. I considered stopping to pick them up, but opted to keep riding. I was here to finish an Ironman.

The crowd of riders started to thin out over the long, single-loop course, but I always had others within sight.

The big climb up to Richter Pass was long and steep as expected, but I felt mentally and physically prepared. I slowly and patiently grinded my way up to the top of the pass.

By the time I reached Yellow Lake, the second big climb, things started to change. My pace dropped considerably, and my legs were tired. My body felt depleted and powerless. I was "cooked." I made the climb slowly, only watching as other riders went by.

Thankfully, the last section of the ride into town was mostly downhill, so I was able to eat and recover my legs somewhat before starting the run. As I entered the transition area, I thankfully and happily handed my bike to a volunteer who returned it to its spot on the bike racks.

I felt confident that I could run the marathon distance. I felt ecstatic to be off the bike and felt much better once I landed on my feet. "I'm two-thirds finished." I optimistically thought so I started running fast. I ran at a 6:30 minute per mile pace which would have put me well under a three-hour marathon. I failed to consider that my best standalone marathon time was 3:14, which meant that

I was running a much faster pace after having just swum 2.4 miles and biked 112 miles. I was stubbornly over confident.

I distinctly remember hearing spectators commenting at the start of my run:

"Look at him go!"

"He's flying!"

I soaked in the glory and the recognition, but I also overheard quieter comments like:

"He's going out way too fast. He'll never hold that pace."

I chose to ignore those comments. I felt invincible…at least in the beginning.

The cheering crowd was euphoric, and I ran the first six miles in under 40 minutes. I felt powerful as I passed many athletes to move into the top 50 overall. I was riding a wave of exhilaration.

At around the eight-mile marker, my pace began to slow and the exhilaration drifted away. The crowds thinned and the energy from the spectators faded as well. I began to feel light-headed and unsteady. My pace per mile dropped to seven-minute then eight minute then nine-minute miles. Maybe I was not taking in enough calories or fluids? Or, maybe I just started out too fast? Perhaps it was a little of both.

I began to panic inside as I recognized the same symptoms that I had experienced during my bonking episode a few months before.

I stopped passing other runners and began to get passed. I felt more miserable and slowed down even more. I started walking through the aid stations. My goal shifted from finishing in under 10 hours to simply finishing. I no longer cared about time or finishing place. I simply wanted the discomfort to end.

I gave up more than 50 finishing positions during my meltdown.

Toward the end of the run, I felt better and was able to pick up my pace. I broke the finish line tape in 10 hours and 14 minutes.

I was an Ironman!

Volunteers handed me the finisher's t-shirt and medal to prove it.

I cannot accurately describe my first time feelings of crossing the finish line and breaking the tape after 10 plus hours of racing and burning through more than an estimated 10,000 calories. I had dedicated six months of my life to that moment and it was euphoric. The feeling became an addictive high—my cocaine—and I would seek it out again and again.

After finishing a solid race as well, Phil spent the next six hours in the medical tent receiving four bags of intravenous saline solution, which made his legs swell up like tree trunks. I think he may have set a record for the most IVs received by an athlete at the race ever. He didn't leave his hotel room for the next two days.

The day after the race, my entire body hurt. My neck and shoulders were tight, and I had a burn on the back of my neck from the Velcro on my wetsuit. Walking down stairs was the most uncomfortable, as my quadriceps in the front of my thighs screamed in pain and quivered as I bore down on them with my body weight. But the pain was sweet because I was no longer just a triathlete, but an Ironman.

By the end of the week, I'd forgotten about the discomfort and suffering I'd experienced on the bike and the run. I only remembered the feelings of euphoria at the finish line. I wanted to feel that euphoria again. I also wanted another Iron distance finisher's medal that I could display on the wall.

Through a friend, I heard about another Iron distance race in Clermont, Florida in October. My excitement ignited after he showed me a home video from the race. I immediately signed up for the Great Floridian.

It was around this time that I switched jobs. I was bored with my job at Lockheed. I was frustrated by my lack of upward mobility, and I didn't feel like I was taking away a sense of self-accomplishment. Perhaps I was looking for the same satisfaction that I felt after finishing a triathlon.

I made a lateral move to another government contractor, Harris Corporation, on a contract that supported the same customer I worked for with Lockheed.

When I moved to Harris, I operated and maintained a remote government communications system that provided important intelligence to senior government leadership. I felt that my contribution was making a positive, tangible impact and that I played a role in troubleshooting and problemsolving to ensure that the system functioned properly. I was again on a time card, but because of the nature of the system, I sometimes had to come back to work late in the evening to make sure that the system functioned properly. I didn't mind this much since I lived five minutes away from work, but I had to schedule my workouts around the new time commitment.

Great Floridian

I wanted to relive the euphoria I experienced in Canada. With six months of Iron distance training under my belt, I figured that my fitness had prepared me for another ultra race with minimal upkeep.

From having lived six months in Orlando, Florida while a student at Nuclear Power School, my perception of Florida was that it was flat as a pancake. There were no hills that I could recall.

When I signed up to race the Great Floridian Triathlon in October, my expectation was that the bike and run courses would be flat since Clermont, where the race was held, was only a short drive west of Orlando. I was wrong.

The Great Floridian course was hilly. Not the few, long, steady hills like Richter Pass at Ironman Canada, but rather many short, steep hills and tight turns. Where the course was not hilly, it was windy and flat.

My training approach to Ironman Canada was defined for varying levels of intensity and duration down to the minute, and I had a training partner for my workouts. When I prepared for the Great Floridian, I trained mainly by myself and followed the Canada training schedule.

Because of near-sightedness I wore contact lenses, so I wore sunglasses to both shield my eyes from the wind and keep the lenses in my eyes. Occasionally during training rides, even with sunglasses, a lens would blow out of my eye. But, I had never lost both lenses at the same time.

Only 10 miles into the bike leg in Florida, my contact lens lifted out of my left eye and landed on my cheek. I managed to place it in my mouth to keep it moist while I keep riding. I soon lost track of it in my mouth as it likely fell out or I swallowed it.

Forty miles later my second lens blew out, and my world became a blur. I couldn't read the road signs until I was almost on top of them, nor could I see anyone ahead or behind me. I was alone in my own little world of me, my bike and the blurry landscape around me. I rode in fear that I would miss a turn and never realize I had missed it until I was miles off course. I was riding near the front of the race where the riders were thinned out so there was no one else in sight for much of the time. I forced myself not to panic, praying that I was still following the course.

I spent the next three hours in uncertainty, except for occasionally passing another athlete or making a turn. About 90 miles into the course, I heard my family cheering "Go David!" as I approached a sharp left turn. I quickly looked up in the direction of their voices and shapes then down again as I entered the turn. Too late! I saw the sand under my wheels as I made the turn. My bike slipped out to the right, and I skidded across the hot, gritty pavement and landed on my left side.

The entire left side of my body was scraped up from the road and my aero bars were tilted at awkward angles. I got up quickly and surveyed my body for anything broken or bleeding excessively. Fortunately, I only had bad road rash. My dad and a couple of volunteers quickly ran over to help me straighten out my aero bars, and I climbed back on my bike. As I rode away, I squirted water from my bottle to rinse off the gravel and blood. I wanted to finish.

I finally pulled into the transition area where I kept a spare lens and quickly regrouped. I remembered the mistake I made by starting the run too quickly at Ironman Canada, so I paced myself more conservatively. I was already exhausted from the bike though and ached from the fall, so I slowed down rapidly and lost minutes through each aid station where I walked.

As I raced, I slowly realized that the desire for more finish line euphoria was not enough to bring me to a faster time goal. I needed proper preparation and execution, plus my body, still new to this distance, had not fully acclimatized to the training and racing demands of the Iron distance. I needed more rest between races, and I needed the right frame of mind to mentally overcome the suffering and discomfort of a 140.6-mile race. I still believed that finishing in less than 10 hours was attainable for me on paper, but it would not come that year.

When I crossed the finish line at Great Floridian, my finish time was half an hour slower than my finish time in Canada two months earlier.

A few months after the race, I paid $5,000 out of my savings for laser surgery to correct my eyesight. Losing my vision during the race scared me. I didn't consult Clare on this decision and the money spent became another source of friction between us.

I had one more significant adventure in 1997 when my body served up an unexpected problem that almost turned deadly the following month. While riding on a warm, sunny Veterans Day, I discovered that I was dangerously allergic to wasps and hornets. This is how it unfolded:

> Veterans Day fell on a Wednesday this year, and I had the day off from work, so I went for a ride in the unseasonably warm November weather. I headed west on the W&OD bike trail in the late morning, turning around in Leesburg after about an hour of riding. Ten minutes later, I felt a sharp, stabbing pain on my right hand.
>
> "Damn!" I said out loud.
>
> A hornet, which was caught between my cycling glove and my thumb, stung me. I shook the hornet off and kept riding. My hand screamed in pain, but I put on my "tough guy" face and shrugged off the discomfort. I had been stung many times in the past while growing up and most recently on the chest less than two months ago during the Reston Triathlon when a bee flew down my jersey. I had never had any problems other than a slight rash for a few weeks afterward.
>
> My hand continued to throb painfully. I kept riding.
>
> I began to feel a little lightheaded and my arms began to itch. Then my whole body began to itch. I looked down and saw hives spreading up and down my arms and legs. Now I was worried as I continued my ride home. I wondered if I was having a bad

reaction. I finally decided that yes, I was having a reaction and needed to find medical help.

I flagged down another cyclist on the trail and told him about my situation, asking him if he knew where the nearest hospital was.

"There's a fire station in Herndon not far off the trail. It's about a 10-minute ride from here," he replied.

He rode with me as we headed toward Herndon.

The hives quickly spread over my entire body. I wondered if I would make it in time. Once we arrived at the fire station, I quickly dropped my bike on the grass and dashed inside.

The room was empty. Something was very, very wrong with this scene. I was in a fire station alone. At that moment, I was again faced with my own mortality and a sense of helplessness that my life was now outside of my control.

My vision blurred and my throat began to itch. I knew that it was going to close. I grabbed the nearest phone and frantically dialed 911.

"I have been stung by a bee, and I think I'm having an allergic reaction. There's no one here in the fire station!" I screamed at the woman on the other line.

"Please, hold on, let me page them." she calmly replied.

She paged the firefighters as I wondered if I would die. Unlike the cancer, this happened extremely fast, and I had difficulty assessing my situation.

Luckily for me, the firefighters were behind the station conducting training exercises and quickly rushed into the room when they received the page. The paramedic immediately gave me a shot of epinephrine (adrenaline) to stop the swelling and prevent my throat from swelling shut. My blood pressure was unreadable at first then read 80 over 50 on the second try. The paramedic hooked me up to an intravenous saline drip and administered Benadryl through the IV. My swelling and hives retracted as my blood pressure slowly rose. I drifted in and out of consciousness from the Benadryl before falling asleep. I spent the rest of the afternoon in the emergency room.

Subsequent testing showed that I was allergic to wasps, yellow jackets, white-faced hornets and yellow-faced hornets, basically everything but honey bees. Doctors told me the allergy may or may not disappear over time.

I could not control the allergic reaction, but I took steps to mitigate future incidents. I began carrying a cell phone, Benadryl and an Epi-pen (self-administered shot of epinephrine) with me wherever I went, but especially when cycling, when I always seemed to get stung the most. I also cycled with my jersey zipped, so that I didn't accidentally scoop up and trap a hornet against my bare skin. I eventually began taking anti-venom shots with the hope that if I was stung, I would only have a localized reaction. So far, so good, as subsequent stings have only resulted in minor local reactions.

In my third year of triathlons, I achieved a new milestone—I had made the jump to the Half-Iron then Iron distance. Racing at the Iron distance provided an incredible feeling of accomplishment and self-satisfaction that I didn't feel in other parts of my life like my relationship or my job.

From a commitment perspective, I put in much more training time than the previous two years, but since I was surrounded by like-minded training partners with similar goals, I didn't think that my commitment to training was unusual. When I talked to family, friends and co-workers outside of the triathlon circle, many couldn't comprehend the training and the distances.

"What did you do this weekend?" asked a co-worker.

"I swam for an hour then biked five hours on Saturday. On Sunday, I ran for two hours."

"Wow! I was happy to make it to the gym on Saturday afternoon." she replied.

© George Chambers

"The next goal I had in sight was to go sub-nine hours. It would take me a few more years to achieve that goal."

Chapter 6: A Turning Point

When I finished my Master's degree in the spring of 1998, I was happy that each class returned six-hour blocks of time during the week that I could then use for exercise. I didn't bother to attend graduation. My classes were held off campus in a hotel conference room, so I didn't feel any real ties to the university.

After Ironman Canada, Phil decided not to do any more Iron distance races because of his experience in the medical tent, so I lost my coach and training partner. Phil was the ideal partner because we were similar in ability, and we lived next door to each other. I continued to run with the Reston Runners and swim with the Reston Masters, so I had other friends to train with but not at the same level of convenience that I had with Phil.

Encouraged by my self-proclaimed potential as an ultra-distance triathlete, I hired a professional triathlon coach to work with me one-on-one.

I first met my coach, Troy Jacobson, at the triathlon clinic I attended at the Maryland bike store in 1995. He spoke about training for endurance events. Troy's name stuck in my memory, and I remembered that he provided a coaching service.

Troy became my coach in June of 1998. I wanted coaching for a full year to learn how to plan a racing calendar year and how to determine the best time for aerobic base training, tapering and recovery in the off-season, each of which I knew had specific purposes to stimulate optimal performance on race day.

From Troy, I learned how to apply more structure and consistency to my workouts without being a complete slave to my schedule. His rule of thumb was that I should complete 80 percent of my prescribed workouts. He had me periodically measure my progress with specific fitness workouts, such as a three-mile hard tempo run on a track, which measured my current fitness level and gave me my anaerobic threshold heart rate. I also learned how to optimally plan out a schedule of races, so I wouldn't compromise my performance by racing triathlons too close together. Most importantly, I gained the confidence and experience to back off my training volume significantly when tapering even though it made me feel like I was losing fitness.

I switched jobs again in 1998. After a year with Harris, I became bored. I was working in an operational role that became repetitive and routine. Every day seemed like the last. Because Harris had a limited presence in Virginia, my only other option with the company was to move to Melbourne, Florida, where Harris was headquartered. This idea didn't appeal to me.

My manager at the time was based in Melbourne. I had gone through four managers during my one-year tenure, and my small team was shuffled within the larger organization. The final straw was when I met my boss for the first time in person, and he gave me my annual review. He said I had done an excellent job and that I would receive a three percent raise. When I asked him how he came up with the raise amount, he said it was pre-determined when I first joined the company a year ago.

I responded, "I'm putting in full work days, plus I'm required to come into work every other night, and I've received excellent feedback from our customer. After all of my hard work, three percent doesn't seem fair." I went on to say that I was exploring other options outside of Harris.

Not surprisingly, he immediately offered back, "How much would it take for you to stay?" I felt cheated and disappointed. If I would have said nothing, I would have walked away with a three percent raise. Because I said that I might leave, he was willing to throw in more money to make me stay. I decided it was time to look for other opportunities.

During my year at Harris, I became good friends with one of the government customers I worked with. He left the government to join EDS (Electronic Data Systems) on a government contract to be a systems integrator. After speaking with my friend and researching EDS, it seemed like a good career move to follow him. My Top Secret clearance could get me in the door. At EDS, I could also move around in the company more easily since they had a much larger presence in the metropolitan D.C. area. I figured that my career opportunities would be more abundant. Plus, EDS was primarily commercial, so I could make the transition out of the government sector at some point in the future as well.

With my friend's referral, I interviewed with EDS and was offered a job supporting a large IT integration project in Reston. I took the job.

Vineman®

"Cancer is my secret because none of my rivals has been that close to death and it makes you look at the world in a different light and that is a huge advantage."
- Lance Armstrong

I can relate to what Lance says. Cancer made me look at life differently, too. I also needed to prove that I had beaten it. Success at triathlon was the proof. I had lost Phil as my primary training partner, but other friends had also made the jump to the Iron distance, so were able to fill the vacancy. During longer bike and run workouts was when I needed friends for support. My typical routine was to swim with the Reston Masters from 7:00 a.m. to 8:00 a.m. on Saturdays at the Reston Community Center then leave for a long bike ride from the Community Center Parking lot. The route was to ride on the W&OD trail out to less populated areas where we could then bike on lightly traveled roads. On a typical Saturday, we would start with eight to ten riders who rode for varying distances and just turned around when they felt like it. I could almost always find someone to ride with me for distances of 80 to 100 miles.

For my long runs, I ran with the Reston Runners on their regularly scheduled 10-mile Sunday runs and either met friends before the run start or stayed later in order to get in the extra training miles.

When I completed my first two Iron distance races at Ironman Canada and the Great Floridian Triathlon, I felt that I was leaving time on the table because of poor race execution and pacing. I believed I could pull off a sub 10-hour Iron distance race. In my mind, 10 hours was the mark separating a good triathlete from a great triathlete. I wanted to prove to myself and others that I could achieve that mark.

I first heard about Vineman, an Iron distance event in Santa Rosa, California, through an online discussion forum. The race name stuck in my mind as one of my "must do" races. Vineman was one of the original Iron distance races in the U.S. and was well known on the West Coast, primarily attracting a West Coast field of athletes.

At the time, Vineman was an Ironman World Championship qualifier and there were two qualifying slots in my age group. Unlike most races, you can't just sign up to race in Hawaii, but there are several ways to get into the race. The first option is to be one of the top male or female finishers from the prior year at the Ironman World Championship. The second option is to enter through the Ironman lottery. Lottery participants pay a fee to enter a pool then a few are randomly selected to participate. The odds are against entry this way given the large number of applicants. The third option is to be a celebrity and be invited. Famous participants have included pro football players and actors. The final and most common option is to earn a slot at a Hawaii qualifying race. Most of the 1,500 entry slots into Hawaii are obtained this way.

Qualifying races are Iron distance and Half-Iron distance races that are allocated a number of qualifying slots depending on the race distance and size. Slots are distributed among the five-year age groups such that each age group receives at least one slot. In the case of races with fewer slots than number of age groups, a single slot might be shared amongst multiple adjacent age groups. The remaining slots are allocated proportionally to the number of participants. Typically, the Men's 30-34 and 35-39 age groups contribute the most participants, so they receive the most slots.

A few weeks before Vineman, I had a brief conversation with a fellow triathlete and Ironman World Championship finisher. If I finished in the top two in my age group, I could pick up a qualifying slot to race in Hawaii in October. My friend asked if I was going to try to get a slot.

I shrugged and replied, "Based on last year's times at Vineman, I would have to finish in less than nine and a half hours in order to qualify for a slot. Even if I did qualify, I don't think I'm ready for Hawaii yet." In the back of my mind, less than nine and a half hours became my goal although I was reluctant to say it out loud.

On the morning of the race, temperatures were cool but were expected to warm up into the 80s during the afternoon. My approach to my race clothing was to minimize the amount I had to put on or take off. The more clothes I had to change in and out of, the more time it would take and the greater the likelihood that I would forget something. I had a jersey from Tri-Speed, Troy Jacobson's company, and some black tri shorts that I decided I would wear throughout the race.

We swam in the Russian River which was dammed during the summer, so the flow was marginal. The out and back made for an easily navigable course.

For the first time at that distance, I came out of the water in just under an hour. Finishing in under an hour became my benchmark for a good swim.

The bike route took us through the Russian River Valley and all around Sonoma County as we cycled past a never-ending line of California wineries. I was cool in my wet, sleeveless jersey for the first hour of the ride, but warmed up after that. Against conventional wisdom, I rode a new bike, a yellow Softride Powerwing®, that I received the week before the race after purchasing it over the Internet. I was nervous because I had been having problems with my shifters, and I spent an hour the day before the race trying to adjust them correctly. I still wasn't sure if they were aligned properly.

I rode steady and consistently spending much of the ride completely alone as I was near the front of the race. My biggest surprise came about three quarters of the way through the bike leg. It was then that I realized I was only five minutes behind the three leaders who were clustered near each other and leveraging each other for motivation. I had no one near me to motivate me or pace off of (I still wasn't using a bike computer), but now I had the three of them to chase down. The three looked at me and then looked at their watches as if they were calculating how far back I was and if I was strong enough to overtake them before the run. I could not close the gap.

When I arrived at the transition area, it was empty except for three bikes. I moved into as high as third place overall during the run when I caught up to one of the three who had beaten me off the bike. He said nothing to me as I pulled alongside, but picked up his pace to pull away. I maintained my steady pace as he moved ahead. A mile later he "blew up," and I passed him for good.

My mom and Clare were there watching me. They had both volunteered to work at one of the aid stations on the run handing out water and food to the athletes. According to Clare, my mom spent most of the time bragging to the other volunteers about her son instead of giving out water cups. She was clearly very proud of me.

Toward the turnaround of the second run loop, a 39-year-old runner from a wave that started five minutes after mine passed me rapidly. I could only watch him effortlessly fly as I dropped back to fourth place. Seeing his age in black letters on the back of his calf made me realize how many years I still had ahead of me to race, assuming I stayed healthy.

Near the end of the marathon, I conceded one more place. "Good job, guy! Keep it up! Don't worry, I'm not going to chase you down." I said to the guy who caught me. I had already blown away my own expectations for the race, and I wanted to give my respect to him for his effort in catching me. I let him go.

I crossed the finish line in 5th overall to finish in a time of 9:29. I had hit my goal and set a new personal record by 45 minutes! I also raised the bar on my own expectations for future races.

At the awards ceremony the next day, I received a wooden wine box with a bottle of Chardonnay for my second place age group finish. That was one of many that I would receive.

Great Floridian (Second Time)

I decided to sign up for the Great Floridian Triathlon for the second year in a row. I had an extra month to recover from Vineman as compared to the timing of Ironman Canada the previous year, so I set my expectations much higher.

The most common mistake that I see triathletes make, especially when preparing for an Iron *Tapering gives the body time to soak in and adapt to training.* distance race, is not tapering enough right before the event. I define tapering as backing off training volume in the days or weeks leading up to an event in order to allow the body to fully rest. Tapering gives the body time to soak in and adapt to training while maintaining a moderate level of fitness in order to "sharpen the sword" so to speak for race day.

I find it psychologically challenging to train at a high volume for a long period of time then suddenly back off to almost doing nothing. When I taper, I feel like I'm losing fitness because I am resting more and exercising less. Quite the opposite is true as I am gaining fitness from more rest and less exercise. It was Troy who convinced me that it's during rest periods and sleep that the beneficial physical adaptations to exercise occur. Looking back, I can honestly say that I have never done an Iron distance race and said to myself afterward, "I wish I had done more workouts in the last two weeks."

Surprisingly, I notice that many athletes don't reduce their training volume that much leading up to a race. I have friends who will ride half the distance of the bike course three days before the event. Yet, if they think the extra training helps them, there's not much I can say but, "Why not take it easy and see what happens?"

From my own experiences, tapering is *Tapering is just as much* just as much an art as it is a science. It *an art as it is a science.* is also highly individual. I am leery of one-size-fits-all tapering schedules. When tapering, I consider variables such as race distance, goals and my ability to recover from training. As a general rule, the longer the race, the longer the taper to allow for a more gradual reduction in training volume rather than a sudden last minute drop. Plus, my body needs ample time to recover from and adapt to the higher training volumes required of longer races.

My goals for a particular race drive the extent of my taper as well. If, for example, the race is a key race where I want to perform at my personal best, I will taper a full taper. For my less important "B" races, I may taper little or none at all in order to use the race as an intense workout on top of a training week to push myself beyond my comfort zone and induce more physical stress and eventual adaptation (with adequate rest of course). Surprisingly, I may still have strong results.

I have experimented with different tapering approaches with different results, but, as a starting point, I approach my tapering with guidelines based on the distance of the race. As an overarching theme to tapering, I have found that less exercise is usually best when tapering.

My taper for Great Floridian looked something like:

Weeks Out	Relative Training Volume (%)
4	100 peak
3	75
2	50
1	25

The irony of tapering is that I usually feel my worst while tapering even though I am working out less and sleeping more than before:

- I feel exhausted all of the time.
- My muscles are tired and sore.
- My motivation is low.

It is usually not until the tail end of the taper that I start to feel really, really good, which, of course, is when it matters the most!

As I approached the final week before Great Floridian, I put my newly formed race week routine into motion. I stayed off my feet and reduced stress as much as possible and just relaxed. With the reduced workout volume of my taper, I engaged in more leisurely activities like walking, reading or just watching movies to take my mind off the upcoming race.

Two days before the race I did an easy, short swim, bike and run to loosen up my muscles and keep the stiffness away. I also began ingesting more fluids. After years of racing, I now know that for me, ingesting sports drinks and carbohydrates is the best way to hydrate. At the time, I made the mistake of drinking only water at the Great Floridian, and I purchased a case of it the day before the race. I drank half the case by force, which caused me to urinate every 20 to 30 minutes.

I drove the bike course and walked though the transition areas, so there were no surprises on race day. This helped me relieve tension and also pass the time.

Check out the course before the race so there are no surprises.

Two nights before the race was my night to get as much sleep as possible; I usually have trouble sleeping the night before a race due to nervousness.

The day before the race was another rest day, I stayed off my feet as much as possible except for another easy swim, bike and run to keep my muscles loose and settle my nerves. I continued to hydrate, and I snacked on mostly carbohydrates throughout the day, eating in moderation and avoiding heavy, spicy or creamy foods that might upset my stomach or create other unpleasant side effects.

In my mind, I visualized each leg of the race in order to become comfortable with my race strategy and execution on the course.

As part of a fitness channel special for cable television, I was interviewed, along with two other athletes about coming back from challenging situations. One athlete had Multiple Sclerosis and the other was missing an arm. I was the cancer survivor. With the small camera crew asking me questions at the race site, I felt a brief taste of what being a celebrity is like (my 15 minutes of fame). I enjoyed both the attention and the opportunity to share my cancer story.

I went to bed early the night before the race, but woke up every 45 minutes to check the alarm clock and make sure that I hadn't overslept and missed the race start. It was a long, restless night.

The swim leg at the Great Floridian went well for me, but during the first half of the bike leg I could not stomach any solid foods or even gels. Every time I ate, whether it was a banana, a gel or a PowerBar®, I vomited a few minutes later. My guess as to what happened was that the excessive amounts of plain water that I drank the day before had flushed out all of the electrolytes in my system causing me to vomit and not absorb fluids during the race. I'm not sure how valid my theory is, but drinking fluids with electrolytes and carbohydrates makes sense to me from a practical perspective as a means to both hydrate and fuel the body.

As I rode, I contemplated whether or not I would even be able to finish the race, but my stomach finally settled about three quarters of the way through the bike course, and I slowly began eating again.

In the final 20 miles of the bike leg after the last aid station, I lost my only remaining water bottle when my bottle cage broke off the back of my seat. This forced me to ride the remainder of the course without fluids on a hot and humid day.

I raced a solid run, with a finishing time of 9:45, which was 16 minutes slower than Vineman. This solidified the thought that my first race of the season would be my strongest and that I should not set higher expectations on following races.

In spite of my slower time, I took third place overall to finish on the podium. I think I made the folks at the fitness channel happy too.

Immediately after Great Floridian, I started thinking about the next year. A new race, Ironman USA®, was opening up in Lake Placid, New York, which was in Adirondack State Park and was also the site of the 1932 and 1980 Winter Olympics. With a couple of friends (peer pressure plus potential training partners), I signed up for the inaugural race.

Another year had ended on a high note. In my mind, I had made a step up in the Iron distance world by finishing in less than 9:30. The next goal I had in sight was to go sub-nine hours. It would take me a few more years to achieve that goal.

My race results bolstered my confidence. I began to entertain ideas of turning pro and picking up sponsorship money, but I had no idea where to get sponsors. I laid out an aggressive schedule for 1999, which included three, Half-Iron distance races leading up to Ironman USA in July. My ultimate goal was to go sub-nine hours at Lake Placid and pick up a slot to the Ironman World Championship in October in Hawaii.

My move to EDS was my third job change since I left the Navy. I was a competitive person by nature, but was unable to satisfy my need to "win" or at least progress at work. My ambitions at work began to shift from promotion with a higher salary to maintaining the status quo to support my active lifestyle, which would give me the sense of accomplishment and self satisfaction that my ego craved. I didn't see myself climbing the corporate ladder at the expense of my active lifestyle.

Yet, at the same time, I found an unexpected ally within the company. I knew that EDS sponsored and employed a professional track cycling team in Plano, Texas. Working with a friend from the HR Department, I approached the business director of my organization with the idea of sponsoring me as a triathlete. The director had formerly been a professional football player until a hamstring injury forced him to retire very early in his career. He had subsequently picked up cycling. I went in to see him and asked for the world—a new triathlon bicycle, reimbursement for race entry and travel expenses and reimbursement for ongoing equipment expenses. He gave it all to me. I would be racing my 1999 season on a brand new Aegis Trident T2® triathlon bike painted in a patriot red, white and blue scheme with EDS logos and "www.eds.com" slapped on the side.

From a relationship perspective, I was pushing my marriage to the breaking point, and I was oblivious to the coming consequences. I had become even more selfish with my time and didn't bother to include Clare in my race scheduling. I just signed up for races that I wanted to do. I was hooked on the sport.

Chapter 7: More Change and Adjustment

In early 1999, my world dramatically imploded. Three and a half years of marriage were suddenly over and my life turned into a soap opera created by my own choices and decisions.

I think what bothered me the most was the reaction other people had to my and Clare's breakup. I noticed people throwing side-glances at me during Sunday runs or at the pool, and I knew that I was becoming a topic of gossip.

Yet, on the other hand, many friends and family members stepped in to show support.

"You're both good people. Things will work out. They always do."

"A few years from now, you'll be able to look back and realize that it was for the better."

Hindsight is always 20/20. From my perspective, marriage had become a chore. We no longer enjoyed spending time with each other. I found myself enjoying spending more time on my own or with workout friends than I did with my wife. There was too much tension in the air when we were together. Perhaps the obvious sign was that I made my choices a higher priority than our choices.

I also met a woman named Jennifer who was going through a breakup with her husband at the same time. We were introduced at a Spinning class that I taught at a local gym. I had always found her very attractive and was impressed by her hard work ethic in class and competitive streak. We quickly became friends, and I learned that we both worked for EDS. Everything clicked between us from the beginning. Being with Jen was exciting, and I wanted to spend time with her.

When my relationship with Clare fell apart, I moved out of our townhouse (leaving Toby with Clare) and quickly into a relationship with Jen. For a few weeks, I lived on an emotional adrenaline high. I suddenly became faster in the pool, biking on the road and running on the trail. I felt like I needed less sleep and began consuming copious amounts of wine. There was a two or three-week period when Jen and I shared a bottle of wine a night. Even when I did want to sleep, I couldn't sleep well because of the mix of caffeine, adrenaline and alcohol in my bloodstream. I stayed up late and lived life large for a short period of time.

My weight bumped up about 10 pounds to the high 170s for the first time in my life.

When I began my relationship with Jen, she knew that I was a triathlete and that exercise and fitness were important aspects of my life. Jen was an avid runner and gym rat. She had trained for and raced in the Marine Corps Marathon, so she better understood the time commitments involved with endurance sport training. We had a more complementary lifestyle.

My heightened state of living lasted for a few weeks before it finally caught up with me, and I reached a state of exhaustion. My workouts became slower as I went from record training times to laggard training times. I backed out of doing the Buffalo Springs Lake triathlon, a Half-Iron distance race held in Texas in June (now called the Buffalo Springs Lake 70.3®), but stayed committed to Ironman USA in August. I ignored the cumulative effects of stress from exercise and stress from my personal life. My body needed rest, but I wouldn't allow myself the luxury of less training. I was still foolishly chasing my sub-nine hour dream, when I should have realized that it was simply too much to tackle during this year of significant change and stress.

Although used somewhat interchangeably in the common vernacular, being "fit" and being "healthy" are two distinct conditions that don't necessarily coexist. Here are some definitions:

Health: Health is a state of complete physical, mental and social well being and not merely the absence of disease or infirmity.[5]

Fitness: The overall cardiovascular and musculoskeletal health of your body. Fitness consists of aerobic capacity, strength, core stability, flexibility and balance.[6]

The most notable difference is that health runs the gamut from physical to mental to social well being, whereas fitness is primarily physical.

Using myself as an example, I was very fit, but when I went through the stress of a break up, my health suffered even while I maintained my fitness. Eventually, my fitness suffered too since I was unable to balance the increased stress with less exercise and increased rest.

Staying healthy can be a challenge during a triathlon season that can stretch eight to ten months and introduce a significant amount of workout and time-related stress. Throwing in relationship or other personal stress fuels the fire even more. One of the greatest challenges I've found leading up to every Iron distance race is staying injury free, not overtraining and not becoming mentally exhausted or stressed. It took me a long time to realize that I had overcommitted myself to training and triathlon in light of everything else going on in my life. It wasn't until Ironman USA that this became clear.

***

Nineteen ninety-nine was the inaugural Ironman USA race. There's something sexy about racing the first race. In reality, I probably shouldn't have done it. My body was tired and I lacked the necessary desire to succeed at the event, yet I didn't want to admit this to myself. Backing out of the race late in the game would have been, in my mind, a sign of weakness that I wasn't willing to admit to. My ego overwhelmed my rational self and I raced.

Nearly 2,000 athletes and I massed behind the starting line at Mirror Lake in Lake Placid, a relatively small lake for the 2.4-mile swim. The athletes in the water and on the shore seemed to dwarf the surface area of the water. In addition to the buoys defining the perimeter of each loop, there were long cables running just beneath the surface on both the out and back legs, which allowed for easy sighting for the athletes swimming close to the buoys.

Even though the swim in an Iron distance race is long, it's only a small portion of the total event and not always a good indicator for the rest of the race. My swim was uneventful and my heart rate peaked as I climbed out of the lake to the transition area which was set up in the Olympic ice skating oval.

Like Ironman Canada, Ironman USA had a hilly bike course. As I had trained for the hilly Canada bike course, I also trained for Lake Placid on Skyline Drive and the Marshall Loop. Even so, I wasn't prepared for the challenging two-loop course. To make matters worse, I flatted on both loops. I was racing on tubular tires, which require a whole new tire to fix a flat, rather than a tube for clincher tires. I had two flats and only one spare. Luckily, the SAG wagon (bike support) was not too far away when I had my second flat and they were able to provide me with a new tubular. Because of the experience with flats on the tubulars (I also flatted earlier in the year at Eagleman), I subsequently switched to clincher tires, which enables me to carry multiple spare tubes in case of multiple flats.

I was 30 minutes slower on the second bike loop than on the first because my legs gave out and I was reduced to a seemingly slow crawl. My physical and mental fatigue compounded the frustration I felt after the two flats. I also likely miscalculated my calorie needs and essentially bonked. Lesson learned, eat more and pace myself better.

In my mind, I had already decided that I wouldn't go to Hawaii that year. I did not feel ready and didn't want to show up without having first conquered the sub-nine hour mark. I was still upset when I missed an Ironman Hawaii slot at Lake Placid by only two minutes. Only having one of the two flats could have bought me a ticket to the World Championship, and I would have been able to say, "Yeah, I got a slot, but I didn't take it."

***

With my newly gained weight, I toyed with the idea of racing as a "light" Clydesdale (180+ pounds) at a new Iron distance race in Ohio called Pineman, but I finally hit the wall of exhaustion. The stress and anxiety of the divorce finally caught up with me. I could no longer force myself to keep going at the pace of training that I needed for an Iron distance race. I had to back off from the all-consuming physical lifestyle for a while.

I became a casual athlete—swimming, biking and running as before but not on a schedule, nor for long distances. My body and my mind needed the rest. I fell out of my routine and stopped being a regular at Reston Masters and Reston Runners workouts.

Because I no longer wanted the structure of being coached nor had a race to focus on, I ended my coaching relationship with Troy. I had worked with him for a complete year and the benefits and knowledge I took away from that experience were well worth the cost, but I needed to step away from the schedule rigidity for a while.

In hindsight, this downtime of low volume, low frequency was healthy. True, I lost some of my peak racing fitness, but the fitness would come back in the spring.

1999 was extremely challenging on multiple levels. I began the year with high hopes of following up my breakthrough year in 1998 with even faster times, but life events interceded.

My personal life changed dramatically as I moved out of one relationship and into another. It became clear to me that other aspects of my life influenced my training

Sometimes stressful life events can compromise an athlete's health as he/she strives to maintain a high fitness level.

and ultimately my racing. From this experience, I recognized that in order to consistently perform at a high level, I would need to reduce outside stresses as much as possible. This experience also forced me to think about the effects of training and racing on other aspects of my life like relationships and my career.

On a positive note, I picked up a sponsor in EDS, my employer, which helped offset costs and allowed me to buy a new triathlon bicycle. Having this type of financial support in a relatively small sport was a luxury that not many triathletes experience.

"When I began racing at the Iron distance, I toyed with the idea of racing at every Iron distance race at least once. This was for no real reason other than it would be cool to say that I had done all of them."

Chapter 8: New Beginnings

"Without change, something sleeps inside us, and seldom awakens. The sleeper must awaken."
- *Frank Herbert, author of the Dune series.*

After spending the latter part of 1999 without focused training, I began to miss the long workouts and sweet feeling of exhaustion at the end of a long training day.

Over the winter, I maintained a nominal level of fitness. I ran sporadically with my running club and swam sporadically at the community center often by myself. I stopped swimming with the Reston Masters during the week because they swam late at night, which impacted my ability to fall asleep. I left practice feeling wired and wide-awake. There was a small fitness center at EDS, where I could exercise at work, and I continued to teach Spinning once a week.

My winter workouts were heavily influenced by the weather and the short amount of daylight. If there was snow on the ground or the temperature was excessively cold, I moved my cycling workouts indoors. I would ride a Lifecycle, teach Spinning or sit in on another instructor's class.

My winter workout routine in early 2000 looked something like:

Sunday:	Run 70 minutes
Monday:	Spinning class for 45 minutes
Tuesday:	Run 40 minutes on treadmill; lift weights for upper body
Wednesday:	Ride Lifecycle for 40 minutes; swim for 30 minutes
Thursday:	Lift weights for legs
Friday:	Off day
Saturday:	Swim for 60 minutes; Spinning class x 2 for 90 minutes

One of my most enduring memories early in the year was from a Relay for Life® fund raiser sponsored by the American Cancer Society. My friend, Bruce Black, who was a fellow triathlete, organized a group of us to participate in the relay on a Saturday night. The following is an account of the event:

Bruce talked me and some friends into an all night "Relay for Life" to raise money for the American Cancer Society. Like me, Bruce is a Naval Academy graduate although he graduated the year before I arrived on campus as a Plebe. Unlike me, Bruce is still in the Navy and is currently stationed at the Pentagon at one of the command centers. He is also married with two young sons.

We joined a larger relay team sponsored by the Reston Runners. Rather than walking the high school track like other relay teams, our team decided to race around the track during a six-hour block of time starting at midnight. We made the run a friendly competition against two corporate teams to see which team could do the most laps.

The Reston Runners team was divided into three sub teams of six to eight runners. Each sub team was responsible for running two one-hour blocks. Within each sub team, we took turns running a single 400 meter loop on the track during each of our two, one hour blocks. This seemed like the most efficient way to complete the greatest number of laps. My team ran the 2:00 a.m. – 3:00 a.m. then the 5:00 a.m. – 6:00 a.m. shifts. Through the night, I ran 16 or so 400-meter intervals. None of us slept that night. We sat around, huddling under a tent in the drizzle, snacking on energy bars and drinking a few beers.

I had never been a night person, so running in the middle of the night when I was normally halfway through a night's sleep felt alien to my lagging body. But it was for a good cause, and we had fun doing it.

I had previously committed myself to riding the Annapolis Bicycle Century immediately after the relay. I finished the relay at 6:00 a.m. then hopped into my friend Jim's car for the one hour drive to Annapolis, Maryland. Jim was a long-time Reston resident and triathlete and is one of those guys who always seems to be off doing some adventure whether it's riding a mountain bike century or racing an Iron distance triathlon.

I managed to catch a few minutes of sleep during the ride to Annapolis, but I was hurting from sleep deprivation when we arrived at the start of the century ride.

The morning was gray and dreary, and, by my own observation, it seemed that most riders opted to sleep in. I tucked in behind Jim and let him set the pace as I followed blindly, numbly lacking the coherent clarity to safely navigate the cue sheet.

Jim was a great friend that day. He patiently kept me on course and slowed down for me as I went on autopilot.

Without Bruce, I wouldn't have the memory of running a relay in the middle of the night. Without Jim, I wouldn't have finished the ride, nor would I be able to say that I had biked 100 miles on no sleep. It makes for a more interesting story!

This ride also confirmed what I had always known—I can't function effectively without eight hours of sleep.

***

My approach to training is one I learned in Boy Scouts. Simplicity is the key. KISS (Keep it Simple, Stupid). I often forget week-to-week

Keep a simple journal to track workouts and use as an early indicator of overtraining, sickness or injury.

(or even day-to-day) what I have done, so I keep a simple journal written on a monthly view calendar and print it out from my computer. The log also serves as an early indicator of overtraining, sickness or injury since I also capture comments on how I feel, minor injuries or sore spots, etc.

Things I record in my journal include the amount of time I spent working out, the distance I covered and my effort. I also indicate how I felt during a workout. Simple!

This is what a typical weekly journal entry looks like:

DAY	WORKOUT	COMMENTS
Monday	S: 60 min.	500 w/u, 5x100 on 2:00, 5x100 on 1:50, 5x100 on 1:40, 5x100 on 1:30; made all intervals, but struggled on last one.
Tuesday	B: 60 min.	Bike easy
Wednesday	S: 45 min.	500m w/u, 100/200/300/200/100 x 2 moderate pace; felt comfortable
Thursday	R: 45 min.	Achilles tight and sore
Friday	S: 55 min.	Easy lake swim
Saturday	B: 180 min.	Elevated heart rate, not enough rest?
Sunday	OFF	Rest day; slept in

Key: S = Swim; B = Bike; R = Run; w/u = warm up

My preference is to log time not distance. It's easy to measure, I only need a wristwatch. It can be hard to measure distance on a running trail or biking on a road without a bike computer. Plus, running for time gives me the flexibility to speed up or slow down depending on how I feel.

***

In April, I finally crossed the most important finish line of my life—the five year cancer-free finish line. After a final full day of exams and scans, the Navy declared me cured of my cancer. I was no longer bound to the Navy, nor were they bound to me.

I didn't celebrate the five-year mark. I think more than anything, I always believed I would beat cancer and so I didn't expect things to go any other way. That day in April was just a confirmation of what I believed to be true.

I did worry a little about what would happen if I had a recurrence since I no longer had access to the Navy's medical facilities, but my civilian doctors were very willing to keep me on a yearly schedule for a chest CT and pelvic MRI which helped reduce my anxiety.

Ironman Austria®

When I began racing at the Iron distance, I toyed with the idea of racing at every Iron distance race at least once. This was for no real reason other than it would be cool to say that I had done all of them. It would be a way for me to separate myself from the pack and do something unique. Plus, the races were in exotic travel spots like Australia, Switzerland, New Zealand, South Korea, and Austria. The idea was not too lofty at the time because there were only 20 or so races at this distance worldwide. The number has increased since then with a few races entering and others exiting the scene each year so it's a moving target.

Ever since I took two high school trips to mainland Europe and the UK, I had wanted to go back. Europe seemed like an ideal racing venue. The climate and terrain on average seemed to suit me better than the hotter, humid climate of Hawaii or Florida. After researching a number of options in Europe, I settled on Ironman Austria which is a relatively small race in Klagenfurt in the south central part of the country. The race was in July and although it didn't have a flat course, it was known to be a fast course.

A month before Austria, I achieved another milestone—I won my first triathlon. I won Spud, a small, local International distance triathlon in nearby Indian Head, Maryland. I came off the bike near three or four others with a single athlete ahead of me by about three minutes. I dropped the others behind and caught the leader about a mile before the finish to win by 30 seconds. This was a big confidence builder leading up to Austria, and I knew my fitness was very good. Going sub-nine hours at Austria seemed very doable.

Jen also made the transition from running to triathlons that year, racing in the Spud sprint distance triathlon. This was a huge milestone for her, as she did not have a swimming background at all. When we first started dating, she used to come and just watch my swim practices with the Reston Masters. When she too started swimming with the group, she began in the slowest of six swim lanes before eventually working her way up to the third fastest lane over many months of dedication and patience.

Jen and I made a vacation of our trip to Ironman Austria, spending a week before the race in Germany driving the Romantische Straße (Romantic Road) to visit medieval towns and castles, and we made a few day trips touring other countries like Italy and Lichtenstein. We both enjoyed driving on the

Autobahn and the efficiency of the European traffic circles, which seemed to keep traffic flowing much better than the traffic lights that we have in the United States. Most everyone spoke English so we had no difficulties traveling around.

Although one could argue that I should have been off my feet watching television in my hotel room instead of standing in line to see castles, I think the touring made the overall trip much more enjoyable for both of us. It didn't make sense to spend so much money to fly to Europe and not enjoy the countries and the cultures.

Klagenfurt, which was a lakeside vacation spot for Europeans, was an ideal venue for a race. From the race website:

> What is the course like? Probably one of the most important questions for the decision of which Ironman to take part in. Catinthia, Klagenfurt and the region around Lake Wörther See provide the perfect ambience for triathlon sport. Nothing better could have happened than the opportunity of racing through Austria's most popular summer-sport area.[7]

I absolutely agree with that description. It was a beautiful and scenic course, with a hometown feel.

By this time I had developed a race morning routine. It varied on a number of factors like travel time to the race site, whether or not I needed to check in my bike on race morning, etc. but typically looked like the following for a 7:00 a.m. start time:

4:30 a.m.
Wake up at least two hours before the race start (three hours before is preferable) which is usually not an issue due to race anxiety since I have dreams about sleeping through my alarm and missing the race start.

Waking up early gives my body the necessary time to cycle through its normal morning functions. I also don't like to rush on race morning since that is usually when I feel the most stress.

Eat a light, easily digested breakfast at least two hours before the race so the food settles. Like tapering, race morning eating is athlete specific.

My motto is "Find something that works and stick with it." My pre-race meal is usually a PowerBar or oatmeal with a little raspberry jam and a banana.

Drink coffee in the morning—this is part of my daily morning routine. The one time I raced without drinking coffee, I felt sluggish and not quite awake.

5:00 a.m.

Mentally walk through each step of the race to visualize my actions.

Last minute check to verify that I have everything I need for the race that has not already been dropped off at the race site the previous day, including my timing chip, swim goggles, wetsuit, swim cap and water bottles for the bike.

5:15 a.m.

Leave for race site.

Bring toilet paper to race start. There is nothing worse than finding a 20-minute line to the port-a-john 15 minutes before the race start. It happens all the time, so I often make for the bushes.

5:30 a.m.

Set up my transition area.

Check tire pressures on my bike.

6:00 a.m.

Warm up for a few minutes.

My typical routine is to run 10-15 minutes easy effort before climbing into my wetsuit and jumping in the water for an easy 5-minute swim before the start. I want to get the blood flowing into my muscles so that my body is better prepared for the transition to the sudden demands of the race start.

6:45 a.m.

Spend some quiet time alone. I find it peaceful and serene. Usually, the sun is just coming up over the horizon. Many of the athletes are already in the water warming up. Everyone is focused on last minute preparations and thinking about the day ahead. I find a quiet spot by myself to positively visualize the race and what I hope to do today. Enjoy the silence and serenity.

6:50 a.m.

Line up for the swim start. Seed myself near the front line of swimmers.

7:00 a.m.

RACE!

I was chasing the sub-nine hour mark at Austria. After a fast swim, my first two laps of the three lap bike course had me on target for a 4:45 bike split, which would have beaten my best time from Vineman by 20 minutes. On the third and final lap of the bike course, I bonked badly and lost about 10 minutes, but still managed to finish the bike leg in just less than five hours which was a personal best for me. The cola that I picked up from the bike course aid stations saved me from losing even more time.

My total time at the run start was six hours even. I needed a sub three hour marathon to achieve my sub-nine time. I made a very good effort at first but, like my experience on the bike, I bonked badly again in the final third of the run. Yet, I still crossed the line in a time of 9:16, a new personal best for me by about 13 minutes.

My finish was a paradox. I was both happy and disappointed at the same time. I had higher expectations for myself as I knew that I could have squeaked out a few more minutes here and there with better choices on pacing. I didn't feel the sweet victory of achieving a sub-nine hour time.

From this experience at Austria, I took away a need to set goals at multiple levels. Rather than picking a single goal to finish in sub- *Set goals at multiple levels.* nine hours, I felt that I should set time goals for a personal best time overall and in each event (swim, bike and run) or set race execution goals like not walking during the run. As such, I could accomplish one or more goals and still walk away with some level of satisfaction.

After returning home from Austria, EDS went through a massive reorganization of the sales and marketing groups where I worked. I picked up a new manager who worked at the corporate headquarters in Plano,

Texas. He was my manager for only a month before I was reassigned to another manager in Texas. After a few trips to Plano, I realized that I didn't enjoy being the only one on my team based in Virginia. I need more face-to-face interaction, so I started looking for a new job.

About a month later, I began a new job as a business analyst at Capital One, a financial services company headquartered in Northern Virginia. If a recruiter asked me when I first left the Navy, "Would you like to work for Capital One?" I would have said, "I have never even heard of Capital One."

I had no experience or desire at the time to work in financial services, I should have been a computer scientist or nuclear engineer because of my computer science degree and nuclear power training. Besides, why work for a company that was predominantly known for being one of the most prevalent originators of junk mail in the country?

Ironically, I first heard about the company through another Academy graduate who took the same graduate program as me. He spoke highly of the company and its culture. I didn't need a background in financial services to be successful, he said. The company was looking for good, smart, self-motivated people that could be trained into their job-specific skills.

Interviewing at Capital One reminded me of interviewing for the Navy's nuclear power program. Both interviews required me to take and pass written tests. Both required me to sit down with interviewers for one-on-one case study problem solving. Capital One also required two behavioral interviews where the interviewers asked me questions about recent situations where I had demonstrated specific behaviors such as self-motivation, problemsolving and getting the job done. Both interview processes were all-day events.

A few days later, I had an offer from Capital One.

Like the nuclear power program, I was in a competitive environment and no longer the top performer. Smarter people surrounded me. In subsequent years, I've submitted resumes to Capital One for friends and friends of friends. Many of these candidates had similar backgrounds and experiences as me. Some even had degrees from prestigious schools like Harvard, yet none of the candidates that I have submitted have been hired. I still wonder how I made it past the interview process.

My biggest fear was that a competitive environment would require me to put in excessive time in order to be successful. EDS was a known entity. I knew what my job entailed and how much flexibility I had with it. When I joined Capital One, like any job, I entered somewhat blindly.

One of the biggest obstacles in my job was that I lived in Northern Virginia and my new business group was based in Glen Allen, Virginia, on the outskirts of

If you tend to travel to the same city for business, join a health club there.

Richmond. As such, I had to drive two hours to Richmond two or three days each week. I quickly sought out and joined the local YMCA in Glen Allen, and I found a local route to ride my bike. I found that it was much easier to drive to Glen Allen on the morning of one day and come back in the afternoon of another day as it gave me enough time to workout both days. The other option, which I have had to do on a limited number of occasions, was to drive down and back on the same day, which usually meant I couldn't squeeze in a workout on that day.

On the plus side, the Capital One office in Northern Virginia was conveniently located near the W&OD trail. My manager, who liked to run during lunch, told me about a small fitness room in the

Commute by bike to fit extra workouts into your busy schedule and kill two birds with one stone.

basement of the building that had showers. I noticed a couple of bikes in the parking garage and after speaking with one of the cyclists in the fitness room, I decided to try commuting by bicycle.

My route to work was just over an hour by bike, with two thirds of it on the trail. This turned out to be an ideal distance for a bike commute. It was long enough that I felt like I had a decent workout, but short enough to not make my workday excessively long. By commuting by bike, I made more efficient use of my time by killing two birds with one stone. My commute by car was 45 minutes, so by taking my bike I only added a half hour to my day while getting in two hours of biking. True, I spent some extra time preparing for my ride, but I found it easier to pack everything for work the night before so I wasn't rushed in the morning.

I didn't have use of a long-term locker, so I carried my clothes each way in a backpack and kept my bag at my desk. Adding my laptop and paperwork to my pack made it weigh more than 20 pounds. I told myself that the extra weight made me stronger. I'm not sure if that's quite true, but I could feel the added weight on a few hilly sections.

Great Floridian (Third Time)

After Ironman Austria, I wanted to reestablish my streak of two Iron distance races per year. Great Floridian was again my choice for an end of season race.

What I remember most about this race was being interviewed beforehand for the race video. I had become a recognized and valid competitor for the podium—one of the race favorites who could steal the win. On race morning, I also heard my name over the loudspeaker announcements: "We have quite a field of competitors joining us today, including David Glover, who placed 5th overall at the Vineman Triathlon."

Unfortunately, I think the spotlight, which might sound appealing, actually hurt my performance by creating more anxiety and more pressure to perform. My quiet personality better fits the underdog than the superhero.

I finished off the podium that year in 7th overall in under 10 hours. Not bad by most standards, but below the expectations of my biggest critic—me.

This was the first year that I experienced end-of-season burnout. The biggest symptom of burnout was that my heart was not in the Great Floridian 100 percent. I had been training all year and peaked in July for Ironman Austria. I tried to hold onto my level of fitness until the end of October, so I was tired physically and mentally and needed a break. Looking back, I could have taken more down time immediately after Austria in order to break up my season more and recharge my batteries.

End-of-season burnout wasn't necessarily bad, it just meant that my body and my mind needed more rest and less intensity. The mistake would have been to keep training hard through the burnout and open myself up to injury or total burnout and possibly even resentment for the sport.

In December, Bruce, Jim, a few other triathlete friends and I were sitting at a Starbucks® talking after a short ride in the winter cold. "Wouldn't it be cool," someone suggested, "If we started a triathlon club in this area?"

Jim spoke up, saying that there was a club in the Reston area in the mid-80s called the Reston Area Triathletes or RATS. In fact, if you look at Dave Scott's 1986 book, *Dave Scott's Triathlon Training*, RATS is one of the few clubs listed in the index with Jim being the original contact.

Jim provided us with the original by-laws and some of the club literature. RATS as a triathlon club was reborn and, by default, I became the new club president.

The purpose of the club was simple: "Provide a means for local triathletes to learn about the sport, find training partners and socialize." We started out as an email list then later moved to an online message board before eventually creating our own website.

The triathlon club provided a way for new athletes to connect with more experienced athletes. The club went from humble beginnings with only a few of us posting messages in order to facilitate discussions, to today where we have an active message board with many members of all ages and experiences participating.

Probably the most rewarding aspect of the club is that it took on a life of its own. I turned over the role of president a few years ago and now play a less active role, only occasionally posting a differing opinion, complementing a discussion thread or sharing information that had not yet been shared.

Chapter 9: The Next Level

Jen and I lived in her townhouse with our dogs, Quincy and Lucy. Quincy was Jen's yellow lab who she had raised since he was a puppy and Lucy was a small, black lab mix who we found by the side of the road.

Pets require a lot of care. Granted, the time and responsibility required pales in comparison to taking care of children, but someone has to be home to feed and walk them and give them the attention they need. This means waking up half an hour earlier in the morning and coming home immediately after work rather than going straight to the gym. I wouldn't trade the responsibilities and hassles of having dogs for the world. They give unconditional love and are always happy to see their owners. But having them added one more priority to my already full schedule.

By this time, I had been my own coach for two years with the caveat that I still heavily leveraged the input and advice of my friends who shared similar triathlon lifestyles and had similar goals. I had learned much from my experiences working first with Phil and the SERIOUS training program for Ironman Canada, then later with Troy Jacobson as a paid coach. When I was relatively new to triathlon and new to Iron distance training, coaching was the right thing for me. The initial coaching both formal and informal taught me how to provide structure and focus to creating my own workout schedule.

The downside of having a coach to provide a structured workout plan was that I felt like a slave to the schedule and was unable to adjust it on the fly. Not being able to complete a workout on the designated day made me feel like I was slipping and created anxiety. Jen and I once spent two hours driving around Northern Virginia to find a high school with an open track in order to do a prescribed track workout—all the tracks were either being used or were locked up. I finally gave up in frustration.

Being my own coach allowed me the latitude to create my own schedule and adjust it without the associated guilt or stress of not being able to complete a paid-for-schedule on a daily basis. I wanted the flexibility to determine what I needed to do on a day-by-day basis. This allowed me to compensate for unexpected events like taking a dog to the vet or spending time with Jen's family.

Build flexibility into your schedule to allow for unexpected events or schedule changes.

Vineman (Second Time)

"Thus I urge you to go on to your greatness if you believe it is in you. Think deeply and separate what you wish from what you are prepared to do."
- *Percy Wells Cerutty, athletic icon.*

After struggling through my divorce in 1999, I rebounded in 2000 to set a personal best time of 9:16 at Ironman Austria. I headed into 2001 with even higher expectations.

On a whim, I bought another triathlon bike. My friend Bruce, who was working part time at Bonzai Sports, a local triathlon shop, was riding a brand new Softride Rocketwing®. My Trident T2 that I was riding was a little too big for me, forcing me to stretch out into an uncomfortable position that hurt my neck and back. I had since purchased a yellow Softride Powerwing®, which I liked very much, so moving to a newer model Softride was an easy decision. I sold my Trident to a taller friend and acquired the red Rocketwing.

The new bike helped me exceed my expectations at Vineman.

Halfway through the bike course, I caught the lead group of three riders at the base of Chalk Hill, the biggest climb in the bike leg. I accelerated past them and pulled away. "I can win this race!" I thought as I took over the race lead.

A few minutes later, near the top of Chalk Hill, I heard the horrifying sound of "pssssssssttttt." felt the shaky wobble of my back wheel and looked down to see my rear tire go flat. I continued to grind up the rest of the hill before pulling off on the side of the road. The long, fast descent after the climb could have been deadly on an unstable airless tire. The three quickly passed me as I changed the flat.

"What happened?" asked one.

"I flatted." I replied.

"Hang in there and don't panic." commented another.

"Easy for him to say." I thought, as I unzipped my small bike bag beneath my seat to remove a spare tube and CO_2 cartridges for air.

"Damn it!" I had forgotten to pick up the cartridges from the race expo. A cartridge would have filled the empty tire in seconds, but I only had a small hand pump. I spent what seemed like eternity (but was only a few minutes) furiously pumping up my tire.

With barely enough air in the tire to ride, I replaced the wheel, tightened the skewer and hopped back on my bike. I feared I was out of contention for the podium.

Ten miles later, I slowly realized that I wasn't consuming enough calories. My mind began to turn fuzzy. I hoped that drinking soda would remedy the situation, but there was none available until the run aid stations.

I muddled through the rest of the bike course, giving up a few more places. My expectations dropped.

I reached the bike-to-run transition area in 7th place overall. My flat tire and calorie shortage had cost me six finishing positions. I debated what I should do. I considered four options:

1. Quit
2. Walk the entire marathon
3. Run slowly
4. Suck it up and race

The first three choices were tempting, but I had not traveled across the country just to finish. I had already finished multiple Iron distance races. These were pretty much the exact words Jen said to me later during the run.

Once I was off of my bike and running, I could consume cola and began to feel better as I settled in at a 7:30 minute per mile run pace, which would give me a 3:15 marathon. The key to recovering lost time would be consistency. I felt confident that I could maintain the pace.

I'm always amazed at the extreme highs and lows that I can experience during a race. Halfway through the bike, I *It's important to realize that there are highs and lows during a race.* was frustrated and down on myself after flatting and bonking. An hour later, I was running strongly, feeling good and reeling in the athletes ahead of me. I think the recognition that the race is full of these highs and lows is important, because I know that no matter how low I feel, I will eventually feel better.

My race became a waiting game as I slowly and methodically reeled in the other runners.

After the first turnaround, I saw the race favorite and past winner about 10 minutes behind me rapidly closing the gap between us. He had won Ultraman®, a three-day event with a total distance equivalent to two Iron distance races, in 1998 by running back-to-back marathons in 2:48 and 2:45. He was a fast runner, and I knew I didn't stand a chance against him in the run if he caught me. Fortunately for me, I never saw him again on the course.

The remaining athletes in front of me began to fade and fall apart. By the turnaround on the second out and back, I had caught all who had passed me except for one as I moved into second place overall.

From spectators and volunteers, I kept hearing, "You're looking a lot stronger than the guy in front. You can catch him." My confidence grew as my patience began paying dividends. I could catch the leader and take the win. I had it in the palm of my hand. I dug deep inside for strength.

I caught the final runner at mile 23 as he cramped. We exchanged greetings and words of encouragement to each other before I quickly pulled away.

Three miles later, I crossed the line as the winner in a time of 9:45 with a victory margin of only three minutes and six minutes over the second and third place winners.

I was an Iron distance winner!

Although I had once again fallen short on my sub-nine hour time goal, I had achieved another milestone at Vineman with the win. Now, I needed to validate that it was not just a fluke by winning again.

A Shift in Perspective

"It never gets easier, you just go faster."
- *Greg LeMond, Three-time winner of the Tour de France*

There is simple truth in Greg LeMond's statement. I think, in some cases though, I perceive that I am working harder or perhaps my body is able to handle a higher amount of physical stress than it could initially handle.

My perspective on "What is a challenge?" evolved significantly from running 200 meters in grade school to running a mile and eventually to winning an Iron distance triathlon. Ten-mile runs were now my base distance run before building up to 18 and 22 mile runs in preparation for a race. I would also bike for six or seven hours at a time during the summer with friends, logging over 120 miles in a single ride.

My body has physiologically adapted to the years of endurance training. I remember suffering through two miles in high school track meets thinking that I was going to die, now I could suffer through a reasonably fast marathon on a whim knowing that it won't kill me. I have also built a higher tolerance to discomfort and pain over the years.

I might be genetically limited to what I can physically achieve, but I can always work to push myself harder mentally. As the saying goes, "Mind over matter: if you don't mind, it doesn't matter."

As a Spinning instructor, I observed that my students had varying perceptions of what a "hard" effort meant. Typically, students who were new to cardiovascular exercise and cycling perceived a "hard" effort as what I would consider a "moderate" effort. The Spinning "veterans" were more likely to exert themselves to a greater extent as evidenced by their higher heart rates, breathing, faster cadence, perspiration and facial expressions. I could always tell who was really working hard. Yet, I gave both newbies and veterans the same verbal guidance.

My goals also evolved with my improved results.

- In the beginning: "I don't know if I can even finish."
- A year later: "I can finish. How fast should I go?"
- A few years later: "I can win. Do I want the win?"

The downside of my changing perspective was that I was chasing more elusive goals. Ultimately, it was up to me to define my success, whether it was "finishing," "qualifying for Hawaii," "finishing top 10," or even "winning." My definition frequently changed from race to race depending on the race, my training, the course, my confidence level, etc, but the success bar trended higher and the corresponding effort and time commitment to achieve that success became higher as well.

Mohican Pineman

Each race becomes its own set of challenges building on previous races and experiences. Can I dig a little deeper in order to go a little faster the next time? Can I adjust my caloric intake to prevent myself from vomiting? As I come face-to-face with my situation versus my own desire and willpower, I have to make a choice.

A month after Vineman in September, I raced at the Mohican Pineman in Perrysville, Ohio. This was a race I had originally wanted to do in 1999, but backed out of after hitting the point of exhaustion. During the race, I almost talked myself into quitting halfway through the run. Following is an excerpt from a race report I wrote after completing the event:

> From a course perspective, Pineman was the toughest triathlon I have ever done. That was also what winner Troy Jacobson (my former coach) said in his victory speech.
>
> The air temperature at the swim start was a cold 41 degrees with a water temperature in the mid 60s and heavy fog. The fog created a very surreal setting for the swim.
>
> Due to the fog, I could not see from one buoy to the next. I'd swim a few strokes, pop my head up, look for a buoy or kayak, redirect, swim to it, stop, look for the next buoy, etc. I popped my head up every few seconds to sight expending additional energy.
>
> Once away from the shore, I had no sense of direction. On the second loop, I came out of the water right behind Troy, and we gave each other a "high five" along the beach before we waded back into the water for our third loop. The kayaks and canoes did a great job of pointing out the buoys whenever possible. By the third and fourth laps, there were very few people around me, and no one to draft off of.

After leaving the swim, I rightly opted for a dry, long-sleeve shirt over my wet race jersey, which I had worn under my wetsuit. I passed Troy in the changing tent, but six miles into the bike, he blew by me looking warm and comfortable in his dry cycling clothing. I shivered and watched him go. I should have changed into dry shorts, tights and gloves, too, as I was miserably cold in my wet shorts during the first loop of the hilly bike course. I eventually gained the feeling back in my toes and fingers by the second loop but then came the "bonk," that nasty monster that strikes and forces you to struggle along slightly delusional with negative thoughts running through your mind. The second loop felt like an eternity.

The bike course was ALL hills, it reminded me of Skyline Drive. There were long hills. There were steep hills. There were long, steep hills. Plus, sharp turns at the bottom of the hills made me lose momentum on descents when I had to slow down to make a turn.

The bike-to-run transition was uneventful. The air temperature rose into the 60s by then, still a little chilly on parts of the run. Dehydration was not really a problem that day. I vaguely remember reading or hearing that the run course was flat. Well, I guess if you compare it to the bike course, it was flat. I remembered the run course as being rolling hills, which by my definition does not mean flat.

I bonked again at mile 10 and nearly talked myself into quitting at the turnaround, as I was miserable and in the process of being run down by someone behind me.

I had to make a choice. Quitting was attractive. I could stop and be done for the day. I had already won a race earlier in the year, so I had nothing to prove to anyone. Yet, I was a cancer survivor. If I quit now, would I quit on myself if the cancer came back? I was afraid that quitting now would set precedence for the rest of my life that it was okay to quit. I needed to finish if only for that single reason.

I waved at Jen, turned around and went out for my second loop.

The rest of the run was much slower and the gap from the next couple of runners behind me shrank. I bonked again at mile 20 and was forced to pick up my pace toward the end. I ran together with a relay runner the last few miles as he slowed down to talk to me and run me in. We crossed the line together.

I had wanted to quit so badly that I lost my desire mid-race. The challenge for me was to turn my attitude around and suffer through the discomfort to finish the race. I was able to change my attitude and finish second.

The feelings of quitting would haunt me again in later races.

I ended 2001 having achieved a new milestone in racing with my win at Vineman followed up by a podium finish at Mohican Pineman. I had earned both, but I also knew that my win at Vineman was one of the slowest times anyone had ever won the race with. The race favorite had a bad day and dropped out. My second place at Pineman was a full 40 minutes behind Troy's win. I felt that I needed to prove that my win at Vineman was not just a fluke.

Chapter 10: Test and Learn

I had lived with Jen for about two and a half years and realized it was either marry her or move out and move on. I loved her, and we seemed to be happy together. One day after work, I surprised her with a trail of rose pedals leading down the stairs where I gave her a ring and said, "Will you marry me?"

She said, "Yes!"

We did not set a date, but talked about getting married in a year or so.

Testing My Way into Success

"Our success is directly attributed to our progressive efforts"
- *Capital One website, www.capitalone.com*[8]

Although learning by experience, and mistakes, is not necessarily a bad approach, I feel that there is a more efficient way to learn about triathlon without having to learn everything by trial and error.

There is a more efficient way to learn about triathlon besides just trial and error.

Capital One employs what we call an information-based strategy (IBS) approach to business decision making. Chairman and CEO Richard Fairbank "founded Capital One in 1988 based on his belief that the power of information, technology, testing and great people could be combined to bring highly customized financial products directly to consumers."[9] The company employs a philosophy called "Test and Learn." We test different marketing strategies in the marketplace, letting the marketplace be the true decider of what products and product features will be successful. We then apply that knowledge to future marketing strategies.

Here is a simple example of how "Test and Learn" marketing might work at a donut shop:

- Each day, make 10 batches each of chocolate, cake, creme- and jelly-filled donuts.

- Sell fresh batches each day.

- Monitor how many of each donut is sold over a one-week period.

- Determine which donut sells the best on which day of the week.

- Make more of the donuts that sell the best and less of the donuts that sell the least on those particular days of the week .

- Monitor sales over time and adjust donut production as consumer preferences change.

By using different data sources and customer preferences, the idea is to identify optimal products for each customer segment by taking into account factors such as the likelihood of a customer responding to an ad, the likelihood that the customer will transfer a credit card balance from another bank to Capital One and the likelihood that the customer will make the required payments on the credit card.

To get to the right product for the right customer, the company makes "mistakes" along the way. For each winning product or product feature, there are losers, but because the company learns along the way it is successful.

The premise behind an Information Based Strategy and "test and learn" is that the marketplace is the true judge of performance, not the limited knowledge, experiences and biases of decision makers.

Applying "Test and Learn" to Triathlon

"Felix qui potuit rerum cogno scere causas."
(Lucky is he who has been able to understand the causes of things)
- *Virgil, Latin Poet*

After working at Capital One, I began applying a similar "Test and Learn" approach to my triathlon *Since we're all different, a cookie cutter-style approach to training may not be optimal for everyone.* training, which I have coined "Learn, Test and Apply." My underlying assumption is that everyone is different. We have different abilities, different goals, different time commitments, different motivations, different likes and different strengths. If you believe that, then it makes sense that a single training plan or "cookie cutter" approach to training, such as what you might find in a book or magazine article, is not optimal for everyone. If you believe that, then it also makes sense that training needs to be customized or adapted to the individual in order to get optimal results. In other words, learn from others and learn from experience then apply sound judgment and common sense to make your own training decisions.

Rather than start with testing, I begin with the tremendous amount of endurance sport information, knowledge and wisdom already out there. The information takes many

Draw on a variety of sources for your training information, including friends and training partners.

forms, much of which is readily available through the Internet. Sources of information include other triathletes, magazine articles, websites, triathlon clubs, race reports and books. As a matter of practice, I draw on a variety of sources to compare and contrast opinions and theories. I find that magazine or online articles are often the best place to start when looking at a particular aspect of training or racing like race strategy, tapering or overtraining. When I train with friends, I bounce ideas or plans off them as they do off me for an additional opinion. We frequently encourage each other against doing things that don't make sense or might lead to injury or burnout.

Starting with a base level of knowledge—some of it right, some of it wrong—I develop a few training hypotheses that I think will work for me. These hypotheses are my tests for

I narrow down the possible training options to those I think are likely to impact my training the most.

what I believe are the actions that I must take in order to achieve my goals. By creating hypotheses, I narrow down the possible training options to the options that I think are likely to impact my training the most. Otherwise, I would potentially create an endless list of "things" to try out. I then test each hypothesis in training or during less important "B" races, so that I can use the knowledge learned during my more important "A" races.

As an example, my hypothesis is that I can improve my performance by focusing a higher proportion of my time on high volume aerobic exercise (less anaerobic) with only a small amount of higher intensity (more anaerobic) training built into the last four to five weeks leading up to an "A" race. In other words, I believe that I will race faster by training at an easier level of effort the majority of the time. My body will become more efficient during endurance exercise. My focus then becomes to build that strong aerobic base with minimal high intensity training until four to five weeks out from a key race. I accomplish this by keeping the bulk of my training time at a relatively easy effort especially in the early part of the season. My less important "B" races become my speed workouts.

The final component of "Learn, Test and Apply" is applying the learning from the testing and knowledge base. After testing, I ask myself a series of questions:

- What worked?

- Why did it work?

- What didn't work?

- Why didn't it work?

- What should I do differently next time?

- What should I try next (i.e., What are my new hypotheses to improve upon next time)?

If something works, I stick with it.

I capture this information in my training log and in my race reports—my personal write up on the race that provides information to others on the race and is also a useful tool for me to remember the past. Because my detailed memories fade rapidly, I write things down. Periodically throughout the year, I read through old notes, race reports and workout logs to distill what I learned from my past experiences to apply to future races.

Conceptually, the process flows looks something like this:

- **Learn** about an aspect of endurance training.

- **Test** what I learned in a practice environment (training or "B" race) to determine what works and what doesn't work.

- **Apply** the knowledge to future training and racing.

- Repeat the process.

The learning cycle repeats as I adapt my training and my racing to new knowledge and new experiences: Learn, Test and Apply. Essentially, I have created a feedback loop as I seek to optimize what works for me as an individual.

Ironman Utah®

Over time, I have come to the realization that there are two aspects to every race and every life event:

- Things that I can control
- Things that I cannot control

I like to think that I only try to influence the things that I can control and not worry about the things that I can't, but this isn't always true. Although I cannot control some things, I can at least prepare. My natural tendency is to stress over the little things in life like the refrigerator that stops working, the traffic that slows to a crawl, or the puppy that won't stop chewing on the furniture. When these little things compound, I have a difficult time maintaining perspective.

Although I cannot control some things, I can at least prepare.

When Ironman North America® introduced a new Ironman in Provo, Utah, I jumped at the chance to race out West, not too far from where I grew up in Idaho Falls. On race day, the weather at the inaugural Ironman Utah® race created conditions outside of my control. My race day composure and those of the other 1,600+ athletes was put to the ultimate test.

Utah would have been my 10th Iron distance race.

I should have realized it was a bad omen when my friend, Steve Smith, and I were walking from the swim-to-bike transition area to the swim start, and we were forced to wear our goggles to protect our eyes from the dust storm that was kicked up by the gusting winds. The wind created white caps in the shallow lake making it look more like an ocean. All other sound disappeared against its howling.

When I jumped into the water to warm up, it wasn't clear to me where the starting line was because the start buoy had blown away. I couldn't hear anything from the announcers from where I was patiently treading water waiting for the race to start.

Ten minutes before the expected start, people began swimming. It was a cascading ripple effect as everyone in the water noticed that everyone else was swimming and started swimming, too.

"What the hell?" I thought. I never heard the cannon go off, but quickly realized the organizers could not stop the race now so I just started swimming, too.

As the winds picked up, it was impossible to see anything while in the trough of a wave. I rounded the first buoy after about 10 minutes. I could barely see the second and started swimming in its direction. I grew tired of having to pop my head out of the water every few strokes to make sure I was headed the right way. The buoy never seemed to get closer; in fact it was drifting away in the high winds. I could only breathe to one side downwind or else I took in a mouthful of water. The athletes were spread out (crowding was not an issue) and there were times when I didn't see more than one or two people in any direction because of the waves.

Just before the second buoy and after about 30 minutes of swimming, a Coast Guard boat came by and a sailor announced that the swim was cancelled because all of the buoys had drifted or blown away and that we should head for the shore. He also said we swam about a half mile too far.

"Which way do we go?" I yelled above the roar of the wind and helicopters flying overhead.

"Swim toward the sun." the Coast Guard sailor said. So I did.

As I neared the shore and started to trudge through the mud in chest-high water, I looked around to see hundreds of swimmers coming out of the water up and down the shoreline and on the jetties. There were still many more hundreds of swim caps bobbing up and down out in the lake. With helicopters flying overhead and boats interspersed with the swimmers, the spectacle reminded me of the chaotic opening scene from *Saving Private Ryan* where the Allied Forces land at Normandy.

I climbed out of the water after 54 minutes of swimming. Upon exiting the water, I was directed back to the transition area where I walked across a timing mat to "check in."

The rumors immediately started flying around that several people drowned. One person actually did die. An hour later the race organizers announced that the race would continue as a duathlon, but with a shortened bike course due to high winds in the canyons. Since the bike was shortened not quite in half, the race organizers correspondingly cut the run in half to 13.1 miles.

A few minutes after 10:00 a.m., we started the duathlon as a time trial with pros going off one at a time at 15-second intervals followed by a steady single file stream of age groupers in numerical order. I wore bib #393 and started approximately 15 minutes after the last pro woman.

I hammered the bike from the start. I figured what the heck, I had trained for a full Iron distance race and now would only be out on the bike course about three hours. My heart rate didn't go below 175 beats per minute (bpm) for the first hour. My max heart rate is ~192 bpm, which is high for me. Likely, the high attitude (4,000+ feet) played a role as well, forcing my heart to pump faster to accommodate for the less oxygen rich air. The course was "relatively" flat, but with high winds. Most of the climbs were false flats meaning you couldn't really tell you were climbing until you realized you were descending at a later point. The only way I could tell whether I was going with or against the wind was by looking down at my gearing.

It was a great feeling blowing by folks and catching the lower numbers one by one. I had to stop at one point to tighten my rear wheel skewer as my tire started to rub. No one with a higher number passed me though, so I knew that I was having a good day.

I finished the bike in a little under three hours and started the run. By then, it was getting hot and there wasn't much shade. The run course was a pair of out and backs from the Brigham Young University stadium. Like the bike course, the run course was also "relatively" flat but there were some small hills in the first out and back. I remember passing a guy about two miles into the run who was sprawled out on the grass due to leg cramps. At about three miles into the run, I caught and passed the lead age grouper and kept the lead until about mile 11 when I was run down by the guy who would win my age group.

I finished second in my age group and as usual, finishing was the best feeling in the world. After all that had happened, I was thankful for only having to run a half-marathon. The pizza afterward hit the spot, and I hung out in the shade waiting for friends to finish.

The next day I picked up a slot to the Ironman World Championship in October. Like most Iron distance triathletes, I wanted to experience Kona at least once.

***

Before I raced in Hawaii, I told myself that I wanted to complete a sub-nine hour Iron distance race. I picked up my Hawaii slot at Utah, but I still didn't have my sub-nine-hour race. I had one more chance to meet this goal. There was a new Iron distance race that had opened up in North Carolina in September called the Blue Devil Triathlon.

I can't remember how I found out about the Blue Devil. When I read about it as a fund raiser for the Duke Comprehensive Cancer Center, I knew I had to do it. I thought to myself, "How powerful is that? As a cancer survivor, I could race with the purpose of helping others with cancer." Because cancer was such a critical aspect of my life, I knew that I could use my experience as a catalyst to push myself beyond what I had done to date.

From the start, I had a clear goal to go under nine hours. I was no longer selfishly racing for myself, but I was also racing for other cancer survivors. I had the opportunity to help others by becoming a symbol of victory over cancer. Because of the tie to cancer, this race became more important to me than racing at Hawaii. I would put all of my energy and effort into the Blue Devil, perhaps at the expense of Hawaii, which was only five weeks later.

I was still traveling for my job at Capital One. I typically traveled to the Richmond area on Tuesday mornings and then back on Wednesday evenings. In the summer when I traveled, I often tried to squeeze in a bike ride with one of my co-workers, Peter Springer, who is a statistician and an avid cyclist.

Peter is an ultra-distance cyclist. He does what I consider extreme cycling events or Randonnee rides, which start at 200-kilometer distances then progress to 300-, 400- and 600-kilometer rides. A rider must complete each distance within the time limit in order to be eligible for the end goal—a 1200-kilometer ride. Randonnee riders must ride through the night in order to finish within the allowable time. As such, Peter is comfortable riding in the dark and introduced me to the experience of night riding. There is something to be said for riding at night with only a small amount of road directly ahead lit up when everything else is dark, it's very peaceful.

Peter and I sometimes met as early as 4:00 a.m. to start a three-hour ride. I would then shower and be in the office before 8:00 a.m.

One weekend, Peter and I decided to try something a little different, we biked from the Capital One office in Northern Virginia to the Capital One office in Glen Allen:

> Peter and I picked a Sunday in July for our epic ride, a Sunday that turned out to be one of the hottest days of the year with humid temperatures exceeding 100°F.
>
> Driving to Richmond is approximately 120 miles or two hours by interstate in a car. We took a somewhat indirect route mostly following "Bike Route 1" for a total of 167 miles. Bike Route 1 is marked by small signs and parallels Route 1 on less-traveled side roads.
>
> We rode conservatively given the distance and the heat. We averaged about 15 mph as compared to a typical weekend road ride where I might average closer to 19 mph.
>
> We both wore fluid bladders and carried several water bottles. I carried in excess of 100 ounces of fluid when topped off, yet the weather still forced us to stop every two to three hours to refill.
>
> The heat was oppressive, my head felt like an egg boiling inside my helmet. I could not keep my body cool. We spent several stops standing in convenience stores and drinking iced cold drinks with the freezer doors wide open to cool off.
>
> To date, the 167-mile ride was my longest. It's hard to find friends like Peter who will do this type of ride on a whim. Naturally, we will plan a follow-on trip, down and back in a single weekend.

I loved my Rocketwing triathlon bike. It was fast, comfortable and cool looking.

However, there was a design flaw. The bike was a beam bike meaning that there was no seat tube supporting my seat and my weight. There were two metal pins that held the beam. One pin was the pivot point from which the beam would raise or lower. The second pin locked the beam into position. I had broken three or four pins in the past year. One of the breaks had occurred during a Half-Iron distance race in St. Croix (now called the St. Croix Ironman 70.3®) causing me to ride 34 miles in a standing position. Needless to say, I wasn't confident that the pin would stay intact.

My friend Bruce had recently switched from riding a Softride® to riding an Airborne® titanium bike. "I can get you a good deal through the Navy sponsorship program." he told me. A few weeks later, I found myself riding a new Airborne Spectre®, custom built with Ultegra® components, not quite high end, but good enough for my use. A few weeks later, I sold my red Rocketwing to a friend who was lighter and less likely to break a pin.

The Other Side

"Volunteers are not paid not because they are worthless, but because they are priceless."
- *Anonymous*

There is one aspect of racing that I did not begin to appreciate until I volunteered at the Reston Triathlon a few weeks before the Blue Devil. I could literally go through an entire race without speaking to anyone except for providing my name at packet pick-up and thanking some of the aid station volunteers. I had no appreciation for the amount of work that went on behind the scenes both before and during the race.

The first time I volunteered at a local run a few years prior, I was assigned responsibility for a water stop, a task that is relatively simple—hand water in paper cups to the finishing athletes. We ran out of water. Where to get more water for the hundreds of finishing athletes? We finally managed to fill a clean trash can with water from a distant spigot and haul it over to the water table by half carrying and half dragging it. In the meantime, I had to listen to complaints of, "Where's the water? I can't believe you guys don't have water at the finish line." The runners were not sympathetic to our logistical challenges. Lesson learned—plan ahead for contingencies.

With my tie to the RATS and its members, I offered to help find race-day volunteers for the Reston Triathlon. As a volunteer organizer, I was invited to attend the Race Captains' meetings. The Race Captains were responsible for coordinating volunteers for major portions of the race such as transition areas, packet pick-up, food, aid stations, etc. Until I attended the meetings and listened to the captains talk, I didn't have an appreciation for how much work went into organizing a triathlon. The planning for the race began almost immediately after the previous year's race ended. There were more than a dozen captains tasked with various aspects of the race including course set-up (swim, bike and run), transition area set-up, food, packet pick-up, medical support, and police coordination to name a few of the responsibilities. Everyone involved was a volunteer.

Blue Devil

"The will to win, the desire to succeed, the urge to reach your full potential... these are the keys that will unlock the door to personal excellence."
- *Confucius, Chinese Philosopher*

From my observations of myself and others, the greatest performance gains seem to come early in an athlete's triathlon career. For example, incremental gains between a second and third race usually far exceed those between race 50 and 51, where improvement can become miniscule, if at all. To restate the economic concept of diminishing marginal utility in exercise-speak, there is diminishing incremental performance or time gains as an athlete approaches a maximum theoretical performance threshold.

Because of past success, I now looked for success as a minute faster here or a minute faster there. To achieve these marginal improvements, I focus on details, especially in race *Since I work full time and don't have the luxury of ample time, I choose my workouts and workout partners with care to maximize my training time.* execution. I pick only a few key races, so that I can perform my best without tiring myself out with a season of endless racing. Since I work full time and don't have the luxury of ample time, I choose my workouts and workout partners with care to maximize my training time. I also don't want to ramp up too quickly and risk injury halfway through the season, nor do I want to drag my season out excessively and risk burnout. I also aim to build a solid aerobic foundation from my training that I can leverage for years to come.

I am attracted to longer race distances because I find them infinitely more complex and challenging than shorter races. Race day nutrition is critical. Pacing is crucial. Perseverance is essential. Race execution is paramount. Motivation can be the difference between first and second.

It is always easy for me to look back at a race and say, "I should have gone a little faster," or "I could have dug a little deeper." When I reflect back on all of my Iron distance races, I think that there is really only one that I raced nearly perfectly, the inaugural Blue Devil Triathlon in 2002. Everything fell into place for me during that race, and I was determined to achieve a personal best time.

I felt comfortable throughout the swim leg although I spit up some oatmeal that I ate two hours before the race. I couldn't find anyone to draft behind because the other swimmers were either too slow or were swimming erratically.

At the start of the second loop of the bike course, the sky started to dump buckets of rain. I had a difficult time seeing since my sunglasses fogged up, but I was afraid to take away my eye protection. I was worried about being hit by a car, missing a turn or hitting a pothole due to the poor visibility, but fortunately, none of those things happened. After my bike started to slide on the wet roads, I backed off considerably on the downhills and the turns. The rain continued throughout the rest of the day although it became lighter at times.

At the end of the bike, I was four minutes behind the leader in 2nd place overall having made up about six minutes since the swim. I left the transition area at 5 hours and 48 minutes into the race; I knew I would need to run a 3:10 marathon to break nine hours. I desperately wanted to see "eight something" on the finish line clock.

The run was a point-to-point course on mostly rural roads from the transition area at Falls Lake to the finish line at the Duke University chapel. The course was hilly (nothing too steep, just lots of them) and one of the tougher marathon courses I had run to date.

My legs felt strong from the start, so I decided to take a risk and push the pace, running just under seven minute miles. I caught the leader at the four-mile marker and bade him a well-intentioned "good luck" then never looked back. As the leader, I picked up a bicycle escort. My pace stayed consistent although

I started to lose some time on the long up hills from the increased effort that seemed to rapidly suck away my energy.

At the 20-mile marker, I estimated my time based on my pace and realized that I could still break nine hours but it would be on a razor thin margin. I could not cross the finish line in "nine- something."

The last six miles were pure hell physically and mentally as I struggled for the strength and courage to keep moving in spite of the suffering. The second place runner dropped back 30 minutes, so I was only chasing the seconds on the clock. I ran the last two miles on fumes before crossing the finish line in a personal best time of 8:57.

I accomplished three goals at the Blue Devil: 1) I won the race as a cancer survivor; 2) I set a new personal best time at the Iron distance; and 3) I validated my win at Vineman the year before.

Ironman World Championship in Hawaii

"My concentration level blocks out everything. Concentration is why some athletes are better than others."
- *Edwin Moses, Olympic gold medalist in track and field*

I rode an emotional high for two weeks after the Blue Devil. I broke the coveted nine-hour mark, something that many professional triathletes never achieve. The downside was that I gave everything I had at that race and saved nothing for racing the rest of the year.

The Ironman World Championship in Kona, Hawaii was next on my schedule. This is the race that most Americans associate with triathlon. Nine times out of ten, when I tell someone that I compete in triathlons, their next question is: "Have you done Hawaii?"

Before 2002, I could only answer, "No, I haven't done it yet, but I will one day."

As Hawaii approached, I didn't feel the typical excitement that I normally feel prior to my Iron distance races. After the Blue Devil, I mentally checked out of racing and began to crave time away from anything that had to do with training and racing. My entire summer had focused on training for Utah and the Blue Devil often at the expense of everything else. I didn't travel, visit family, or go out during the week with friends. My mornings began with 6:00 a.m. workouts, six days a week, especially on the weekends when I started my long rides and runs early to beat the heat and the crowded W&OD Trail. I had maintained a hectic, exhausting tempo of wake up, eat, workout, eat, go to work, eat, workout, eat and go to bed. I wanted some downtime away from the structure and commitment of training.

At one point, my motivation was so low that I seriously considered pulling out of Hawaii except that I had already paid the $425 entry fee when I took the slot at Utah plus I had paid for two non-refundable $800 airline tickets.

My attitude shifted from "I want to win the race and go sub-nine hours at the Blue Devil" to "I want to vacation in Hawaii and just finish the race."

Jen and I arrived on the Big Island the weekend before the race and were joined a few days later by a couple of friends. My parents donated timeshare points to us so that we could stay at a resort about six miles from the race start. We wanted to enjoy the island, so we spent time snorkeling, kayaking and lying on the beach. The race still loomed in the back of my mind as something that I would eventually have to face, which prevented me from taking a complete vacation.

One of the most exciting aspects of the Ironman World Championship is that it's a "who's who" of the triathlon community. All of the American and international stars whom I had read about in magazines or heard about in locker room conversations were there. It was not uncommon for us to grab a cup of coffee in town and end up sitting next to world-class triathletes drinking their coffee too.

Everywhere around town, there were sponsor banners and athletes. Articles I read frequently made fun of the European athletes who paraded around town wearing only Speedos and t-shirts. It was often true and made for an amusing sight. To drive this point home, there is an annual underwear run. Athletes gather near downtown Kona in their boxers or briefs (the women also wear tops) and warm up with calisthenics. They then proceed to jog around town in their underwear. Besides the underwear run, one of my most memorable pre-race sights was a leather-clad biker who paraded up and down the main drag on his Harley with a small Schnauzer tucked against his chest. Both dog and owner wore goggles, or in the dog's case, the dog wore appropriately named Doggles®. We saw the motorcycle every day.

I woke the morning of the race to a dark and rainy sky, the rain was a first for the race. I hoped that the weather would remain overcast and wet, so that I would not have to endure the heat that the Hawaii course is famous for. The sky remained overcast and drizzly during the swim, but the sun broke through the clouds during the bike leg.

All along the bike course, the sun perched unmercifully high overhead and its heat radiated up from the black lava fields and asphalt. I saw the cool, wet ocean to my left on the way out of town and on my right on the way back, but everything near me was hot.

During the run, I remember thinking how nice it would feel to stop and lie down on the side of the road. My body was overheated, dehydrated and sunburned. I felt depleted of energy and I ached from soreness and dehydration. The muscles in my legs threatened to seize numerous times. I slowed to a walk when I reached each aid station. I grabbed a drink in each hand then slowly began running again.

Soon I found it harder to move back to a run. I eventually walked the entire length of each aid station then started walking between aid stations. I wanted the heat to end. I picked up ice and put it in my cap to cool my head, but the ice quickly melted.

I felt so miserable during the run that I stopped at a port-a-john to not just use the bathroom, but to also give myself few minutes to stop the discomfort in my legs.

I finished the race in ten and a half hours, but I lost the competition with myself. I could not keep my concentration or my motivation to drive myself faster through the discomfort.

***

After finishing Hawaii, I felt different than I had after other races. I lost the feeling of euphoria that usually stays with me for a few weeks post race. I'd been humbled and disappointed after finishing an hour and a half slower than my finish time at the Blue Devil only five weeks earlier. I'd already signed up to race the inaugural Ironman Coeur d'Alene®, Ironman Utah's replacement, the following year, but I wasn't excited about the thought of having to prepare in early spring for an end of June race.

Upon returning to Virginia, I needed a break from triathlon. I stopped working out altogether for two weeks. When I returned to exercise, my workouts lacked desire, and I felt like I was just going through the motions to maintain a minimal base level of fitness, so that I would not lose everything I had gained that year. I stopped reading triathlon articles and stopped posting answers to newbie questions on the RATS message board. I no longer showed up for the weekend RATS rides, preferring to sleep in or just ride on a stationary bike at work.

In hindsight, I should have called it quits after the Blue Devil in order to finish the year on an emotional high. Rather, I finished at Hawaii on an emotional low, bordering on what I believe was depression. Add in daylight savings time and not being able to see the sun driving to and from work, and my attitude turned to gloom and doom.

My job performance suffered slightly, and I allowed myself to be stressed out at the slightest hint of re-work or change. It probably didn't help that my team at work went through several reorganizations in a period of only a few months where I involuntarily changed jobs four times with four different managers. I kept my head down and did my job, but I didn't enjoy it. Simply earning a paycheck was enough for me at that time.

Jen and I were still engaged, but had not made any firm commitments about a marriage date. We talked about selling her townhouse and buying a house, which gave us a reason to push off the marriage and associated costs until after we moved. In hindsight, I think I was afraid to get married and be locked into another commitment that might end as it had with Clare.

After looking for a place, we settled for a single family home in a new community in Ashburn, Virginia, west of Reston.

The post-Hawaii feeling of glumness stayed with me through the holidays and into the New Year. It wasn't until February when the air warmed above freezing and the days became longer that my motivation and desire slowly returned.

Time heals and forgets.

Chapter 11: Flexibility

Jen and I moved into our new house in March. In addition to my training schedule and full-time job I now had yard work to do.

When we moved to Ashburn, my commute to work nearly doubled. I compensated for this by driving into Reston in the morning and parking at my gym. I would then go for a swim, and from there ride the rest of the way into work, which took just under an hour. I tried to do this commute twice a week.

Schedule flexibility is important for early season training in Northern Virginia when the weather can be unpredictable. It's not uncommon for temperatures to fluctuate 30 degrees from day to day or for there to be snow on the ground in March. Adding wind and rain to an already cold day makes for a miserable ride, especially when caught in a thunderstorm more than an hour ride away from home. Sometimes, it's best to just pull the plug and try again another day.

Sometimes it's just best to pull the plug and try again another day.

A bike ride along Skyline Drive in Shenandoah National Park in March with my friend, Steve, nearly proved deadly for both of us:

> The weather was cool, in the low 40s and overcast when we started biking. We parked just outside the park entrance to take advantage of the first six miles of climbing and to warm up in the cool, moist air. This decision came back to haunt us.

> We climbed.

> After an hour of climbing we had only reached the 10-mile marker. The rain began falling as a slow, steady, drizzle. We were both dressed with rain shell jackets covering several lighter layers so we kept riding. It was cold on the downhills, but we warmed up quickly on the climbs.

> A few miles later, the rain falling on my jacket froze due to wind chill created by the descents. I stubbornly said nothing and kept riding.

> At mile marker 22, a park ranger in a truck signaled for us to pull over.

"You need to turn around. The roads may freeze over."

Steve and I realized what should have been obvious an hour before. We were both stubborn in that neither one wanted to be the one that cried, "Uncle!" and gave into the weather.

The ranger drove off as the rain began to come down much harder. I soon discovered that my shell jacket, which was water resistant, was not waterproof. My clothing underneath was soaked.

How can I describe the trip back except to say that it was pure hell, but from a frozen frame of reference? I've never been as cold in my life as during the 1.5 hour trip back to the car.

As we rode back, I could see the ice building up on my bicycle fork and on my brakes from the wet road, forcing me to feather my brakes every few seconds to clear them. A few seconds later, they glazed over again with ice. Eventually, ice built up on my rear cog set, and I could no longer shift into any other gears. I was stuck in a mid-range gear for the remainder of the ride.

Because I was wet and cold, I started shivering uncontrollably on the descents, my handlebars shaking dangerously as I fought for control. I fearfully wondered if my wheels would slide out from under me as the roads approached the freezing point, but I was more afraid to stop pedaling for fear of hypothermia.

During the last six-mile descent to the park entrance and the warmth of our cars, we could not ride fast for fear of sliding on the questionably slick road, thereby prolonging the suffering. My muscles convulsed to generate heat, and my teeth chattered uncontrollably. I prayed that the roads wouldn't freeze until we were out of the park.

When we arrived at the park entrance after what seemed like a lifetime, the road was closed to cars. No one was allowed into the park.

Still shaking, Steve and I loaded our bikes into our cars with fumbling and numb hands, cranked up the heat and drove to a small diner to drink hot coffee and eat. We both shivered for another 30 minutes, spilling our hot coffees on our trembling hands and on the table.

Thankfully, the park ranger had pulled us over and suggested we turn around. If he hadn't stopped us, we likely would have ridden at least another three or four miles to the bottom of the hill and would have had to spend that much longer in the wet and cold.

Disappointment

"After all, tomorrow is another day."
- *Margaret Mitchell in* Gone with the Wind

The 2002 race season ended on a low note with Hawaii. Unfortunately, the 2003 race season also began on a low note with the Desoto American Triple-T®, a four-race triathlon held over three days in May, which added up to the equivalent mileage of an Iron distance triathlon. I figured that this race would help me prepare for Ironman Coeur d'Alene in June, and I planned to overload my body with racing, and then get enough rest to absorb the benefits between the two races. Triple-T nearly ended in tragedy for my team.

Steve, another friend named Mark, and I entered the race as a three-person team. Mark was of similar speed to Steve and me. This was the second year of the Triple-T, and we believed we were contenders for the podium with our fast, well-balanced team. Steve was a faster swimmer than both Mark and me, but in biking and running we were a perfect match.

Each team member had to finish all four of the triathlons for a total of 12 races. The first two races were scored as cumulative individual times and the last two were scored at the slowest individual team member's time. At the end of the weekend, the team with the lowest overall time won and each team member would take home a brand new $2,500 bicycle.

As we drove to the race site in Portsmouth, Ohio, we excitedly talked about strategy and pacing. Steve had analyzed the other teams and identified the teams to beat, including the previous year's winners. We believed we had a strong chance for the win.

Here is how the race played out:

Race #1: Short Prologue (Friday evening)

The short prologue was an individual event with a time trial start. Athletes started at five-second intervals based off of each team's initial seeding. The top five overall finishers would each receive a 30-second time bonus for their teams. Our team was seeded third overall before the start. I was in starting position number seven, thirty seconds behind the leading athlete.

Like most of the athletes that day, I opted for my wetsuit in spite of the short swim distance—400 meters—since the water felt very cold.

I mashed the gears on my bike from the start and managed to catch and pass a few other cyclists before hitting a mile long hill. I pumped my legs up and down like pistons. My lungs burned, feeling like I had literally ripped a hole in them through exertion, and I spit up stomach bile over my right shoulder every minute. At the top of the hill, I turned around and headed back down.

The one mile run was fast, and I jumped on the heels of two athletes who had passed me on the bike leg going downhill. The pace hurt and my heart rate stayed near maximum the entire time. I was unable to recover enough from my effort on the bike to pass both. The single mile stretched like an eternity, and I had no kick at the end.

After the race, my lungs still hurt and I coughed excessively.

As a team, we finished 6th overall.

Race #2: International Distance (Saturday morning)

Like the first race, the morning International race was also a time trial start, and I once again started in position number seven. I woke up that morning with a little soreness in my legs from the previous night. I wondered how I would feel at the beginning of the final Half-Iron distance race on Sunday after two more races on Saturday.

Reflecting back on my experience in the prologue, I decided that I needed to pace myself a little better, especially on the swim. Because there were no aid stations on the bike leg, I opted to carry two water bottles (one half full) plus a couple of energy gels. This turned out to be a smart decision.

The swim was uneventful, although I was cold in my sleeveless wetsuit. My zipper broke on my full-sleeve wetsuit during a training swim a few weeks prior, so the sleeveless was my only option unless I wanted to buy another wetsuit. I wasn't quite prepared to do that until I tried fixing the broken one.

The bike route was a challenging course. I kept my leg tempo high, but steady on the flats while driving my heart rate up on some of the steeper hills. I felt strong throughout and was able to move up several positions, coming off the bike right on the heels of the second place bike finisher. As we approached the transition area, we were both confused and almost collided because the bike dismount area had moved from the previous night's race.

The run was along a dirt fire road for three miles before the turnaround. After a brief conversation with the second place bike finisher, I picked up my pace in pursuit of the leader. After an initial flat section, the next two miles were mostly uphill followed by a relatively steep descent to the turnaround. I pushed myself on the run but was unable to take the lead.

We moved into second place overall as a team.

Race #3: International Distance (Saturday afternoon)

The third race nearly proved deadly for Mark.

The race was the same distance as the morning race but with a twist. Rather than a typical triathlon swim start, the race began with a mass bike start from a neutral moving peloton on an out-and-back course followed by the swim then the run. I tried to take a nap after eating a light lunch, but couldn't fall sleep. I was feeling more and more soreness creeping into my muscles from the first two races.

The peloton left the transition area following the official race vehicle, a pick-up truck. As a group, we established a relatively slow pace for the first mile or so until we passed through a construction area, which had the road closed in one direction. The pace accelerated, but it still felt relatively easy given the allowable drafting benefit. Steve, Mark and I positioned near each other and close to the front of the peloton. Because the three of us were strong riders, our strategy was to stay near the front and go with any complete team that tried to break away.

About mid-way through the first half of the ride, Steve rode up next to me and asked, "Where's Mark?"

"No idea." I replied.

We slowed down to wait for Mark in case we would need to work together to bring him back to the peloton. The peloton pulled away, and we couldn't find Mark.

We decided to close the gap on the peloton that had opened up on us as we continued to look for Mark. As we passed the peloton going the other direction after the turnaround, one of the riders said, "Come catch us."

So we chased. I told Steve that I thought we ought to have some fun and burn up the other riders' quads. Steve and I hammered at near maximal effort, rotating the lead every minute to take advantage of each other's draft and allow the trailing rider to recover before pulling again. We caught the tail end of the peloton at the bottom of a long climb, sat at the back for a few minutes to recover, then methodically moved up to the front.

The leading rider commented that he saw a cyclist hop into the back of the official race vehicle carrying a bike with a disk wheel. We reasoned that it was Mark as there was still no sign of him on the course. Without Mark being able to finish, we would be disqualified from the event. Steve and I had nothing to lose by going fast now. Even if we destroyed our legs before the run, it wouldn't matter since we were unofficial.

Now the real fun began as Steve and I continued to push the pace, with a select group of four or five that broke away from the main peloton.

I made a sprint for the finish line and crossed first, edging out one of my competitors for the win.

Back in the transition area, we met up with Mark who had ridden back in the truck. His rear disk wheel came apart with the rim separating from the carbon disk while he descended a hill at 40 mph. Fortunately, he was able to stop safely without crashing or taking out other riders or hurting himself. This could have been a deadly disaster and a terrible tragedy for his family and young children.

After dilly-dallying in the transition area, we decided to finish the race even though it would be unofficial.

Race #4: Half-Iron Distance (Sunday morning)

The final race was the Half-Iron distance on Sunday morning. We woke up to tired and sore legs. The excitement of racing was gone, and we all sluggishly dressed and headed down to the lake for the final event.

Because we were disqualified, Steve, Mark and I started at the very back of all the other teams, about 40 minutes behind the leading group. As we finished the first loop of the swim, which brought us back to the swim start, the "Little Smokies Triathlon," a Half-Iron distance event that took place at the same time was just beginning. We dove back into the water with the Little Smokies starting horn in the background. A few seconds later, we were surrounded by fresh triathletes who were only doing a single race that weekend.

Exiting the swim, we began the bike together, taking turns drafting off of each other. We passed many of the slower teams and moved up in the overall time rankings although unofficially. Toward the end of the second loop on the bike, we saw the first "Little Smokies" rider behind us.

"There's no way we're going to get lapped when we're drafting off of each other. Let's pick it up."

We beat him into the transition area, but were quickly passed by his fresh legs at the beginning of the run.

After three days of racing, the half marathon leg felt like an eternity. We finally crossed the finish line unofficially in 2nd place overall.

We hopped in the car and headed home. There was no need for us to stay for the awards ceremony.

Keeping it Simple

"Our life is frittered away by detail...Simplify, simplify."
- *Henry David Thoreau, American Author*

After being both coached and self-coached, I reached the conclusion that training should be simple and straightforward. *Training should be simple and straightforward.* Why build in unnecessary complexity? Besides, I didn't want to spend a lot of time creating a schedule that I knew that I wouldn't be able to follow without constant rewrites.

I find it amusing when I hear other athletes talk about their detailed workout schedules. I hear things like, "My coach told me to ride in zone 1 for 10 minutes then zone 2 for 50 minutes then back to zone 1 for 10 minutes" or "I'm doing 6 x 1 mile repeats in zone 3 while recovering at 2 minutes in zone 1."

My first question is, "What is zone 1 and why are you training in zone 1?"

The typical response I receive back is: "Zone 1 is keeping my heart rate between 1XX and 1YY because my coach told me to."

"But why?" I ask.

"Because my coach says so." they reply.

Hmmm…that still doesn't explain why they should be keeping their rate between 1XX and 1YY.

In 11 years of competitive racing and training, I haven't come across a standardized definition of "zone 1" in any triathlon training book.

Ironically, my comments to them later in a ride tend to be something like, "I thought you were supposed to ride in zone 1. This is a hard effort."

"Uh, yeah." They gasp and pant as they are hopelessly out of breath. "I guess, uh, I'm not, uh, following, uh, my coach's, uh, advice."

I am amazed at the level of complexity that many people build into their training schedules. For example, a workout might look something like this:

- Bike – 15 minute warm up at [heart rate] zone 1; 45 minutes at zone 2 with 3x2 minute repeats at zone 4; 15 minute cool down in zone 1.

- Run – Warm up for 10 minutes. 4 x 800 on the track with 2-minute recovery between each interval followed by 4 x 400 with 1-minute recovery. Run at AT (anaerobic threshold) + 5 bpm.

I have concerns with this level of rigidity and structure for a number of reasons.

What if I desire to ride with a group on a ride that doesn't follow my training schedule? Should I miss the group ride, so that I stick to my planned workout even if it means riding alone?

What happens if my heart rate is elevated due to stress or overtraining? What should I do instead of my workout?

What if I'm on the verge of catching a cold after waking up with a sore throat in the morning? Should I do my track workout that is scheduled for today? What are my other options?

The weather forecast is calling for rain tomorrow. It might make more sense to do my long bike ride today instead of tomorrow, but my schedule says I need to do it tomorrow.

Perhaps if I didn't have a full-time job, had a wide open day without other commitments, had access to top of the line facilities, and had around-the-clock access to a good coach who could customize and adapt my plan real-time, I could more easily follow workouts to a "T" while training in the prescribed heart rate zones for the prescribed times. Hmmm…sounds nice, unfortunately, I have a limited amount of time, dynamic work and personal schedules plus friends that I train with who are not usually interested in swimming, biking or running in zone 1 if my schedule says to ride in zone 1.

Consequently, I attempt to simplify my training as much as possible. If my planned workout needs to change, I change it. Life is complicated enough without worrying if my heart rate is five beats too low or five beats too high.

My workout schedule looks more like this:

Monday: Off

Tuesday: Swim 60 minutes; Drills, Bike 120 minutes easy

Wednesday: Run 45 minutes easy

Thursday: Swim 60 minutes (4x500 meters); Bike 60 minutes easy with 15 minutes hard effort

My desire for flexibility in my schedule and balance in my life has pushed me away from working with a coach. Although I enjoy the structure of being told what to do, when to do it, how long and how hard, I resent the rigidity. It creates stress for me when I attempt to meet the schedule as there are always conflicts and competing priorities. I would rather set up loose training guidelines developed from my own experiences.

I create simple training guidelines (keyword "simple") as a framework for planning and scheduling my workouts. By establishing guidelines upfront, I also enable more flexibility in adapting my workout schedule around my somewhat dynamic life rather than the other way around.

Examples of training guidelines:

1. Minimum of two workouts of each event (swim /bike/run) per week.

    Rationale: To ensure adequate frequency to maintain fitness and form. Three of each (more ideal) is possible with a full-time job assuming that I can squeeze in back-to-back workouts during the day to minimize the prep time associated with exercising. If I have to choose between biking or running, I will almost always choose biking as I have historically learned through experience that the biking seems to help my running, but not necessarily the other way around. There are some advantages to be gained by increasing frequency, but they need to be matched by the need for increased rest plus there is a higher likelihood of injury or overtraining.

2. One "off day" per week to do something besides swim, bike and run.

    Rationale: To recover mentally and physically. This is my day to sleep in as long as needed, take the dogs for long walks (great low impact aerobic workout), complete any nagging projects around the house or run errands. I don't do too many things, of course, or I am defeating the purpose of having a rest day.

3. 10 minutes of stretching after every workout.

    Rationale: To improve or at least maintain flexibility. I stretch after I workout when my muscles are warm and full of blood rather than before a workout when they are tight and more susceptible to injury. If I'm not working out that day, I will warm up with a brief walk or run prior to stretching.

Armed with my training goals and training guidelines, I begin with an empty calendar to help me visualize the weeks in the training year.

Applying my guidelines, I start filling in my planning calendar in pencil taking into account things like:

1. Known personal events (weddings, vacations, etc.)

2. Key "A" races. For each racing season, I focus on two or three Iron distance events as my key races with one race in early summer and the other race in either September or October to break up the season into two smaller chunks.

3. Less important "B" races, which provide anaerobic training, help me gauge my current fitness level and force me to break up my high volume training weeks with short pre-race taper periods. Early season races also give me a "feel" for racing intensity after a winter and spring of aerobic workouts.

4. Tapering period.

5. Recovery time post race.

6. High volume weekends five to eight weeks out from a key race.

7. At least three months of aerobic base building before racing while minimizing high intensity work. My "base volume" long workouts are: Swim- 60 minutes; Bike- 3 hours; Run- 10+ miles (or 80 minutes).

8. Balance hard weeks with easy weeks (e.g., three hard weeks to one easy week) for recovery, so the body can adapt to the effects of the harder weeks.

With these guidelines as a starting point, the calendar almost fills out itself. I adjust and tweak it several times during the year until I have something that aligns to my goals, other commitments and passes the "reasonableness" test. If I need to change it, I change it. Simple!

Ironman Coeur d'Alene

"Train the distance. Train the course. Train in similar conditions." I tell myself. "Training teaches the body to understand what it can expect on race day and allows it time to adapt to the future demands of the race."

Even with proper preparation for distance, course and climate, races can serve up unexpected conditions as I found out in the inaugural Ironman Coeur d'Alene in Idaho in June where the weather conditions caught me completely by surprise.

Because of the northern latitude and summer solstice being at the end of June, the days were very long in northern Idaho. At the time of the race, the sun was up before 5:00 a.m. and didn't set until after 10:00 p.m.

The weeks prior to the race had temperatures in the 70s or 80s during the day and 50s at night, which would have been perfect racing weather. As the race drew closer, the temperatures crept up into the low 80s then the mid 80s. Jen and I flew into Spokane, Washington on the Thursday before the Sunday race day to find temperatures in the mid-80s with a forecast for race day in the 90s—not good. Granted, the heat was a dry heat, not the wet, humid heat of the East Coast, but temperature would play a significant role in the race.

I woke up race morning with a scratchy, sore throat.

The swim began on the beach near the host resort in downtown Coeur d'Alene. The water temperature on Lake Coeur d'Alene was in the mid 60s, cool but comfortable with a full wet-suit, and water visibility was excellent. The course was 2 x 1.2-mile triangular loops broken up by a quick dash out of the water and over the timing mats before wading back in for the second loop.

BOOM! Everyone rushed into the water. Chaos! Confusion! Arms and legs flailed everywhere.

In addition to providing buoyancy and warmth, my wetsuit also served as body armor to protect me from the swinging arms and legs. My swim goggles were knocked loose in the first minute, and I scrambled to quickly put them back on my face before the swimmers behind me could swim over me.

After a few minutes, the pack thinned, and I was able to settle into a groove. I kept my pace steady and manageable, and I occasionally popped my head out of the water to sight the buoys and adjust my direction if necessary. I intermittently bumped into other swimmers and constantly felt people brushing against my feet. I exited the water in just over 56 minutes having evenly split both laps.

I aggressively pushed a fast pace on the bike leg from the beginning. I felt strong and systematically passed other cyclists. I steadily powered up the hills, although I remembered thinking to myself on the second big climb that I wished I had swapped out my rear cog set for one with easier gearing.

As temperatures climbed into the 90s, I began to overheat. I observed the salt caking on my arms and black shorts from my sweat. I ingested salt tablets to replace the lost salt and TUMS® to settle my stomach. My heart rate dropped below what I wanted to maintain, but I was unable to do anything about it except to focus on keeping it from going even lower. I was miserable and was not prepared for the heat.

I drank what seemed like gallons of fluid, both Gatorade and water, averaging about 1½ water bottles between every aid station (approximately 36 ounces every 10 miles or 25-30 minutes). I was unable to stomach any solid food like energy bars, so I consumed mostly GU® provided at the aid stations and the gel I carried.

My brain cooked in my helmet from the heat generated by my head.

"Damn!" My inner thigh cramped. I slowed down, stood up on my pedals, ingested more salt and the cramp went away in a few minutes. Ten minutes later, the muscles seized again. Not fun.

"Damn!" I said again as the glute muscle in my right butt cheek cramped next, but I kept riding.

There was little to no shade on the open asphalt roads. The heat seemed to radiate down from the sun as well as up from the black road. This could have been a fast run course for me if it were not for the heat. I heard later that the temperature reached a high of 98 degrees during the afternoon.

After finishing the bike in about 30th place, I passed a few more athletes in the transition tent. My unrealistic pre-race goal was to run the marathon in under three hours, so I stubbornly started the run at a sub seven-minute-per-mile pace, but quickly backed off the effort as I realized the heat would turn this race into a race of attrition. I dropped my pace down to a more conservative and realistic eight minutes per mile, which I thought I could sustain until the end. I also opted to walk the aid stations to ensure that I could consume enough fluid as well as pick up ice to cool my overheated body. My routine for each aid station became:

- Slow down to a walk
- Take a sip of water
- Take a swig of Gatorade
- Take a gulp of soda
- Dump ice down my shirt
- Place a cold, wet sponge under each shoulder of my race jersey
- Start running again

I said, "Good job" and flashed a thumb's up to two friends on the run; both looked like they were in good spirits. As I headed out for my second run loop, I glanced across to see another friend on the sidelines cheering me on with his arm in a sling. He had been racing, but fell on the bike and broke his collarbone. Bad luck!

The second loop of the run was pure hell. I was seriously overheated and felt lightheaded. I struggled to stomach food, and managed to force down a few gel packets. I involuntarily emptied my stomach on the side of the road four or five times. My right glute muscle tightened and threatened to seize up again. I massaged the muscle, which loosened it for a few minutes before tightening back up.

I reached a point mentally where I no longer cared about anything except the next aid station, so I could grab the cooling ice and refreshing fluid. I threw my pre-race goals completely out the window as my thoughts turned simply to survival. My walks through each aid station became longer and longer as my willpower to keep running slowly faded. Although I still passed a few more people, others passed me as well. I graciously walked through every bit of cool water from the sprinklers that residents had set up in the streets.

At mile 24, I calculated that I could still break 10 hours, so I forced myself to pick up my pace. I crossed the finish line in 9 hours and 54 minutes (17th overall), falling well short of the sub-nine hour race that I hoped to achieve.

As I crossed the finish line, a volunteer handed me my finisher's medal while two other volunteers half carried me to the medical tent. The medical team covered me in ice bags to cool my body down and gave me a saline IV to replace fluids and electrolytes. After an hour in the medical tent, I felt better and limped over to the massage tent for a massage. I later heard that 20 percent of the participants didn't finish the race.

I took away several key lessons from Coeur d'Alene.

1. Pre-race goals and expectations are good for motivation and planning, but they need to be flexible depending on the conditions of the race. Ninety-eight-degree heat is not meant for a personal best time.

   Pre-race goals are good for motivation and planning, but they need to be flexible.

2. A positive attitude, especially when race execution starts to unravel, can mean everything. Every race will have ups and downs at different points for everyone. The key to success is moving forward in spite of the downs and realizing that everyone else is experiencing the same race conditions.

   A positive attitude can mean everything.

3. For extremely hot weather races, hydration and electrolyte replacement are essential. In hindsight, I should have eaten more salty foods like pretzels in the days prior to the race to increase the salt in my body while also ingesting more salt tablets during the race. Although I drank lots of fluid, I was still dehydrated at the end. Realistically, there was no way to avoid dehydration given the conditions, but I should have tried to take in more fluid on the bike.

I felt like I had adequately prepared for Coeur d'Alene. However, in this case, the weather conditions created an unpleasant experience. I was able to re-adjust my goals and strategy on course to deliver a satisfactory race to finish in the top one percent overall. Had I wanted a Hawaii slot, it would have been mine for the taking, but I passed.

Reston Race Director

In 2003, I took on a much larger role than volunteer coordinator at the Reston Triathlon as one of several race directors. I took responsibility for the two transition areas—the swim-to-bike transition area at the lake and the bike-to-run transition area at a high school a mile away from the lake. The course necessitated two transition areas for safety reasons given the dense suburban population of Reston and road width. The two transition areas created more than two times the work of a single transition area.

As a group, the directors organized the Race Captains, attracted sponsors, acquired the necessary approvals, made the business decisions and ran the race on race day.

The race directors were always looking for opportunities to improve the race. As an active and experienced triathlete, I offered my perspective. For example, we moved to chip timing and 100 percent online registration as a means to provide results more quickly and accurately, as well as ease the registration process for both athletes and organizers.

We met multiple times in the month leading up to the triathlon, but the real work kicked in three days before, when we stuffed race packets with race numbers, safety pins to hold the race numbers, energy gels, sponsor literature, swim caps and swim-to-bike transition bags. The packet stuffing process, once properly organized, turned into a large assembly line.

The day before the race, a cadre of volunteers, Boy Scouts and I set up both transition areas starting at the lake at 8:00 a.m. A local piping company had donated long narrow sections of pipe, which we laid out in the lakeside parking lot, and then attached wooden supports on either end to create bike racks. The racks each held 10 bikes. We set up 50 racks to handle up to 600 bicycles. We also set up an orange snow fence around the perimeter of the parking lot in order to limit access to athletes only. We repeated the transition area setup at the high school.

The night before the race, I couldn't sleep. I felt as nervous as I had before I did my first race. Like the night before a big race, I ran through scenarios in my mind of what might go wrong although this time the scenarios were from the perspective of a race director, not a participant.

The morning of race day, I arrived before 5:00 a.m. at the lake to set up water hoses and power cords. Once the athletes began arriving slowly thereafter in the dark, my volunteers and I directed the flow of people into the transition area and to their bike racks. I spent half of my time chasing down family members who were not supposed to be in the athlete only area.

Once the race began, my volunteers maneuvered the athletes through the swim-to-bike transition area by helping them find their bikes and directing them out onto the road. We also gathered all their personal items in trash bags to transport to the other transition area at the high school for the athletes to pick up after the race. By the time the last swimmer exited the water; we had broken down the transition area and loaded the truck with the transition area gear (swim buoys, bike racks, snow fencing and tables).

In parallel, another crew of transition area volunteers was over at the high school maneuvering people through the bike-to-run transition to begin the last leg of the race. It was the same drill as before, helping athletes find their gear and directing them out of the transition area to start the run. As people finished the race, I spent the majority of my time locating their belongings. The biggest challenge with two transition areas is logistics. We had to move everyone's swim-to-bike gear from the lake to the high school before they finished the race. We provided participants with numbered trash bags for swim gear. Unfortunately, the gear did not always end up in the bags and my volunteers had to make as assessment as to which athlete the item(s) belonged.

After the race, we broke down the bike-to-run transition area and loaded the truck to take all of the gear from both transition areas back to the storage shed.

With the intent to improve the race in future years, I solicited feedback from local triathletes. Most of the feedback was positive with many good suggestions, but I also received a few complaints. In the spirit of sharing feedback and also having a little fun, I shared this information by creating a list of things to consider during the race:

1. Know where your bike-to-run transition gear is. Please don't yell or swear at the volunteers if you can't find your stuff. Honestly, no one wants to steal your stinky running shoes that are hidden under your transition towel where you placed them.

2. Please don't place valuables in the swim bags. An athlete put his keys, his wallet and his wedding ring in his bag that had been accidentally put by someone else's stuff. Needless to say, he was very upset at me.

3. Please put your swim items inside the swim bag, not alongside it. If it's not in it, we have to try to "guess" which bag the goggles and wetsuits belong to, and sometimes we're wrong.

4. Please put your name and phone number in your wetsuit and on other items you would like to keep. Chances are, if someone does pick it up by mistake, you'll get it back if it has your name on it.

5. Please check that the bag you grab has your stuff in it, not someone else's. Unfortunately, we can't check inside every transition bag to make sure that each item belongs to the person who is taking it out.

6. Please clean up your trash when you leave the race. We picked up several bags of trash in the transition areas. We are volunteers, and none of us get paid to clean up. Picking up half-used, leaking, hot gel packets is not a pleasant experience, especially for someone like me who is allergic to the hornets and bees that it attracts.

7. Know the rules. Make sure you have bar end plugs. Thankfully, the local bike shop Bonzai showed up to provide 70 bar end plugs. That equates to at least 35 athletes who would not have been allowed to race had Bonzai not been there.

Every year, the other directors ask why I volunteer instead of racing. "I like volunteering." I reply. "This is my opportunity to give something back to the sport." It feels good. I also have the opportunity to offer my perspective as an athlete to make a great race even better.

Now when I race, I make a conscious effort to give a quick "Thanks" to every volunteer that I come into contact with over the entire course. Sometimes, it's just a simple thumbs up or a nod if I can't find the strength to speak.

Blue Devil (Second Time)

"I am giddy, expectation whirls me around.
The imaginary relish is so sweet
That it enchants my sense."
- *William Shakespeare in Troilus and Cressida*

With better results came higher expectations. I reached a point where I expected to be a top finisher in any race that I did—either age group or overall depending on the size and competitiveness of the race. I also had dreams of winning one of the bigger races like Ironman USA or Ironman Coeur d'Alene.

This meant that I was less likely to do a race unless I was really ready to do it. It was hard for me to compete in a race knowing that I was not in excellent racing shape. If I had a bad race, people questioned my ability. If I had a great race, people said it was to be expected. Maybe I was racing too much in the court of public opinion.

Two and a half months after Coeur d'Alene, I competed in the Blue Devil Triathlon in October for the second time as the returning champion. My expectation and my goal were to win again.

At race registration, a volunteer handed me bib number "1."

"You must be David Glover." she said.

I smiled.

I was honored to wear the number, but I also realized that I was now a marked target as the "One to beat."

My biggest pre-race stress was deciding which type of clipless pedals to use during the race. I had recently switched from Speedplay® to a newer pedal with less float. Float is the amount of lateral rotation of the back of my foot which the pedal allows and a broader contact platform for the shoe. After a week of mentally flip-flopping back and forth between pedals, I finally decided to use the Speedplay pedals for the race even though I hadn't used them in the past month. I made this decision for two reasons:

1. I suspected that my new pedals may have caused a recent pain in my right leg that I was experiencing.

2. I could simply step down on either side of the Speedplay pedals to attach the cleats on my shoes to the pedals. The other pedals required me to carefully align the front of my cleat with the front of the top of the pedal and step into it, and sometimes I missed.

The buoys were nearly invisible in the dark as I seeded myself at the front near my friend, Mike Guzek, who I refer to as my "locomotive." My goal for the swim was to tuck in behind him in the water like a boxcar to be pulled along by his large frame. The race was scheduled to start at 7:00 a.m., but was delayed by about 10 minutes until the sun appeared over the horizon. It was October and a few weeks before daylight savings time ended.

The starting horn blew, and I dove straight for the back of Mike's feet. A few times Mike veered to the left before correcting back to the right while I swam a straighter line between the buoys. My stroke was relaxed, and I was able to sustain Mike's pace comfortably, which meant I was having a great swim. I exited the swim 7th overall, a few seconds behind Mike.

My plan was to take over the lead of the race by the end of the first loop. In my first race at Blue Devil, I had lagged the leader by 10 minutes at the start of the bike leg and didn't take the overall lead until mile four of the run. This year, there were five people ahead of me at the bike leg start with the gap to the leader at only five minutes. I quickly passed three of the five within the first 10 miles.

There were three aid stations on the bike course, all of which were on the loop portion of the lollipop-shaped course. I caught the second place rider just before the second aid station. At one point, he re-passed me, forcing me to temporarily drop back out of his drafting zone. My heart rate dropped as he slowed down in front of me. I picked up my pace and passed him again.

I caught the remaining rider just before the end of the first loop. Starting the second loop, only one rider behind me was within sight so I pushed my pace even harder on the next set of hills. Five minutes later, I glanced back. I was alone.

As the lead cyclist, I now had the benefit of a race escort vehicle ahead of me, which was easily identifiable by its flashing light. I also picked up a motorcycle police escort. No worries about angry motorists! The only riders I saw on my second loop were those I passed who were on their first loop. It was good to be alone.

My pace was steady although my heart rate had fallen off from what I hoped to maintain. I excitedly thought to myself, "I can win this," but dampened my overconfidence with, "Yes, but not if you blow up on the bike or run. Pace yourself!"

Half an hour later, my stomach became queasy and unsettled. I had spit up a few times earlier in the day (which is normal for me), but I suddenly and violently heaved multiple times, projecting orange-colored liquid over the right side of my body and onto the pavement. I estimated that I coughed up the equivalent of two water bottles of fluid, which had been sitting in my stomach. I wondered if the folks in the lead vehicle 50 yards ahead of me were oblivious to my situation. This was not a good omen with the marathon still ahead. The nausea quickly faded away, and I forced myself to begin consuming fluid and food again while ingesting TUMS to settle my stomach.

I believed my fitness on the bike was better than the previous year, however:

1. I was no longer driven to break nine hours, I had already achieved that goal.

2. Unlike the previous year when I was chasing the leader until mile four on the run, I led off the bike and had built a gap on the following athletes.

3. I recognized a need to ride conservatively after vomiting, as I was concerned about loss of nutrition and saving myself for the hills on the run.

I finished the bike leg in just under five hours, eight minutes slower than the year before but the only rider to go under five hours that day.

As I exited the transition area to start my run, I only had a three-minute lead, which was not much in a marathon. To give perspective, I competed in a Half-Iron distance race five weeks earlier where I had started the run with the eventual winner. We had a solid five-minute lead on the next athlete, and I finished 5th.

The run is where the Iron distance race truly begins and ends. Unlike most of my past races, I didn't feel good at the start of this run.

The run course was different than the first year's point-to-point course back to the Duke University campus. This year's run was five identical loops within a park. The race website described the course as "rolling" with four "significant" hills. Doing the math in my head, five loops with fours hills each equaled twenty "significant" hills. This year's course was undoubtedly the toughest marathon course that I had done. There were few flat sections. Thankfully, the day was relatively cool with a cloud cover so heat wasn't a factor.

My initial pace fell short of my goal to maintain sub-seven minutes per mile, so I began drinking cola immediately to bring in the simple sugar and caffeine for energy. I felt better and was able to pick up my run pace.

The run course layout was ideal for several reasons. Five loops broke down the full 26.2 miles into five more manageable segments. I now had five 5.2-mile mini-goals to chase. Because there were many out-and-back sections plus parts of the course overlapped, I could keep track of my trailing competitors on every lap. The five loops also made aid stations available about every half mile as compared to a typical mile between aid stations. I never had to worry about reaching the next aid station because it was literally just around the next corner.

I met many folks out on the run course as we exchanged encouraging words:

"Good job, buddy, keep it up!"

"You look strong."

"Hang in there, man."

"I'll see you at the finish line."

"Man, you're really smoking the run!"

The interaction broke up the monotony of 26.2 miles.

I felt better after drinking the cola, so my plan for the run was to quickly build a margin of time on the nearest runners. If I ran too hard, I would "blow up" and start walking. I didn't want to run too slow and give up any time gap as it might give the closest runners the motivation and confidence to close the distance. I wanted them to run hard to catch me, so that they blew up. I built up my lead from three minutes to six minutes over the first few miles and held that gap for much of the race before picking up a few more minutes toward the end.

I started the final lap. The last 20 percent of the run was where I felt 80 percent of the pain and discomfort. My quadriceps screamed in agony on the downhills. My legs burned with lactic acid, and my eyes glazed over on the up hills. I was lightheaded, but I kept moving.

As I approached the turn for the finish line, I pumped my hands in the air with a big smile on my face. I've done it again! I was now the two-time winner of the Blue Devil Triathlon!

With three Iron distance wins, I contemplated pursuing a license as a professional triathlete, but before I added the tag "Professional Athlete" to my biography, I wanted to be able to commit 100 percent and represent the sport at the highest level. I couldn't commit 100 percent with a full-time job that required me to travel. For now, I was content to race as an amateur. As an amateur, I did enjoy finishing faster than many of the professional athletes in races. This boosted my self-confidence and proved that I could possibly compete at a professional level.

Sustained Power

I often see questions on message boards like: "How hard a heart rate effort should I go on the bike when racing?"

My response, "The quick answer on heart rate: as hard as you can maintain without bonking or blowing up."

My friend, Aaron Schwartzbard, gave an outstanding explanation expanding on my simple response. Aaron is about five years younger than me, but is probably the wisest and most well-read person I know in regard to training theory and practice, so I value his opinion greatly. He also works full time and has dabbled in a vast number of events including marathons, triathlons, ultra-distance runs (from 50-kilometers up to 100-miles) and even a double Iron distance race (4.8-mile swim, 224-mile bike, 52.4-mile run). I would not be surprised if he qualifies for the marathon Olympic trials one day. Here was Aaron's response to my post and the original question:

> Although it might appear to be trivially true, that bit of Dave's advice is probably the best advice you'll get about the bike of an Iron distance race. Speaking as someone who has been known to show up at a race or two with a high level of general fitness, but a low level of bike-specific fitness, I'd say that any other general guideline might not be applicable to your particular constraints. For me, the bike portion is usually a low intensity affair. The muscles in my legs responsible for turning the pedals over just aren't developed enough to put a heavy load on my cardiovascular system for all those hours.
>
> Steve [another friend of mine] mentioned 75 percent of maximum heart rate (MHR) as a reasonable intensity level. For him, and probably for most people, that's a reasonable suggestion. But during my last two or three Iron distance races, there's no way I could have done that. From a cardiovascular standpoint, I'd have no problem operating at 75 percent of MHR for six hours. I'd be more than happy to go for a six-hour run at 75 percent MHR. But on a bike, at least during my last race season, I'd be surprised if my legs could have done that on a bike for TWO hours. It's not just that I can't go as fast as folks like Steve or Dave, it's that I really can't maintain that kind of INTENSITY, specifically on the bike.
>
> During my last Iron distance race, which was on a flat course, from the first hour of the bike to the last, I was hardly breathing heavily. I couldn't go any faster, but I was hardly breaking a sweat.
>
> I realize that my case isn't representative of the standard case, but it does serve to illustrate a point. That point is this: fitness is a multidimensional concept. Increased fitness doesn't just allow you to go FASTER, it also allows you to maintain higher INTENSITY for a longer time. So the mathematicians out there will recognize this as an optimization problem: higher speed has higher cost, and you need to spend just the right amount on the bike to leave you with enough "currency" in your legs,

stomach and lungs to get you through a marathon as fast as possible. All that is just a long-winded way of saying go as hard as you can maintain without bonking or blowing up.

But in your specific case, you've done a few Iron distance races, and you have some idea what it's like to run a marathon off the bike. If, as you claim, you haven't figured it out yet, I see two possibilities of what might be going on. Either you feel that your run is too slow or you feel that your ride is too slow. If the former is the case, back off on the bike. If the latter is the case, then ride faster until you reach the former case, then back off on the bike. Remember, it's not just a 112-mile bike race. As I read Iron distance race reports, I notice two thoughts often come out. One is, "I had a great race, but I think I could go faster on the bike." The other is, "I had an awesome ride, but I blew up on the run." Based on the number of times I've read those two sentiments, even if I had never done an Iron distance race, I'd come to the conclusion that if you don't finish the bike thinking, "I could have gone faster," then you're in trouble.[10]

I call this ability to go faster at a higher intensity "sustained power." At longer distances, absolute maximum speed becomes less relevant than the ability to maintain consistent, steady speed delivered over a longer period of time.

Great Floridian (Fourth Time)

"Ful wys is he that kan hymselven knowe!"
(Very wise is he that can know himself)
- *Geoffrey Chaucer, English Poet*

Before each race, I ask myself:

- Why am I here?

- What do I want to achieve?

- How deep am I willing to dig to achieve it?

- How much suffering am I willing to endure?

These are simple questions, but ones that I must ask and answer before and during my races. The answers to these questions fundamentally drive whether

I try to win, push myself for a personal best, just finish or quit. Yes, I've been tempted to quit many times, as it is an easy choice to fall back on mid-race when conditions deteriorate.

If I want to perform at my best, I need to put on my race face and, more importantly, establish a committed and positive attitude. If I cannot commit totally, I cannot hit my potential. Iron distance racing is a long and uncomfortable day, but the race is only a single day. I need to commit myself for that entire day to perform at my best.

If I cannot commit totally, I cannot hit my potential.

Occasionally when I race, time becomes irrelevant. There is no past, no future, just now. As I learned in scouting with my cistern project, a difficult task can be accomplished with adequate preparation and by breaking down the task into smaller, more manageable sub-tasks. My race becomes a race of sub-goals: swim to the next buoy, bike to the next five-mile marker, run to the next aid station, etc. Even with multiple Iron distance races under my belt, I still have a difficult time comprehending 140.6-miles all at one time. I need to break it up into smaller, more manageable chunks.

Instead of envisioning the entire race, break it down into smaller, more manageable chunks.

When I returned to the Great Floridian Triathlon in 2003 for the 4th time, I didn't have a good reason for doing the race other than I was curious to see what it would feel like doing an Iron distance race two weeks after my repeat victory at the Blue Devil. I had no grand illusions about hitting a personal best time, but thought I could still pull together a solid race and maybe even finish on the podium. I also wanted to test my resolve in adverse conditions as I pushed into unfamiliar territory.

I decided to do the race three days after the Blue Devil. In the back of my mind, I had toyed with the idea of signing up before the Blue Devil, but I wanted to see how the Blue Devil played out and, more importantly, how I felt physically and mentally after the race before I committed to another one only two weeks later. My legs were still sore, but I felt that I could recover physically, at least on the surface, within two weeks. After a few email exchanges, two friends, Mike Guzek and Aaron Schwartzbard, were racing the Great Floridian as well.

My attitude toward this race was different than other races. My expectation was only to finish. No pressure. No time goals.

As a kid playing tag, I remember chasing a friend who always seemed to be just out of reach. That described my swim. From the start of the second swim loop, there was a small pack of swimmers about 30 meters ahead of me, who I just couldn't catch, and they stayed always within sight. It was very frustrating!

I considered dropping out after the swim, as my body felt tired, and I didn't have a compelling reason for doing the race. I refocused my thoughts as well as I could and kept going.

Similar to my race at Blue Devil two weeks before, I had stomach problems shortly past the halfway point on the bike. My stomach was not digesting all the gel, fluids, fig bars and bananas that I had crammed down my throat. At some point, my stomach released its contents onto the pavement as I kept riding. I was back to an empty stomach and losing calories. I lost more time and gave up a few places in the race as my power output dropped, as evidenced by my lower heart rate. Again, I considered dropping out of the race, but stubbornly chose to keep going.

The sun was high in the mid afternoon sky when I started the run with temperatures reaching the 80s. There was almost no shade on the run course, which, when coupled with a black asphalt running surface, made for a hot run course. I felt miserable and my motivation was low, but I kept moving.

After the first run loop, I let my concentration slip and talked myself into just walking the rest of the marathon. My legs were still tired from the Blue Devil, and I was feeling miserable. I estimated the time to complete the remaining distance if I walked and realized I could still finish in around 12 hours. As I passed through the transition area to start my second loop around the lake, I walked. Over the next couple of miles, I gave up four or five finishing positions and was quickly on my way out of the top 10 overall. I didn't care.

Another triathlete ran by and encouraged me to start running again. I ran for about a mile with him then decided I wanted to walk again, saying, "Thanks, but I think I'll just walk for now." despite his encouragement to keep going. He kept running.

After several miles of walking, I struck up a conversation with another walker. We then ran together for the rest of my second loop (his first loop). At the start of the third and final loop around the lake, I felt a little better so picked up my pace. At some point, I caught up with Mike, and we chatted for a mile. He wasn't feeling so well either.

Toward the end of my third loop, I was somehow still in the top 10 so I decided to suck up my feelings of self pity and finish strong. I crossed the line in ten and a half hours to finish in 6th place overall. I grabbed my dry clothes bag, lay down on the grass and waited for Aaron and Mike to finish.

After the awards brunch on Sunday, Mike and I headed to nearby Epcot® at Walt Disney World® to take advantage of the food and beer. As we approached "The Rose and Crown," a British pub, a young lady asked us if we were interested in some free beer "from around the world." We smiled and plopped our tired bodies down in front of a bucket of beers. We spent the rest of the afternoon and evening eating and drinking back the calories we burned off the previous day. It was heaven!

Sometimes it's the challenge of pushing myself beyond what I have ever done before that makes me race. Sometimes it may be simply to do it because it's there. That may be a good enough reason to finish a race, although not good enough to win a race, at least from my perspective.

Beginning with the End in Mind

"In absence of clearly defined goals, we become strangely loyal to performing daily acts of trivia."
- *Unknown*

Even before the 2003 racing season ended, I started to think about what I wanted to do the following year. For some races, I needed to commit a year ahead of time since they filled up very quickly. Being forced to sign up for races a year in advance can be somewhat frustrating on the one hand but forces commitment and early planning on the other.

I wanted to race at Ironman USA again, so I pitched the race to Jen a year in advance by telling her a bunch of our friends were signing up for the race the following July and it would be fun to go to Lake Placid again. I suggested we make a vacation of it and rent a house in the Adirondacks for a week. She agreed.

I needed buy-in to reduce some of the race resentment that had built up in the past since training and race schedules had again overshadowed personal vacation plans. With commitments from a group of friends to rent a house together, our mid-summer vacation for 2004 was set, and I would return to Lake Placid five years after racing in the inaugural race in 1999.

Remember to include significant others while making race plans and travel schedules.

I needed goals. My personality is such that I like to have a list of things to do, so that I can check them off as I do them. As I check things off, it makes me feel good. As list items pile up, I begin to feel overwhelmed. I think the worst possible job for me to do would be one that did not enable me to accomplish any goals. This is likely one of the reasons that I struggled with my first civilian job out of the Navy as a systems integrator with Lockheed Martin. I worked on a long-term project. By the time I left the project 18 months later for a new position, I felt like there had been very little forward progress in what I was doing. I had nothing significant to show for my time.

My goals for racing become the end state of what I'm trying to achieve, for example, finish in less than nine hours in an Iron distance race or finish three ultra races in a season. My goals are both near-term focused (this season, so that I can check things off my list) and long-term focused (within five years, so that I maintain a longer perspective). Realistically, I will need to re-adjust my goals as the year progresses due to unforeseen events or opportunities, but I want that initial stick in the ground in order to have something to sight off of for the future—perhaps analogous to sighting off of the next buoy in the swim leg. As I reach a buoy, I sight the next buoy and so on until I reach the finish.

As I thought about my goals for 2004, I asked myself a series of questions:

1. What distances do I want to race? Okay, the obvious choice for me is to try to do at least two Iron distance races each year, but what else? As a general rule, the longer the distance, the more training time required and the fewer number of races that I will physically be able to do. One trend that I have noted over the years is that I now race

much less frequently than I used to do. I have some friends who still race every weekend or sometimes even twice in a single weekend, often with great success. Sometimes they are not so successful and end up injured or burned out midway through the season. Although I love the challenge of racing, I have come to enjoy training for itself and the lower intensity workouts.

2. When do I want my race season to begin and end? This may be driven by location, weather, and outside commitments among other things. In the mid-Atlantic where I live, the racing season is typically from late April through October. There are opportunities to race in the other months, but they require travel.

3. Where do I want to race? Driving to races is much easier logistically than flying or shipping a bike, but flying opens up more options. Do I want to vacation as well?

4. How much time do I have to train? What other commitments do I need to meet?

5. What other goals do I want to achieve by the end of the season?

I attempt to pick goals that are measurable, otherwise, how will I know if I have achieved them? For example, "running a mile in under six minutes" and "finishing *Pick your goals based on your own performance, not the performance of others.* a marathon" are measurable goals. In the first instance, the goal is time, in the second instance the goal is just to finish. My bias is to pick goals that are dependent on my performance rather than others' performance. For example, "finishing in the top three overall" is a measurable goal, but somewhat dependent on who shows up to race that day.

My primary goals for Lake Placid were to finish in under nine hours and in the top 10 overall. I have twice finished in the top 20 overall at the larger races (Utah Duathlon and Ironman Coeur d'Alene), but a top 10 finish had alluded me so far. Naturally, my goal after two successive wins at the Blue Devil Triathlon was to win again.

My goals were set for 2004, but 2003 ended on a rocky note with regard to my relationship with Jen. We had been engaged for nearly two years and life at home had become routine. I made a mistake when I became emotionally attracted to another woman who was also in a committed relationship at the time. The appeal was euphoric, but not rational and ended up seriously jeopardizing my relationship with Jen.

© Paul Stackhouse

"For me, a race was as much a mental and emotional challenge as a physical challenge."

Chapter 12: Rely on Change

"Imagine that a new wonder drug has been created. It will prevent illness and disease, including cancer. It will help you lose excess weight and keep it off. It will slow the aging process, making you look and feel younger than your years. It will give you energy and increase your self-esteem. It will reduce stress, fight depression and anxiety, and put you in a better mood. It will make you stronger and healthier. It will improve your posture, your flexibility, your balance and your endurance. It will even help you sleep better.

Now imagine that this drug doesn't cost a penny and that you can take it several times a day or just once a day and still see results. In fact, you'll start seeing results within two weeks of your first dose.

Sounds pretty appealing, doesn't it? Would you take it?

The miracle drug is available right now and you can start taking it today. It's called exercise."
- *From the opening chapter of* Mayo Clinic: Fitness for Everybody, *Rochester, MN*

I agree 100 percent. I think that many of the potential benefits of regular exercise, as called out by the Mayo clinic above, are known by the general population but just not followed. I also think an understanding of what *Exercise needs for an endurance athlete are different from those of a power lifter or soccer player.* actually happens when you do exercise is not well understood. It is also a fair statement to say that my exercise needs as an endurance athlete are different from the exercise needs of a power lifter or a soccer player.

As a triathlete, I need to understand some things about exercise in order to make the most effective use of my training and my time.

I like endurance athletics guru Dr. Phil Maffetone's definition of endurance:[11]

- A steady-state level of activity where one can develop and sustain relatively high speeds at sub-maximum effort over time.

- The ability to develop higher speeds while remaining predominantly aerobic.

- Increasing the percent of fat-burning and decreasing the dependence on carbohydrate utilization with training.

The goal then with improving in endurance sports is to improve the body's ability to efficiently operate at higher intensities during that period of prolonged activity.

Fundamentally, in order to improve as an endurance athlete, I need to:

- Become more efficient at using oxygen (i.e., increase my ability to utilize my aerobic system).

- Increase the level of my glycogen stores as a source of energy. Although I want to draw primarily on fat stores as fuel, I need the glycogen to use the fat.

- Push my anaerobic threshold higher in order to maintain a higher intensity without the accumulation of lactic acid in my muscles.

The general wisdom seems to be that an endurance athlete should develop an aerobic base before engaging in any anaerobic exercise. An aerobic base is the foundation upon which one can add the speed via higher intensity, more anaerobic workouts.

Training for Endurance Sports

"The purpose is to push your threshold up, and I believe the only way to push it up is to train below it. If you train above it, ultimately you're going to push the threshold down."
- *Lance Armstrong on his training philosophy*

When I first started exercising again after my cancer treatments, I was essentially starting over from scratch with my level of fitness. My initial workouts were long walks on nearby trails. As my body healed over the next few months, I gradually added in more variety and more intensity to my routine. I wanted my fitness back quickly but, because of my incision, I was forced to regain it slowly. In hindsight, the slower approach may have been better for me in the long run as I did not suffer any setbacks on the way to my first triathlon later that summer.

My friend and fellow ultra-endurance athlete Aaron Schwartzbard posted an online message describing the effects and benefits of aerobic training (below anaerobic threshold - AT) versus anaerobic training (at or above AT):

> In essence, for any endeavor in which you exhaust your muscles' Adenosine Triphosphate (ATP) stores (molecular level units of energy), you need to focus on the base aerobic fitness to cause adaptations (increased red blood cell count, increased capillary density, improved Type IIa muscle fiber recruitment, etc.) that allow you to process your body's energy stores most efficiently.
>
> So why do so many people insist on doing large amounts of anaerobic work? Because when you start doing anaerobic work, you can see improvements quickly. After just a couple of weeks of doing one or two anaerobic workouts a week, someone might notice that they're getting faster. Well, if a LITTLE bit of speed work can produce such immediate results, then A LOT should be even better! At least, that's the natural way to look at it. Unfortunately, it doesn't work exactly like that.
>
> A good anaerobic session, one in which you are REALLY pushing yourself anaerobically, is tough on the body. It might require a couple of days of recovery before your aerobic workouts are back at the level where they were before the anaerobic workout. So there's this conflict: anaerobic workouts stress your body in ways that aerobic workouts don't, causing improvements in speed and efficiency, but at the same time, they interfere with your ability to perform the aerobic workouts that are the bread and butter of any endurance athlete's training regime. What's a triathlete to do?
>
> The answer is that a triathlete is to learn from the mistakes of many, many athletes that came before him or her. The two important lessons that have been learned "the hard way" many times in the past are these:
>
> 1. If you do high-intensity workouts too frequently, then you aren't going to be sufficiently recovered from one to reap the benefits of the next. If your legs are feeling heavy, and your resting heart rate is elevated, then it

doesn't matter how hard you push yourself around the track. You're just wasting your time and suffering unnecessarily. Not only that, but you're setting yourself up for burnout or injury.

2. If you carry on with high-intensity workouts for too many weeks in a row, the detriment from missed or low-quality aerobic workouts is going to exceed the benefit from the high-intensity workouts.

With this in mind, we can set up some parameters. One or two anaerobic sessions a week is sufficient. Do that for something in the neighborhood of four to eight weeks. Cut out the specifically anaerobic sessions a few weeks before your first key race of the season. During this phase, you need to cut back on the total volume of your workout week. With those parameters in mind, you can start playing. That's when you need to figure out what works for you (or find a good coach to help you figure it out).[12]

From my own perspective, I have found that anaerobic workouts, when done at a high enough intensity, are physically and mentally tough. The workouts are not enjoyable because they are so uncomfortable.

Why build an aerobic base? A good analogy to building an aerobic base is building a road. Let's assume that I start with a two-lane road with one lane in each direction. When traffic is light, the road easily handles the traffic. As the road becomes congested and the traffic starts to back up, travel times increase until the traffic eventually stops. Similarly, without an aerobic base, the body can perform at a low level of intensity for a prolonged period of time. As time and intensity of activity increase, the body is unable to handle the prolonged and increased workload. Lactic acid, like car traffic, builds up in the muscles and slows the body down more.

If you do high-intensity workouts too frequently, then you aren't going to be sufficiently recovered from one to reap the benefits of the next.

Now, if I take the same road and add more traffic lanes, the road can now handle an increased traffic volume. The key is to build the lanes before the traffic becomes unbearable, so that when it does increase, the road is able to handle the volume. Similarly, if I build a solid aerobic base, which increases the ability of my body to handle increased exercise stress, my body will have the extra capacity (i.e., more traffic lanes) to sustain prolonged intensity (i.e., more traffic) during a race. If I wait until the traffic becomes great, I am fighting against the traffic to also build the road.

In the months leading up to a key race like Ironman USA, I frequently find myself asking:

- How fit am I now?
- How is my training progressing?
- Am I improving?
- Am I ready for my race?

I like to use non-key "B" races as progress checks leading up to my key races. I compete in these races with the primary intention to test my fitness level

I use non-key "B" races as progress checks leading up to key races.

and practice race execution. I try to not invest any emotional capital that might lead to disappointment if I have a less than stellar race. Local races that I have completed in the past make for good "B" races and they also give me a basis of comparison for my fitness relative to previous years.

The Spud Triathlon (International distance) in June was my "B" race before Ironman USA in July. I had raced in Spud five times prior, so I knew what to expect from both the course and myself. The swim sometimes varied by plus or minus several minutes each year (my guess: varying river current in the bay), but the bike and run course were always the same making a race-to-race comparison easy. I also signed up for Triple-T again in May.

The week before Triple-T and four weeks before the Spud Triathlon, I pondered whether I would run or bike the rest of the summer (or if ever for that matter). While commuting to work one day on my bike, I developed a painful soreness behind my left knee. After riding home that evening (unwise, but I didn't have an option since my car was at home), the soreness became a sharp, shooting pain. I couldn't put any pressure on the leg while bent without wincing. I played through several scenarios in my head and pessimistically thought that I might no longer be able to bike or run. Maybe I could become a great swimmer or I would need to pick up a new, less physical hobby or two.

After consulting with a physical therapist friend, we ruled out bursitis and a meniscus tear. She thought it might be tendonitis, which I confirmed with my doctor a few days later. While discussing my treatment options, my doctor asked if I depended on triathlon as a source of income. When I said that I didn't, he advised me not to race the following weekend. He said if I did, that might be it for the rest of the summer.

So that's why I didn't do Triple-T again in 2004. My doctor prescribed a knee brace, ice, rest and up to 2,400 mg of Ibuprofen a day to reduce inflammation.

I took a week off from biking and running completely then slowly added easy spinning on an indoor Lifecycle, then easy outdoor riding after the two-week point. I didn't run at all for almost three weeks. I did get a lot of swimming in, but had to use a pull buoy to support my legs to prevent aggravating my knee by kicking. I also couldn't push off the pool wall with my left leg.

With all of the downtime from training, I had low expectations for Spud. I was pleasantly surprised with what actually happened at the race.

In spite of my knee troubles, Spud was one of the few races where everything seemed to click and nothing seemed to go wrong. I had won this race for the first time a few years prior, but never managed to pull together another win at this distance—until 2004. Following is an excerpt from my race report:

> The drive to Spud was an hour from my and Jen's house. The drive was uneventful until our friends, Tom and Veronica, who were also driving to the race, honked at us to grab our attention. A few seconds later, we saw Tom's bare butt plastered against the rear passenger window. Ugh!
>
> Spud was a low-key, no frills affair (interesting factoid: Spud Triathlon was named after the race director's deceased cat). Transition racking for bikes was first come, first serve. I tactically racked my gear near the exit for the run start, taking advantage of the theorem that "a straight line is the shortest distance between two points."
>
> The swim was uneventful although the preceding sprint race started 20 minutes late due to trouble getting everyone in through the park entrance. I made a mental note that

trying to force 1,000 cars into General Smallwood State Park in a one-hour block of time was not a good idea. When the race was finally about to start, I seeded myself at the front of my wave near Tom and another friend who were both strong swimmers.

I exited the swim literally on Tom's feet and sprinted up toward the transition area removing my cap and goggles and unzipping my wetsuit as I ran. I arrived at the bike rack, exchanged greetings with Tom who was putting on his socks, removed my wetsuit, put on my bike shoes; positioned my helmet and glasses; pulled my bike off the rack; and said "Bye" to Tom who was still messing with his socks.

"That was a fast transition! Good job! You're #2 leaving the transition area." commented a volunteer.

Now, I just need to catch whoever is ahead of me.

There was a steady line of Sprint athletes to chase and pass until the courses diverged and the sprint course made a turn to head back toward the transition area. I attempted to give words of encouragement to each Sprint athlete as I passed, but was sucking wind to get the lead. My words came out something like: "Good, uhh, job, uhh, gasp, Keep, uuh, it, huh, up!"

I caught another friend, Dave, at mile five. We exchanged "Hey, Dave" to each other and I kept pushing my harder pace.

Throughout the rest of the bike, I never knew who else was behind me or how close they were. I wanted several minutes of lead time on the next person for the start of the run, as I was not too confident in my running legs given my recent knee problems. I kept throwing glances back, but couldn't see anyone behind me.

My bike-to-run transition was slow as I stumbled while

trying to put on my running shoes. No socks for me for the run either, I would take my chances with blisters.

I left the transition area for the second time through a long, narrow, convoluted chute marked off by plastic tape. As I left the grass and stepped onto the road, I saw Tom biking in for second place and estimated I had at most a two-minute lead.

Once I left the park for the highway, my running felt exceptionally smooth and controlled. My heart rate was high but I was "in the groove."

After the turnaround, I passed Tom coming toward me. We "high fived" each other then gave each other a "buddy hug" as a joke. "Sorry, gotta go," said Tom. He was running scared with only a small gap on the next two runners.

The last mile or so was through the park with twists and turns and not much of a chance to see who was behind me. I made the final turn to run across a creaking wooden footbridge to the finish line where I flashed the "V" sign with both hands. "V" for victory and for peace. I had won my second Spud race!

At Spud, my fitness level was good across all three events in spite of my recent injury. With the win my confidence was boosted, and I was able to rekindle focus on my key race, Ironman USA. The big unknown was still my run as I had not built and maintained a strong, steady base of long runs.

Ironman USA (Second Time)

"A bad day for a cyclist is quite different than a bad game for a football player. With the exception of crashes, almost all the pain a cyclist endures is self-inflicted. To win a bike race, a rider must be willing to suffer more than his rivals. To create more pain, he must push the pedals harder and faster."
- *Sal Ruibal in* USA Today *article about Lance Armstrong, February 17, 2004*

Cycling's time trial event is often referred to as the "race of truth." Each rider starts the race one after another at a specified time interval to compete for the best time. The time trial race is simply a rider racing the clock. Triathlon is also a race against the clock.

There is something pure about racing against the clock. Time is objective and treats everyone the same. I love the challenge of pushing myself over a sustained period of time to go longer, faster and harder. In an Iron distance event, the distance is long enough that the little choices I make early in the race can play out significantly later in the race. The race is both a tactical and strategic challenge. At the end of the day (literally), what matters is the final time. Everything else feeds into and leads up to that.

What is it that truly sets the great endurance athletes apart, the triathlon legends like Mark Allen and Dave Scott or cyclist Lance Armstrong? Natural ability is a given. The reality is that some individuals are genetically inclined to be better endurance athletes than others. Lifestyle definitely plays a role: eating healthy, staying active, getting adequate rest, etc. are important lifestyle factors. However, I think there is something else that separates the "good" from the "best" assuming all other factors are equal.

The "something else" is commitment *The true competition is* and attitude, which are reflected in the *really oneself.* comment Lance Armstrong made to author Sally Jenkins: "It's not a good day if I haven't suffered a little." I think that this simple statement by Lance points to an ability and a need to push oneself beyond the point of comfort in order to be successful. In short, the true competition is really oneself.

There were seven weeks between Spud and Ironman USA. I did my best to stabilize my home life with Jen during that time, although we both knew there were problems in our relationship. We put our issues aside and headed to Lake Placid with friends in July for the race and a week of vacation.

I had to overcome physical and emotional setbacks to get to Ironman USA. The mountain scenery and fresh air of the Adirondacks were a temporary distraction but during the race, I faced more challenges.

My swim went well, but during the bike my lower back hurt, my butt hurt and my neck hurt from holding a stretched out aerodynamic position for hours. I was covered in my sweat, snot and sticky energy gel that were running down my chin, my jersey and my legs. My eyes and neck, chafed from my wetsuit during the swim, burned from the salt of my sweat. My inner thighs cramped uncomfortably, but I wouldn't pull over to stretch them out, as I knew the cramps would go away after a few minutes. As expected, the cramps went away only to return half an hour later. I ingested a few salt tablets in an attempt to alleviate the cramping.

Every few minutes on the bike, I stood up to stretch out my aching lower back and legs. At one point on the second loop of the two loop course, I pulled my bike off to the side of the road in order to plant both feet on the ground because I was throwing up so violently that I couldn't ride a straight line and worried about crashing or causing someone else to crash. My stomach emptied itself repeatedly of the sports drink and gel that I had consumed during the previous four hours. When I started forward motion again, I had depleted all the calories and fluids that I had in my stomach. I felt miserable and my mind was muddled from the effort and the loss of calories and fluids.

My pre-race goal for Lake Placid was to finish in the top 10 overall in less than nine hours. I painfully realized that my time goal was no longer realistic or even possible given my condition. I had to choose whether I should keep going as part of me desperately wanted to stop. I was competing against myself and no longer cared about what anyone else was doing.

Every Iron distance triathlon gives its own challenges and discomforts to the participants. The challenge may be simply to keep moving forward even when the discomfort becomes unbearable or race execution slowly unravels. The longer the race, the more time there is to dwell on the discomfort and the more difficult it is to stay mentally focused and "in the game."

After vomiting in Lake Placid, I was in a bad state physically. I believed that I had lost most of the calories and fluid I ingested over the previous two hours, so I was bonking and dehydrated with 30 miles on the bike course and a full marathon remaining to race.

"Why am I here?" I asked myself again and again over the long hours of the race. I struggled to find a powerful answer.

"I am a cancer survivor." I finally answered back.

I suffered through the bike after giving up several places and eventually recovered enough to run a decent marathon and finished in a respectable time although far short of my pre-race expectations.

I could have picked up another slot to the Ironman World Championship in Hawaii, but I passed. I left Lake Placid feeling disappointed and unfulfilled.

The Return on Training Investment

From my observations, most new triathletes seem to come from single sport backgrounds. My background was running. I ran consistently since high school, so I initially excelled in the running portion of triathlons relative to my non-running peers.

I have a friend, Katie, who is a swimmer. She's in the pool almost every day and will always default to swimming if given the choice of workouts. Not surprisingly, she will be one of the first athletes out of the water in any triathlon she races. She is a decent cyclist, and running is her weakness. She doesn't really enjoy running and has struggled with recurring leg injuries. She seems willing to sacrifice time on the bike or run in order to spend more time in the event that she loves the most. I think this works for her and keeps her happy in the sport.

It took me a few years to bring my cycling performance up to the level of my running. My swim lagged both, but I was working on closing the gap. Until I brought my biking up to par with my running, I preferred running since it was easier and more enjoyable for me than the other events. I looked at swimming as a "necessary evil" that I had to do to compete in triathlon. I didn't hate swimming or cycling, but I never really loved them like I did running.

As I improve over the years, my time goals become more and more challenging. Realistically, I might squeeze out more time from the bike or run given the relatively longer time interval spent in those two disciplines relative to the shorter swim interval. As an example, "typical" Iron distance times (% of total race time) for me are:

- Swim – 0:57 (10%)
- Bike – 5:10 (55%)
- Run – 3:15 (35%)

As such, a one percent improvement in performance in a single event would give me five minutes on the bike compared to only one minute on the swim. Therefore, I tend to put more effort into biking.

Vineman (Third Time)

"In preparing for battle I have always found that plans are useless, but planning is indispensable."
- *Dwight D. Eisenhower, American General and President*

I try to approach each race with the desire to progressively push myself just a little harder or to dig a little deeper each time. I know that I am physically limited in reaching the pinnacle of the sport, but I can maximize the abilities and fitness that I do have. At the end of the day, I want to be able to say that I gave everything I could. I want to be able to walk away and look back with contentment.

When I raced Vineman for the third time in August of 2004, I was coming off of a disappointing finish at Ironman USA only three weeks prior. In spite of near perfect weather conditions at Lake Placid, my race execution and stomach issues left me feeling like I should have been able to go much faster. I wanted to do Vineman in order to prove to myself that I could do better.

I needed a pre-race plan, something in writing that would force me to critically examine my training and my race day execution. Racing a second Iron distance race only three weeks after the first was a risk I was willing to take.

I sat down at my desk and typed out a plan.

My plan for race week was to relax, reduce stress, stay off my feet as much as possible and get lots of sleep. I would clean my bike the weekend before the race and ensure that everything worked properly by test riding it in race configuration (i.e., race wheels, aero bottle, gearing).

Weather conditions in Santa Rosa on race day were expected to be warm with low humidity. I would ingest a little more salt in my diet and drink more fluid two days before the race. I would stay away from anything spicy like Mexican food or acidic like tomato sauce, that might upset my stomach before the race.

The day before, I would hydrate with a sports drink that contained carbohydrates and electrolytes, not just plain water. I remembered my mistake at the Great Floridian a few years before when I drank water all day the day before the race and had stomach problems on race day.

I would snack throughout the day before, but eat in moderation. Lunch and dinner would be a mix of simple and complex carbohydrates with some protein. Subway® sandwiches make a good lunch for me the day before a race. They are easy to find, and I can plan my meal no matter what city I'm in. I would avoid alcohol, which promotes dehydration and might impact my already fragile sleep.

I would do an easy swim, bike and run the day before the race to loosen up my muscles. The short bike ride would also allow me to test my bike reassembly after the plane ride so that something as simple as a slipping saddle midway through the race didn't force me to stop. After my workout, I would drive the course for familiarity and confidence.

My plan was to be in bed by 7:00 p.m., which I didn't think would be an issue with the time zone change. My body would feel like it was going to bed at my normal bedtime of 10:00 p.m.

On race morning, I would:

1. Wake at 4:00 a.m., three hours before race start. Again, this shouldn't be an issue with the time zone change

2. Eat oatmeal with raspberry jam and drink a cup of coffee which is my normal routine.

3. Plan on a 30-minute drive to the swim start.

4. Warm up for a few minutes in each event (if possible).

5. Eat a PowerBar then a banana later in the morning if needed.

6. Consume an energy gel 15-30 minutes before the start.

Ultimately, the race would be me against me. I have no control over anyone else's race, fitness level or luck on race day. At the end of the day, I wanted to be able to know that I gave my best, independent of anyone else's performance. I needed to run my own race but I still might leverage others to push me.

I targeted 56 +/- 1 minute for my swim leg, which was in the Russian River. The river was narrow, so it would be easy for me to sight the buoys and swim a straight line. The first loop would give me an opportunity to check my watch as an indicator of total time. I intended to push myself, but at a reasonable pace so that I wouldn't slow down more than a minute or two on the second loop.

I targeted 5:10 +/- 10 minutes for the bike leg. The bike leg was a two-loop technical and challenging course. There were multiple rolling hills and one long, steep climb at Chalk Hill near the end of each loop. My intent was to maximize my sustainable power using perceived effort, heart rate and pedal cadence to monitor my effort and pace. As a basis of comparison I rode a ~5:05 on this bike course in 1998 and a ~5:20 in 2001 (including changing a flat tire) so my expected time was reasonable.

On the bike, I would carry a weak mix of Cytomax, two flasks of energy gel (approximately six servings each), a half dozen fig bars and a small bag of gummy bears. Carrying my own food allowed me to be selective in what I picked up on the course (if anything) and gave me options in the case of an upset stomach or a missed hand off at an aid station.

Carrying your own food provides flexibility and security in the event you miss a handoff at an aid station.

I would alternate taking Gatorade and water at a ratio of two bottles of Gatorade to one bottle of water to dilute the concentration of sugar in my stomach to aid absorption. In addition, I would chase the gel with water for the same reason.

If the weather warmed up later in the ride and I began sweating excessively as evidenced by salt caking on my bike shorts, I would start ingesting salt tablets every 30-60 minutes to mitigate potential cramping.

I targeted 3:15 +/- 15 minutes for the run leg, which was on rolling hills on paved roads. The run leg is where I would really feel the effects of racing Lake Placid only three weeks before. I had run a 3:16 marathon at this race previously although the run course had since changed.

My plan was to set a reasonable seven-minute per mile pace and maintain it as long as possible. I might tweak my pace more or less aggressively depending on both air temperature and where I was placed during the run. I still planned to race my own race against myself, but I might make an aggressive (and risky) pace change if I had a chance to win.

For run nutrition, I would begin the run carrying a full gel flask. I had good luck drinking water and flat cola at the aid stations without too many stomach problems previously in the year. I would pick up bananas or oranges from the aid stations as needed, and I would continue ingesting salt tablets as needed. My target finish time for the race was 9:15 +/- 15 minutes.

Following is an excerpt from my race report, describing how the race actually played out:

> At the pre-race meeting, Russ Pugh, race director and Vineman founder, told a story about his hobby—growing giant pumpkins. His prize pumpkin was already almost 500 pounds and on pace to exceed 1,000 pounds. Russ wanted faster pumpkin growth, so he applied a powerful fertilizer, a fertilizer that worked well, too well. The pumpkin grew an amazing 25 pounds in seven hours, then it cracked. Russ became too greedy in his desire to grow a prize-winning pumpkin.
>
> After listening to Russ speak, I drew the analogy that racing an Iron distance race was like growing pumpkins: be patient and don't be greedy by starting out too fast. It's a long race. Otherwise, like Russ' pumpkin, I might crack.
>
> Were three weeks enough time to recover physically and mentally? The previous year I raced Blue Devil and Great Floridian only two weeks apart. I painfully found out on both the bike and the run legs that two weeks was not enough time to recover between races. Would the extra week make a difference?
>
> **PRE-RACE**
> The week before the race, I found out that I am "Brad's guy" in the Vineman office pool. Brad Rex, the announcer for this race as well as the Blue Devil Triathlon, was "betting" on me to take the win.
>
> "Great, more pressure on me." I thought to myself. I decided it best to tame Brad's expectations since he was there at my meltdown at Great Floridian the previous year. I told him about racing Ironman USA three weeks before, "But, I feel great." I added trying to sound confident.

At registration, I was handed bib number "2" since I had previously won the race in 2001. Once again, I was an easily identifiable target for the rest of the field.

SWIM
The swim start was a little chaotic but quickly thinned out due to the small athlete field. I quickly latched onto the draft of a taller swimmer who stroked effortlessly ahead of me, but he was fishtailing back and forth as I swam a straighter line. I finally passed him near the end of the first lap then spent the second half of the swim by myself in "no man's land" with small pockets of swimmers ahead of and behind me, but not near enough for me to either speed up or slow down.

My swim time was slower than expected, but times seemed to be slower across the board.

Swim split: 1:00:30 (Estimated time: 56 +/- 1 min)

BIKE
The weather stayed cool due to cloud cover, so I was happy to be wearing arm warmers from the start. Right away, I passed a few athletes then settled into a steady pace to slowly reel in the few riders ahead of me. "Patience. Don't crack the pumpkin." I thought.

After stomach distress at Lake Placid, I paid more attention to what I ingested. More water and less sport drink to dilute the sugar coming into my stomach. Because of cooler weather, I didn't need to carry more than one bottle at a time between aid stations. I picked up a new bottle of either water or sports drink at each aid station, dumped half of it into my aero bottle, which rested between my aero bars, then tossed aside the half empty bottle.

Throughout much of the bike, I experienced a caffeine headache from no morning coffee. My only coffee option on the drive over to the race start at 4:45 a.m. on a Sunday morning was the 24-hour gas station along the interstate. No coffee seemed like a better option at the time. In hindsight, I should have stopped.

The good news was that I experienced an upset stomach 90 miles into the bike, not at mile 70 like at Lake Placid. The bad news was that I vomited once again. I managed to swallow a few gummy bears, but that was it. "Just get to the end of the bike so that you can start the run and get some cola," I thought to myself.

I finished the bike near my expected time. So far so good, except for the vomiting.

Bike Split: 5:07:10 (Estimated time: 5:10 +/- 10 min)

RUN
The transition from bike to run went smoothly as I shed my bike shoes and helmet for a pair of running shoes and a visor. I left the transition area 11 minutes behind the sole athlete ahead of me. "I can reel him in." I thought to myself. I knew that he had expended significant effort on the bike and might be weak on the run. I only needed to run 30 seconds per mile faster to catch and pass him. Stay patient. Game on.

As hoped, I felt good at the start of the run. My goal for the past few years continued to be to run a sub-three hour marathon in an Iron distance race. I had come close several times with a personal best of 3:10 at the inaugural Blue Devil. I figured that I would need to run a 3:10 marathon in order to win Vineman. I set out running seven-minute miles which put me well under a 3:10 pace, yet that was a pace that I believed I could maintain for the full distance.

My strides were fluid. My leg turnover was rhythmic and smooth. Thump. Thump. Thump. Thump.

A third of the way through the run, I had already made up six minutes. "Pass him at the start of the third and final lap." I schemed in my mind.

Halfway through the run, I was only three minutes back and was maintaining my faster pace. The win was in the bag.

Then suddenly, at mile 14, things changed. I heaved heavily and was forced to stop on the side of the road bent over holding my knees. This time it was the cola and water I drank at every aid station that upset my stomach. I bonked hard and started to stagger as my mile splits slowed dramatically.

I contemplated curling up in a fetal position by the side of the road until someone drove by to pick me up. Like Russ' pumpkin, I had cracked. Maybe I was being too greedy by racing only three weeks apart and trying to go for a win.

My focus shifted from taking the win to simply survival. Time became irrelevant, and I only cared about trying to end the suffering. I had come so close to a win, but fate stuck a cruel jab in my side. I finished the second loop at a slow jog, swigged some more cola and water then headed back out for the final loop.

I slowly felt better during each mile of the final loop and my mile splits begin dropping: 10:30, 8:50, 8:25 and 7:52. With only five miles to the finish, I crunched the numbers in my head and realized that I could still finish in under 9:30, but it would be tight.

Cliff Bar® sponsored a $2,000 prize purse to be split amongst any male athletes who finished in under 9:30 with a similar purse to be shared amongst any women going under 10:30. I had to choose: dig deep for the second place finish and the money or just finish second. I chose to dig deep.

Reflecting back a few days later, I couldn't remember much about the last five miles other than my entire body felt utter discomfort and suffering. I was literally chasing seconds on the clock and constantly in danger of falling down from exertion and fatigue. With a half mile to the finish I saw Russ riding toward me on a small scooter. He slowed down when he recognized me, checked his watch and then excitedly mumbled something about me running, before turning his scooter around on a dime and speeding back to the finish line.

In the final stretch, I saw the clock. I only had a minute and a half to spare. I savored the finish, flashed the victory sign with both hands and walked across the finish line in sweet exhaustion.

Run Split: 3:18:21
(Pre-race estimated time: 3:15 +/- 15 minutes)

Total Time: 9:28:58
(Pre-race estimated time: 9:15 +/- 15 minutes)

POST RACE
I walked away with my hunger for racing well satisfied, two boxed bottles of wine and $1,000 in my pocket.

I had a pre-race plan for Vineman, and I executed it. I was very pleased with my results given the short time since my previous race, but I still had issues with my stomach. I went back to the drawing board for race day nutrition.
I needed to find a proper mix of foods and liquids that wouldn't make me sick during my races as it was rapidly becoming the norm for me to throw up during both the bike and run.

I came up with three possible reasons:

1. I was taking in too many calories at one time.
2. I was ingesting the wrong types or wrong mix of liquids and solids.
3. This was an inherent issue with my stomach, which I would just have to live with on an ongoing basis.

I hoped it was one of the first two that I could correct, but in the back of my mind I didn't rule out the third.

I started researching exercise nutrition from multiple angles looking for that golden nugget of wisdom that might alleviate my stomach distress:

*   I subscribed to a monthly nutrition newsletter on Active.com.

*   I reviewed several of the many triathlon training books that I have on my bookshelf.

*   I reviewed my past race reports for notes for what I consumed while

training and racing. I wish that I had taken the time to capture more detail.

- I asked my triathlon friends about their nutrition, trying to discern what they did differently and what worked for them.

- I reached out to my friend who owns an online sports nutrition store called Personal Best Nutrition (PBN) to leverage his knowledge of endurance sports nutrition.

Not surprisingly, there was varying and sometimes conflicting guidance about endurance exercise nutrition from a myriad of sources.

One shared observation was that the pooling of simple sugars in the stomach causes gastric distress. There is a limit on the concentration of simple sugars in fluid that the stomach can readily absorb in a fixed period of time. In concentrations above that limit, the stomach is unable to absorb the fluid and the sugar pools. In reviewing past race reports, I observed that when I was sick, those particular races provided drink mix with only simple sugars like glucose at the bike and run aid stations. This seemed to be a likely culprit as once I had divested my stomach contents, thereby reducing the sugar concentration in my stomach; I felt much better within a few minutes and was able to successfully ingest food and fluids again.

Unfortunately, this explanation did not account for why I had stomach issues during shorter races. Because International distance races were usually self-supported on the bike, I wasn't ingesting any fluid other than what I carried with me. I still vomited during these races, but could not blame it on simple sugars alone because I was ingesting a drink mix with a complex carbohydrate (i.e., not simple sugars) and a protein blend that I added to my water bottles. The research supporting a blend of protein with carbohydrates in the drink mix seemed legitimate but, as I noted in my race reports, the protein didn't sit well in my stomach. I realized that this was a possible cause of the feelings of nausea and vomiting that I was experiencing during my shorter races.

I again approached my friend who owns PBN and he suggested a new product on the market called CARBO-PRO® that is entirely complex carbohydrates with no simple sugars. The white powder was tasteless and dissolved quickly in water. He also suggested mixing in a small portion of simple sugar drink mix for flavor.

Assuming I could alleviate some of my stomach distress by reducing the concentration of simple sugars in my stomach, the next issue to solve was how to carry the volume of fluid that I would need during an Iron distance race if the race only offered a simple sugar drink mix at the aid stations. Because the 112-miles takes me around five hours to finish, it would be impractical for me to carry that much fluid and weight especially on a hot and hilly course where I might need one to two water bottles every 10 miles.

After reading another friend's race day nutrition strategy, I surmised that I could carry two bottles mixed with a super concentrated mix of CARBO-PRO and Cytomax, which I could then supplement with plain water from the bike course to dilute it back to a consistency recommended by the manufacturer as suitable for stomach absorption. I could also place two concentrated bottles in my bike special needs bag, which would then be available for me to pick up at the half way point. As a result, I was no longer dependent on what the aid stations provided other than plain water.

I would try this method out at my next race, the Blue Devil Triathlon.

***

Jen and I had lived a cautious existence since the beginning of the year. In August, I finally realized that I was uncertain about marrying her. We had been together for more than five years and engaged for more than two years of that time. In all fairness to her, I should have made up my mind much earlier. I moved out in August and rented a one-bedroom apartment. She remains a wonderful person, and I hope that she finds happiness in a relationship one day.

Suddenly I felt alone. I was used to having activity in the house with Jen and the dogs around and my apartment felt empty. Slowly, I started dating. I felt like a newbie on the dating scene all over again as I had not dated since just after college. I had no idea where to go to meet women. Bars didn't seem like a great option given my "early to bed, early to rise" lifestyle. By the time many people were going out to party, I was in bed asleep. Plus the thought of standing and drinking in a smoky bar didn't appeal to me as a healthy, non-smoker who knew that staying up late would impact my ability to wake up early for my workouts. My workouts were still my priority.

My first dating event was as a participant in a bachelor auction sponsored by

Team in Training® to raise money for The Leukemia & Lymphoma Society.

I am shy around girls that I don't know and the prospect of standing up in front of a room full of women who were bidding on me for a date scared me. Rather than go alone, I brought a female friend along.

"Why did you bring sand to the beach?" my friend Tom said to me after the event.

"I wasn't really thinking." I snapped back.

Like many of my triathlon races, I made a few tactical mistakes at the event. First, I started drinking mixed drinks right after my first beer. I tend to stay away from mixed drinks since beer will typically fill up my stomach and keep me from drinking too much too soon.

Second, I only ate one small appetizer the entire evening. Granted, this was only partially my fault as I didn't see any food until much later in the evening after I had already consumed copious amounts of alcohol.

I woke up the next day in my hotel room fully clothed. I had no idea how I got there or what had happened after the auction. I knew that I had raised $500 for The Leukemia & Lymphoma Society and that I had won one of the silent auctions, although I couldn't find my auction winnings.

I later found out that a few of the other participants and I got smashed and were dancing late into the night before we finally got sick and were driven back to the hotel by one of the other bachelors.

I decided that bachelor auctions weren't such a good idea for me.

My friend, Rob, who was also single at the time after going through a messy divorce, told me about an online dating service that he thought provided a great means to meet women. I figured what the heck. I really had nothing to lose. Rob had some great stories to share—some good, some bad and some altogether frightening, but I figured I would be selective in screening any women that I pursued.

I signed up online and created a profile to share my interests, likes/dislikes, activities, favorite foods, etc. I answered the prompted questions truthfully and thoughtfully, giving what I thought was a fair assessment of who I was and what I was about. I checked my profile daily for messages and "winks." Winks were from women who had expressed an interest by winking at me. After receiving a few winks and dropping a few more, I began trading emails with a few dating prospects.

My first date was with "Singer32." She described herself as athletic and toned, outgoing, a few years younger than me, and she displayed some promising pictures. She worked as a singer part-time, but her "real" job was at a local consulting firm. After a few email exchanges and a phone call, we made a date at a restaurant in a nearby mall.

When I met her, she was outgoing and appeared to be the same age as her profile indicated. However, she did not live up to the promise of her pictures, as she seemed to have gained about 50 pounds since they were taken. Call me shallow, but I'm only attracted to slim, fit women. I have always been this way. I believe it's a reflection on my own commitment to exercise and my high standards of keeping myself lean and fit. By all means, this is not to say that I want to date someone as exercise-obsessed as I am, but rather that shape and self-respect count greatly in my book of desirable qualities.

I acted the gentleman, plus I needed practice with the dating thing, so I sat down and had a drink with her. We talked. She clearly was the extroverted opposite of my introverted personality. I explained my situation and how I was just out of a long-term relationship to which she shared her own recent break up with a longtime boyfriend. We had dinner, but I stopped drinking wine after three or four glasses, while she kept drinking until she had consumed seven or eight glasses. I was feeling tipsy after consuming half the amount of alcohol she had consumed, so she must have been drunk. After eating dinner, I glanced at my watch and decided that this was going in a direction that I didn't want it to go with someone I didn't want to go there with, so I stood up to leave.

"Are you okay to drive home?" I asked cautiously, not enthusiastic about the thought of either driving her home or allowing her to drive herself home in her current state.

"I have some friends who are coming over to meet me." she replied.

"Cool." I thought. "I'm out of here."

I dropped her an email to make sure she had made it home the next day.

Fortunately, she had. The date was not a complete loss, as I think it helped me talk through my situation with someone who had gone through a similar situation but from the opposite side of a relationship.

My second date was with "SeekingHarmony," who was nine years younger than me. She was also athletic and toned, and she seemed to fit the description much better than my first date. In spite of her youth, I think she was only 24 at the time, she came across as well educated in the ways of the world and insightful. Plus, she loved to exercise and seemed to care about what she put into her body. I think she would have been a cool girl to date except for two reasons. The first being that she seemed very closed-minded to any opinions other than her own, and she voiced many during our brief conversation. Never mix politics and religion should apply to first dates. The second reason was that she was an occasional smoker. I couldn't understand smoking, especially for someone who seemed so committed to fitness, so I asked her, "Why do you smoke?" To which she replied, "I need some vice. I know it's bad for me, but it helps me relax. Besides, I'm not going to live forever."

After dinner, she gave me a quick hug and said, "I had a good time. Call me tomorrow."

I called her back the next day. No response. Oh, well, it was probably for the best.

Blue Devil (Third Time)

Mike Guzek, Brady Dehoust and I drove down to Durham, North Carolina two days before the Blue Devil.

Brady is another friend who, like Mike, is a few years younger than me. Brady will forever be known as the triathlete whose wife went into labor while he was in the middle of the swim leg of the Columbia Triathlon (in Maryland) that year in May. Upon exiting the swim, my friends and I tried to stop a focused, dashing Brady as he made his way out of the water to the transition area. He had a great swim and didn't want to stop his race. It took a few moments before it finally registered in his head what was going on with his wife.

Although he jokes about his skinny legs which he inherited from his father, Brady is a strong biker and very strong hill climber who has put me in duress numerous times trying to stay with him on long, hilly rides. Brady has a full-time job, but also has the added responsibility of a new baby at home. Yet, through dedication and careful time management, he is able to compete successfully at the Iron distance and keep up a full and happy home life.

Mike described how we tried to ease our nerves two days before the race:

> I traveled down with two-time winner (and cancer survivor) David Glover and another training partner and friend Brady Dehoust. We made the four-hour drive from D.C. to Durham on Thursday just in time to register and get in a lake swim before the pre-race pasta dinner. I'm not sure what all the key race week activities should be, but if you were with us three it involved attempting to swim to the bottom of Falls Lake in a wetsuit and trying to learn the "egg beater" from Glover. I learned from Glover that the egg beater is a water polo technique where you raise your body out of the water with an alternating breaststroke kick while pushing up with your hands and then waving them around (as if you were going to block a shot). When Glover first attempted this with no warning I thought he was being attacked by a shark. I suddenly saw him flailing around and rising high out of the water. Of course, the ever-present grin gave it away—a shark was not attacking him. As for touching the bottom of the lake, all I can say is that the lake is deep and scary.[13]

At the Blue Devil, I would test my theory to alleviate my stomach distress.

"It used to be that you would go to the pro racks to see the latest and greatest equipment and high end bikes. Now, you go to Men's 50-54 age group," commented race announcer Brad Rex on race morning. His words seemed to ring true as I had observed over the years. Brad and I went back many years to my earliest Iron distance races at Great Floridian where he announced the races. Since then, I have looked on him as a symbol of luck for me. He's my rabbit's foot that I have kept in my back pocket as he was there for all three of my prior Iron distance wins at Vineman in 2001 and Blue Devil in 2002 and 2003.

What I remember most about the swim was the sun rising up from the horizon as a beautiful and subtle blend of purples, reds and oranges. It's amusing to me what little and insignificant details I notice and later remember during races.

I was a triathlete for 10 seasons and this was my 17th Iron distance race. What amazed me were the Blue Devil athletes like Chris Coby, a fellow cancer survivor, who was competing in only his second triathlon ever. His first triathlon was the Blue Devil the previous year. From my perspective, this was analogous to someone who learns to read by starting with Tolstoy's *War and Peace* instead of Dr. Seuss' *Cat in the Hat*—it's just not done. Chris was always smiling when I saw him and would finish the Blue Devil one hour faster this year.

There were two athletes at the Blue Devil who had done multiple back-to-back Iron distance races leading up to the Blue Devil. One athlete had finished four Iron distance races in the previous five weeks and the other had finished seven Iron distance races in the previous seven weeks. Both planned to race again the following weekend at the Great Floridian Triathlon in Florida.

When I saw one of them after the race sitting in the medical tent, I had to ask him, "How do you do it? I mean, you are literally racing an Iron distance race from one weekend to the next. What do you do between races? How do you recover?"

He smiled, shrugged with a look of self-satisfaction on his face, and said, "I take it real easy on the biking and swimming for a couple of days. By mid-week, I will try a little aqua jogging. I also need 10 or 11 hours of sleep a night."

I couldn't comprehend, nor would I have the confidence to attempt multiple back-to-back Iron distance races like that. I had completed the Blue Devil and the Great Floridian races two weeks apart, but the effort left me exhausted physically and drained emotionally. Maybe someday I would think differently and want to attempt something like that, but not now.

The wind felt exceptionally strong on the bike course and always seemed to work against me. I kept my head down, tucked my body into a tighter aerodynamic position and grunted through the course.

Throughout the race, I dwelled on my cancer experience and choked up with tears as the emotion of the event overtook me from racing in an event dedicated to finding a cure for cancer. I swallowed the emotion as best I could, refocused on the race and kept riding.

For me, a race was as much a mental and emotional challenge as a physical challenge. Every second, every arm stroke, every pedal stroke, every breath was a decision point where I constantly asked myself:

"Should I sight the buoy or stay on the legs of the swimmer ahead of me?"

"Do I breathe every stroke or every other stroke?"

"Do I pick up my cadence on the bike or push a bigger gear?"

"Do I eat solid food or gel?"

"Do I jog, run or walk up the hill?"

"Am I running too fast or too slow?"

"Do I quit or keep going?"

I didn't always make the wisest decisions, but I had never yet quit.

With about five miles to go before the end of the 112-mile bike, I felt my rear tire wobble unsteadily, so I veered over to the shoulder of the road and stopped. Flat tire. "Damn!"

I lost the lead changing my flat and entered the transition area in 2nd place overall.

"Way to go, David!" I heard from an anonymous spectator as I quickly retook the lead in the transition area to start the run in first. "So far so good." I thought, although I wished I had a larger margin on the guy behind me.

Each run aid station had a theme. The most elaborate theme was the Wizard of Oz aid station, which was staffed by a Team in Training group costumed as Oz characters. Interacting with Dorothy, the Wicked Witch, the Tin Man and other Oz personalities brought a smile to my face every time I ran by their aid station. They seemed to become my own personal team, calling my name and anticipating my every need. If a drink hand off didn't go smoothly, Vicky Yeingst, as Dorothy, chased after me to bring me the drink so that I didn't need to stop. Vicky, who was a triathlete and a Team in Training coach, would become the volunteer coordinator for the Blue Devil Triathlon the following year.

Every time I ran by the finish line to begin another loop, I heard Brad comment: "Here comes David Glover. He was a cancer survivor before it was cool to be a cancer survivor."

I flashed my big, toothy smile and gave a double "thumbs up" to the crowd as I soaked up the energy and their cheers. I felt like a celebrity.

To which Brad responded something to the effect of, "David Glover has discovered that it takes less energy to smile than it does to frown. Just look at him smile."

I passed Brady going the opposite direction. He looked smooth. He had overtaken several runners already and was making up additional time on the remaining runners between us.

"The guy in second place is starting to fade, and I think he's about to blow up." I commented to him. He seemed to smile through his expression of determination and focus but didn't break stride.

A few miles later, I commented, "Brady, dude, you have a good shot at second. Keep it up!" I told him. No smile from Brady this time.

At the start of my third lap, I saw the former second place competitor lying on his back off the side of the road surrounded by volunteers and medical staff. He had, as I would later find out after the race, expended too much energy on the bike and blew up on the run. I have to give my respect to him for his determination and perseverance.

Bill Scott, the race director, rode on his mountain bike in front of me during the third loop. "How cool is that?" I thought. I have the race director escorting me.

On my final lap, Vicky (Dorothy from the Wizard of Oz aid station) handed me her small, stuffed dog Toto to run with. I saw event director Dorrys McArdle drive by in a golf cart with some of the race staff, and she gave me words of encouragement and a smile.

As I made the final right turn for the last downhill stretch to the finish line, I grinned at the cheering spectators, threw my hands in the air for applause and crossed the finish line in a time of 9:34:59.

I was now the three-time winner of the Blue Devil.

My racing season was over for the year. It was now time for me to kick back for a few months and toast the end of a long racing season with good food and good beer. I was looking forward to being able to relax. I didn't want to even think about training or racing again for a while.

***

After Blue Devil, I once again found it hard to relinquish my hard earned fitness even though I recognized the need for time away from racing and serious training to enable my body to recover both physically and mentally. I had come to expect the feelings of malaise and disinterest in triathlon training at the end of the season. By no means did I stop exercising, but I worked out less frequently and less often. My attitude shifted from "What do I need to do?" to "What do I want to do?"

I recognize the need for time away from racing and serious training to enable my body to recover both physically and mentally.

I needed to turn my back on triathlon for a few months. My training routine dissolved, as did my regular interactions with my training partners. All of us seemed to drift off in different directions, as we spent more time on other activities besides worshipping the warm weather sport that calls us out to the lakes, roads and dirt trails in the spring, summer and fall.

Somewhere, I lost some of my desire to race and sometimes my desire to even exercise. My attitude became blasé toward triathlon in general. I felt like I was just going through the motions. I began to doubt my fitness and myself.

I found myself unable to get up in the morning for early morning workouts, and I frequently hit my snooze bar for over an hour before I rolled out of bed. The sense of urgency to get out the door in the morning was no longer there. Rather than swim in the morning, I skipped out of work to swim at lunch. My body shifted from early to bed, early to rise to later to bed, later to rise. I discovered I needed less sleep because the physical demands on my body were no longer as demanding.

My workout efforts became easy and low in intensity. As I heard about friends running in local races, I was happy to just watch as a spectator, thinking to myself, "I'm glad that I'm not out there running." as I sipped my coffee.

My lack of discipline toward exercise spilled over to other aspects of my life. I stopped shaving my legs and let the hair on my chest grow back. I shaved my face every other day rather than every day.

After living by myself for several months, I thought it might be nice to have some company at home, so a dog seemed like a good option. I missed having a friendly face to always greet me at the door and having someone that I could pal around with and who needed me to take care of them.

After a week of Internet searches of local animal rescues and shelters, I decided to visit Friends of Homeless Animals (FOHA), a nearby no-kill animal rescue. My first choice for adoption were two hound puppies named Hansel and Gretel. After an apartment visit by a FOHA volunteer, I decided that instead of adopting two young puppies that would need constant attention and be potentially destructive to my rented apartment, I would look into adopting an adult dog.

I noticed a deaf dog on FOHA's website named Princess, who was also available for adoption. When I saw Princess in person, I thought to myself, "What a beautiful Dalmatian!" She had the most beautiful light blue eyes and her spots were separate and distinct. When I noticed that she had been at the shelter for more than seven months, I decided I had to have her.

Living with a deaf dog is a little different than living with a hearing dog for two reasons. The first is that a deaf dog doesn't know when you come home and the second is that you can't call its name to get its attention. The advantage of this is that I can make several trips to and from the car for groceries without having to worry about the dog knocking the bags out of my hands from excitement or running out the front door.

***

My third Internet date was with Emi. We actually "dated" for a few weeks although I am fairly confident that she was playing the field on other nights. Like my first date, Emi had recently moved out of a long-term relationship after finding out that her husband was cheating on her. She and I seemed to hit it off quite well.

Emi was attractive, worked out on a regular basis, liked Princess and seemed like a cool girl.

One day, she simply stopped calling me back. I called a few more times and left messages, but eventually gave up.

After a few more adventures, or rather misadventures, I came to the logical conclusion that although Internet dating was more convenient on some dimensions in that I could screen potential girlfriends by reading their online profiles, dating was still time consuming and somewhat of a crapshoot because one person's definition of "active" wasn't the same as another person's. I also thought that the dating process was too time consuming as it interfered with my routine. I eventually pulled my profile off the Internet.

I ended the year tired after a roller coaster ride of ups and downs. After a disappointing race at Lake Placid, I pulled off a come-from-behind performance at Vineman to capture half of the prize purse then went on to defend my title at the Blue Devil Triathlon for the third year in a row. My personal life was once more in a state of rapid change as I moved out of my long-term relationship with Jen to be back on my own again.

"Time away from the sport provides perspective on myself, my relationships and even on my training. The lesson, which I am still striving to achieve, is to fit triathlon comfortably into my life, rather than fitting life into triathlon."

Chapter 13: A Year of Reflection

Like all things, my lack of structured training eventually came to an end. I think more than anything, I just got tired of not having the sense of purpose in my life that training for triathlons gave me. Besides, I couldn't disengage myself from the training and the exercise for too long. I loved being fit, and I loved the discipline that exercise forced upon me.

I also knew that once the days became longer and the temperatures warmed, that my motivation would come back as the ground thawed.

I had high hopes in 2005 as it was meant to be my year in triathlon. I had made a number of significant changes in my life in 2004 and now I had no one to answer to and I could focus as much of my time toward training as I wanted. I should have a stellar year.

In January, I decided I needed to purchase a house. Jen had bought me out of our joint mortgage and paying rent each month for something I didn't own in a rising real estate market didn't appeal to me. Besides, I was getting tired of apartment life and the late night noise and cigarette smell from my neighbors.

I liked the convenience of Reston both from the perspective of being close to work as well as having easy access to facilities like pools and other amenities like the W&OD bike trail and running paths. The downside was the premium I had to pay to live there relative to other areas further west of Washington, D.C. Lifestyle versus price, I chose lifestyle.

In March, I bought a townhouse on a lake in Reston. I paid extra for the lakeside lot, but I wanted the serenity of the view, the privacy of having no one immediately behind me, and easy access to the lake for swimming.

I also splurged and bought another triathlon bike, a Kuota Kalibur®, which was the same frame that Norman Stadler rode to victory at the Ironman World Championship in Hawaii in 2004. I had no real reason to buy it other than vanity as my titanium Airborne worked fine. I wanted something new. I knew that a new bike wouldn't make me faster, but I would draw more attention with a sleek new Kuota than I would with my Airborne, so I bought the Kuota.

A few weeks after I moved in, I heard from my friend Veronica. "I have a roommate for you." she said.

"I don't want a roommate." I replied. "Besides, I already have a roommate. I have Princess."

Veronica insisted that her friend Laura would be the perfect roommate for me. After several weeks of back and forth, I finally agreed to meet her. Her goal was to evaluate my townhouse as a place for her to live and mine was to evaluate her as a suitable roommate.

Our initial meeting turned into dinner then lunch then more dinners. I was taken by her beauty, her unassuming personality and the great conversation we shared.

That's how I met Laura and why Veronica jokingly says that I owe her a finder's fee for bringing us together.

***

Since I began racing Iron distance races, I had my eye on a race in Roth, Germany.

The Quelle-Challenge® in Roth is, in my mind, the pinnacle of what the sport is really about. Roth is a small town in Bavaria, about 90 miles north of Munich. Roth used to be an Ironman World Championship Qualifier with slots to Hawaii, but a few years ago the race went independent, lowered their entry fee and no longer served up Hawaii slots. The race has continued to flourish, in spite of the change, and hosts more than 2,000 athletes each year. Roth is known for its extremely fast times (athletes have gone under eight hours) and amazing crowd support. The whole countryside seems to turn out to volunteer or cheer for the athletes as crowd estimates are 100,000+. There is energy at Roth unlike any other place in the world.

I set aggressive triathlon goals for 2005:

- Quelle Challenge Roth in July: < 8:45 (<8:30 stretch).

- Vineman in August: <9:15 (<9:00 stretch).

- Blue Devil Triathlon in October: <9:15 (<9:00 stretch) plus win.

My goals were based on times *I have no control over who* rather than position (except for *enters a race—I can only* the Blue Devil as I was to defend *race to my own potential.* my title) given my assumption that I have no control over who enters the race - I knew I could only race up to my own potential.

I expected Roth to be my fastest race that year because it was the earliest race of the three when I usually have the "freshest" legs. It was also the fastest course in the world (a world record time of 7:50 was set there by Luc van Lierde). Historically, my first race of the season tended to be my fastest, since I am usually more focused and less likely to be overtrained so early in the year.

I knew that my race at Vineman would depend heavily on race day temperatures and my post-Roth recovery, as the races were six weeks apart.

The Blue Devil Triathlon would be my final race of the season. I was returning as the three-time champion with the intent to win for a fourth time.

To meet my time goals, I planned to do the following:

- Three months of aerobic base to develop an aerobic infrastructure to meet the demands of heavy training volume and the higher intensity of racing.

- After building a base, I would introduce one, high-intensity workout per sport per week at most (i.e., still focus on aerobic workouts but work in a little bit of high intensity efforts). Given that I am doing a large amount of volume, too much intensity will be counter productive leading to burnout, excessive stress and potential injury.

- One epic training week to put in a lot of biking and running miles to shock my body into adaptation to the Iron distance.

- Three long training weekends: 6,000+ meter swim, 130+ mile bike, 3+ hour trail run prior to Roth as confidence boosters and to also prepare my body for Iron distance racing.

I would need to follow the epic training week and long training weekends with easy recovery days (or a full week) in order to allow my body the rest for the adaptation to occur. Rest (sleep and downtime) would be absolutely critical to enable my body to adapt to the demands of my training. I would need eight hours of sleep per night and would take at least one day off per week.

Staying healthy while training for an event that results in a tremendous amount of stress creates ample opportunity for injury. I wanted to take proactive steps to head off issues and nagging problems that might lead to a season ending injury. I began taking yoga a few years before to improve my flexibility, strength and ability to relax. I committed to doing yoga twice a week through the 2005 season which meant giving up an extra run or cycling workout during the work week. I also committed to massage (deep tissue sports massage) and chiropractor adjustments on a regular basis. The proactive treatments would help me minimize and mitigate the likelihood of an injury sidelining me from training. Finally, I began taking multi-vitamins to supplement my diet, provide anti-oxidants and give my body the building blocks it needs to recover from and successfully adapt to training stress.

Fitness Optimization

I believe there is a theoretical limit of potential fitness (what I call "optimal fitness") that each of us can approach but never quite achieve. As we attempt to achieve optimal fitness, we approach a theoretical limit. Although we never quite reach it, we can do everything as reasonably and efficiently as we can to deliver the best possible performance given our abilities. The key to being successful, therefore, is to come as close to that limit as possible.

I believe there is a theoretical limit of potential fitness that each of us can approach, but never quite achieve.

In order to strive for my optimal racing performance, I need to see the "big picture" of fitness. Borrowing on mathematical formula nomenclature, I propose a simple formula to represent one's fitness:

$$\text{Fitness}_t = f\left(\sum_{0 \text{ to } t\text{-}1} \text{Stress} + \sum_{0 \text{ to } t\text{-}1} \text{Adaptation}\right)$$

This equation states that fitness at any time "t" (today) is a function of all the prior stressors (both workout related and non-workout related) and all the adaptations to the stressors over the time period before as a precursor (t-1) to the fitness event at time t. Another way to think about it is that stress (both exercise and other stress) and rest today impact my fitness in the future.

I define stress as a culmination of all the demands that are placed on the body (both positive and negative) and how the body responds to the demands. Stress is taking the body to a heightened level of awareness and function. Excessive stress exhausts and ultimately damages the body.

The human body needs to balance stress with rest/recovery. Stress includes both exercise stress and other stressors like job, family, etc. *The human body needs to balance stress with rest/recovery.* If the total amount of stress increases beyond a manageable level, backing off of exercise (volume, intensity and frequency) while increasing rest may be necessary. Too much stress of any kind can lead to symptoms of overtraining like sleeplessness, irritability, mood swings, feelings of depression, soreness, change in appetite/weight and general feelings of malaise. I have felt all of these when I've experienced too much stress.

Like many people, I have dealt with events that cause elevated and sustained stress levels many times in my life including cancer, divorce, home buying, home selling and sick and dying family members. I am sometimes slow to recognize the symptoms of too much stress and tend to keep pushing forward with my workouts in spite of all the stress. When I went through my divorce in 1999, I actually experienced short-term elevated performance levels induced by my high stress levels--I was charged with energy. Initially, the stress seemed to enhance my fitness, but after a week, I became tired. After another week I became exhausted and the effects spilled over into other parts of my life and affected my overall health. I finished with a mediocre season in 1999, which I had to cut short after a single Iron distance race in July. My body and motivation forced me to stop racing.

Adaptation is the body's ability to compensate for the stress placed on it. Adaptation takes place primarily through rest or recovery. Rest includes sleep and *Adaptation is the body's ability to compensate for the stress placed on it. This takes place through rest or recovery.* easy recovery workouts, which are light workouts that improve circulation without strain or discomfort.

When I'm under a lot of stress, I have trouble falling asleep and staying asleep at night. Realistically, I can only expect to induce a moderate amount of incremental workout stress at any given time in order for my body to adapt to the stress through rest. Once my body has adapted, I can add more. I need to balance increased stress with increased recovery. If I add too much stress too soon, my body cannot successfully adapt and I risk injury and overtraining.

To summarize, the benefits of exercise are stimulated by exercise, but only realized through rest and ultimately adaptation. Without adequate rest (along with numerous other factors like nutrition and hydration), the body will not optimally adapt to the exercise stimulation. My experience has been that inadequate rest and recovery lead to increased likelihood of injury or even illness.

The benefits of exercise are stimulated by exercise, but only realized through rest.

The physiological benefits of training through adaptation manifest themselves through physical indicators like improved endurance, increased muscle strength, lower body fat, and lower resting heart rate. The irony of the situation is that during a prolonged high volume training weekend, I am competing more rest time against other priorities but actually have less overall time due to the longer workouts.

In some cases, endurance training may seem counterintuitive. By training slower and easier, can I get faster? Remember the body adapts to stress not during the exercise, but during rest and recovery. Completing most of my workouts at a lower intensity helps prevent overloading my body with too much stress at a given point in time. If I expand that concept to a training season, I need rest days to give my body adequate time to recover from and adapt to a long training season. Once my body has adapted, I can then load progressively harder, longer, and more frequent workouts. Without that time to adapt through recovery, I am limiting my potential.

Even though I try not to spend extraneous time on activities like watching television or going out for late nights, I still need downtime, which I consider as my time to waste.

Even if I had more time and didn't have to work a full-time job, I doubt that I could train much more than I do now, as I would likely risk more injury. With the extra time, I think I would rest more (sleep more at night and nap in the afternoon) and participate in more relaxing activities like reading or painting.

Ultimately I need moderation and balance in my life, otherwise, I'm a slow burning fuse on a stick of dynamite.

***

Early in the calendar year, I shifted my workouts from no structure and planning to some structure and planning. I bumped my workout frequency up to my desired level of three workouts in each sport each week (three swims, three bikes and three runs). Daylight was still short, so my workouts during the week were primarily indoors. If there was no snow or ice on the ground, I biked outside on the weekends. I absolutely hated to ride indoors on my bike trainer. I am uncomfortable plus the trainer wears through tires quickly. So, I spent my biking time on either a Lifecycle or Spinning bike at the gym. Occasionally, I would drop into a Spinning class but the workouts tended to be too intense for me at that time of the year. If I did take a class, I faked the "all out efforts" to keep my heart rate under control.

Physically, I had been plagued since the prior year by recurring and nagging leg injuries that seemed to migrate back and forth between different locations on both legs for no apparent rhyme or reason, although I suspect that they were all related somehow. One week, my right hamstring was tight. The following week, my right hamstring felt okay, but my right calf muscle cramped while my left knee ached. The pain or tightness moved somewhere else the next week. Because I spent so much of my day on a computer and sat with a poor posture, I also had recurring issues with tight shoulder and neck muscles. I took a week or two off of running, signed up for several massages and even tried aqua jogging. Nothing seemed to fix the problem, although the symptoms often disappeared temporarily.

Once the time changed in early April (Daylight Savings), the days became longer, enabling daylight bike rides during the week. My focus shifted from maintaining an aerobic base to increasing my aerobic training duration.

One thing that I have learned is that it's much easier to recognize the symptoms of overtraining and burnout in others than it *It's much easier to recognize the symptoms of overtraining and burnout in others than it is in myself.*

is in myself. Rather than admit that I'm tired and need rest, I tend to push myself harder to "stretch" my limits and over compensate for my lackluster performance. This creates a vicious cycle of overtraining to compensate for lagging performance leading to possible illness, injury or burnout.

Symptoms of overtraining that I have experienced are:

- Limited ability to focus on an activity. My mind runs in many different directions, and I have a short attention span.

- Chronic soreness. Something aches all of the time.

- Loss of interest in normally interesting activities.

- Social withdrawal. I prefer to be alone.

- Difficulty sleeping, restlessness, waking up in the middle of the night and not being able to fall back asleep.

- Irritability.

- Loss of appetite.

- Feeling tired or "run down" all the time.

- Elevated heart rate during and after working out. My heart is working harder than it should for a given level of effort.

- Feelings of negativity toward normal activities. The consummate pessimist.

The best course of action is simply rest. I know that. In some instances, a few good nights sleep and a day off are adequate. In other cases, it may take a few weeks to recover. I believe the key is to catch the symptoms early and take the rest sooner rather than later. In many cases, others that are close to me observe these symptoms before I realize them myself.

I experienced many of the symptoms of overtraining in early 2005 while I also dealt with the stress of buying a new house and moving. Because of nagging injuries, I aggressively pulled back on my early season racing plans by opting out of three Half-Iron distance races and a marathon all of which I had signed up for and paid for in advance. I entertained the idea of not doing any additional races after Roth except for maybe Vineman and the Blue Devil Triathlon. I also entertained thoughts of freeing up my summer to pursue other more leisurely activities like hiking, traveling and visiting family, all things that I had neglected the previous few years.

Triathlon again won out over other activities in my life.

With my goals in mind, I pulled out a pad of paper and began crafting a high level training plan for Quelle-Challenge in Roth:

Weeks Out: 24-14
Focus: Establish an aerobic base
Comments: All aerobic intensity workouts – breathing comfortably; minimal accumulation of lactic acid in the muscles; consciously focus on form. Shift into a regular routine targeting 3x swim, bike and run per week. Bike outside (weather permitting) every weekend and commute by bike to/from work 1x per week.

Weeks Out: 13
Focus: Fitness check
Comments: Same as above plus Cherry Blossom 10 Mile Run. The purpose of the run is to test my fitness relative to previous years of doing this same race. I will not specifically taper for the race so my legs will be somewhat tired from the training week.

Weeks Out: 12-11
Focus: Maintain an aerobic base
Comments: Increase long bike time to 4+ hours and long runs to 1.5+ hours in preparation for Iron distance.

Weeks Out: 10
Focus: Half-Iron distance race
Comments: First "non-key" triathlon of the season to "test the waters" and practice execution. Kinetic 1/2 Half-Iron Distance race.

Weeks Out: 9
Focus: Epic training
Comments: Epic training week at my parents' lake house in South Carolina. Goal is to get as much biking volume as possible during the week plus swimming and some running (6-8 hours of exercise per day). After completing this week, subsequent long workouts will seem easy and less extreme.

Weeks Out: 8
Focus: Easy week; long weekend
Comments: Easy during the week to recover from Epic Week. Sleep as much as possible to soak in the training benefits. Long bike (100+ miles); long run (2.5 hours).

Weeks Out: 7
Focus: Race, Half-Iron distance
Comments: Taper during the week. Walt Disney World Triathlon® is the second "non-key" race and the final tune-up before Roth.

Weeks Out: 6
Focus: Aerobic base
Comments: Moderate volume aerobic base; recover from Half-Iron race before the last hard stretch before tapering. Long bike (80 miles); long run (2 hours).

Weeks Out: 5
Focus: High volume
Comments: Long bike (100+ miles); longest run (3 hours)

Weeks Out: 4
Focus: High volume
Comments: Longest bike (100+ miles); long run (2.5 hours)

Weeks Out: 3
Focus: Taper for Roth
Comments: Long bike (up to 80 miles); long run (1.5 hours)

Weeks Out: 2
Focus: Taper for Roth
Comments: Long bike (up to 60 miles); long run (1 hours)

Week Out: 1
Focus: Race - Roth
Comments: Very easy week includes travel to Germany (travel day is off day); easy aerobic workouts during the week with a few brief tempo efforts built in.

I "tested the water" for my fitness level in early April with the Cherry Blossom 10 Mile Run in D.C. I had not done any speed work that year yet and my running had been somewhat sporadic, but I still desired to finish in less than 60 minutes—my benchmark for running fitness.

As I was running the race, I kept reminding myself how much the intensity of racing 10 miles hurts. I much prefer the long, slow suffering of an Iron distance race over nine hours than a one-hour pain session.

Surprisingly, I bettered my 2004 time by 25 seconds.

I tested the water again two weeks later at the inaugural Kinetic Half-Iron distance race.

I made a serious tactical error at Kinetic by leaving my full flask of energy gel in the transition area. To my chagrin, I discovered that the bike aid stations only gave out water so my calories for the two plus hour, 56-mile ride were limited to what I carried in my water bottle. I needed more calories.

I equated my ride to "death by a thousand paper cuts." My energy level dropped after only an hour as I gradually slowed down and bonked one paper cut at a time.

As I entered the transition area at the end of the bike, I grabbed my gel flask from where I had left it on the ground and sucked down several gulps of gel. I then grabbed a second flask and headed out of the transition area to start the 13.1-mile run. My friend, Mike Guzek, was startled to see me only a few minutes ahead of him after I had left him in the swim-to-bike transition area following the swim.

Like the beginning of the bike leg, I started the run at an aggressive pace, hoping that my body could quickly absorb the calories that I missed consuming during the bike. I scooped up a cup of sports drink at every aid station for the fluid and the additional carbohydrates.

My run was uneventful except for my right calf, which tightened up at the start of the run. The tight calf had been a nagging problem but not bad enough to stop me from running. I moved within about two minutes of the second place runner but I ran out of pavement before I could catch him. I crossed the finish line with a smile on my face then walked over to congratulate the first two finishers.

High volume training commenced at the end of April, starting with the "Tour de Skyline." A few friends of mine started this two-day, out-and-back, go-at-your-own-pace 100+ mile ride along the length of Skyline Drive three years before. This year's ride started with temperatures in the high 40s with rain forecasted for both days. Brady and I began the ride with a few dozen others, but at the 25-mile mark we were cold and wet so contemplated whether to keep going or turn around. I flashed back to the ride Steve Smith and I did on Skyline Drive the year before where the roads almost froze and ice built up on our brakes. Steve's comment to Brady and I, "You guys have nothing to prove." hit home so Brady and I turned back at mile 26.

Steve, Brady and I spent the following week in South Carolina at my parents' lake house. It was an entire week dedicated to triathlon training. Beginning in 2002, I had taken a week of vacation each year in late April or early May to seriously train without any of the usual life distractions that take time away from the exercise and the much needed rest.

Because of the importance of this week and probably also because working out was the only thing I did besides sleeping and eating, I took the extra time to jot down notes on each day's workouts:

Workout Log South Carolina Training Week

Day: Saturday
Workout: Off
Comments: Cold and wet outside. Rest day before high volume training week.

Day: Sunday
Workout: Swim 60 minutes (lake)
Comments: Travel day from Virginia to South Carolina. Lake swim at moderate effort focusing on good form and staying relaxed.

Day: Monday
Workout: Bike 375 minutes (hills)
Comments: Hilly course with 8,400 feet of climbing (~113 miles). I felt good although my legs fatigued toward the end of the ride. Nutrition intake: HammerGel/Carb-boom (2 flasks), Cytomax mixed with CARBO-PRO. 3 colas during the ride. No stomach problems or cramping.

Day: Tuesday
Workout: Swim 60 minutes (lake); Run 90 minutes (trails); Bike 195 minutes (trails).
Comments: Legs are tired from bike yesterday. Swam early for an hour easy. Run from Lower Whitewater Falls along Foothills Trail (~1,500 feet of climbing). Legs tired especially feeling it on the downhill sections of the trail. Effort-moderate. Wrenched left knee slightly, need to watch.

Training with others, like Steve and Brady, who were as strong or stronger than me pushed me beyond what I could easily do by myself. Case in point was a long trail run we took that week:

> Brady, Steve and I drove from my parents' lake house to nearby Oconee State Park, which is the start of the Foothills Trail. I had run numerous times on the marked dirt trail, which meanders up and down along the Cherokee foothills and across streams. I led the three of us at the beginning of the run, which initially brought us to Hidden Creek Falls where we paused for photos before starting back to pick up the main trail again.
>
> Steve took the lead, followed by Brady with me bringing up the rear as we slowly headed uphill. My pace was somewhat beyond what I would run alone, but I consciously forced myself to keep Brady in sight although Steve was soon out of view ahead of Brady. At some point, my left knee started to ache which forced me to be a little more cautious on the down hills after I wrenched it earlier in the week when I tripped on a tree root. Brady was now out of sight, too.
>
> The effort to keep up with Steve and Brady became greater and greater. I was starting to zone out into my own little world and rationalized to myself that I didn't need to keep up with them. I slowed down even more and entered my own private woods. At the turnaround, they were waiting for me.

Once we hit the turnaround, I ran my own slow pace back behind them. With my knee aching, I had already pushed myself further than expected. I was happy to be able to run at all. I made a mental note to start lifting weights with my legs back home in order to strengthen the supporting muscles as a way to mitigate further injury.

After a few minutes, I was alone again, plodding along at my slow, but steady pace. The run was peaceful and the only sounds I heard were the wind and occasional cracking of a tree. At one point, I heard a soft jingling of bells. Bizarre. I think I imagined the noise. Steve and Brady stopped to wait for me several times before we finally made it back to the car almost two and half hours after we started.

The three of us were exhausted from the week of training, but we each pushed each other physically and mentally a little further than we could have stretched ourselves alone.

Occasionally, spend some days away from everyday life to train.

After the trip to South Carolina, the mental and physical challenges of training coupled with the demands of my job soon became a vicious downward cycle from which I couldn't escape. I found myself needing more and more coffee in the morning to wake up which then created more challenges falling asleep at night. Once I finally fell asleep, I couldn't sleep through the night. I would wake up the next morning still feeling tired, and I would counter that feeling with more caffeine. I entered a state of perpetual exhaustion.

My body weight unexpectedly bumped up five pounds almost overnight from 165 to 170 pounds; I hadn't weighed that much in two years. My diet hadn't really changed much other than I drank more beer resulting in dead alcohol calories. Reflecting back, the beer and the caffeine were poor substitutes for rest.

My workouts were no longer enjoyable. I did them because I had to maintain some minimal level of fitness for Roth, not because I really wanted to. I no longer felt the endurance exercise "high" that I was used to feeling during and after long bike rides, but rather I felt nauseated during the workout. Not the kind of nausea associated with being sick, but more like a feeling of being unsettled.

In the last few months leading up to a key race like Roth, I typically experienced "breakthrough" workouts such as:

- I swim an exceptionally fast set of 200-meter intervals in the pool;

- I repeatedly bike a series of steep climbs with my legs turning much faster than normal; or

- I "comfortably" run 15 miles at a 10-mile race pace.

I didn't experience any breakthrough workouts in the months leading up to Roth. My confidence waned.

With the exception of the Cherry Blossom 10 Mile Run, my early season race results only sunk my confidence even more. I entered two consecutive swim races, a one-mile race and a two-mile race (both lake swims) two months before Roth. I had a decent one-mile swim but was "crushed" on the two-miler as my arms loaded up with lactic acid and my pace slowed to what felt like a crawl. On the second mile, I was passed by packs of swimmers from later start waves. I left frustrated and exhausted.

I worried about my upcoming race at Roth. I feared that I was on a path of self-destruction, a downward spiral where the only possible outcome was injury or absolute hate for the sport from total physical and mental burnout. There was no longer a light at the end of the tunnel.

But then something happened.

Five weeks before Roth, I was riding with two friends on a five-hour ride with two sets of tough climbs. On the first set of climbs, I lagged behind and could only watch them as they pulled away. I rationalized that I was just not feeling well and simply couldn't match their rapid, fluid pace up the hills. They continued to ride and I continued to fall back even more as I wallowed in my own self-pity. I felt like I was doomed to mediocrity.

"I'm 50/50 right now in not doing Roth. Maybe I will just go watch the race and make it a nice vacation." I told them. "Maybe I'll just call it a year right now and not do any more racing."

An hour later in the ride, I began to wonder if this feeling of "feeling bad" was really only in my head. I self diagnosed. My legs actually felt fine. They weren't tired or loaded with lactic acid, which would have meant that I had overextended myself physically, and my heart rate wasn't abnormally high on the climbs (per my heart monitor). Physically, I had no excuse for falling behind.

As we started another climb, I again lagged back, watching both friends pull away from me once more.

"No, not this time." I thought.

I willed my legs to turn over faster to accelerate my bicycle up the hill. The gap lessened and lessened as I quickly gained on them. My legs were moving like synchronous pistons: thump, thump, thump, and thump as I drove my bicycle up the hill. I quickly caught and passed both to move to the front. I kept driving and started to open up a small gap. They remained close as we finished near each other at the top of the climb.

At the base of the next big climb, I needed to prove to myself that my feelings of despair and self-doubt were all in my mind, and that I wasn't losing my edge and my fitness. I stomped on my pedals to accelerate and attack the hill. Stomp on one pedal and pull up on the other pedal. Stomp and pull. Stomp and pull. My legs whirred furiously as my heart rate approached maximum. "Push harder." I told myself, "Don't slow down." My legs and lungs were screaming fire. I hurt. I wouldn't look back. My mind was only on my making my legs move faster. Nothing else mattered. The road twisted and turned as I climbed higher. As I approached the top, I shot a glance backward. No one was in sight. I smiled to myself as I embraced the wind on the steep descent. I had achieved a breakthrough workout! Perhaps, my fears, self-doubts and poor attitude were simply in my head. My fitness and my raw desire were back.

Two weeks later, my attitude had turned around positively. I felt good when I worked out instead of feeling nauseated and unmotivated. I slept better at night and was more rested during the day. I grew excited about racing in Germany. I began reading through the messages on the RATS message board to see what the board members were writing about and offered my opinion on a couple of topics.

Three weeks before Roth I felt a need to push myself one more time.

On a Saturday morning, I did a three-hour bike ride with Brady. Later the same day, I met up with the Pedalshop team (Pedalshop is a local bike shop who had become my sponsor). This second ride was a road ride with a twist as it took place predominantly on dirt and gravel roads. For an added challenge, I opted to ride a fixed gear bike.

A "fixie" was my new toy that I had bought used from my friend, Tom. I like it for its simplicity. There are no gears to change and if the wheel moves, the pedals have to move with it. In other words, there is no coasting. The legs never rest – they are always in motion. Gearing choice is critical to the ride as there is only one gear. Pick poorly and your legs either spin out on the flats or grind to a crawl before forcing you off the bike to walk up the remainder of a hill.

My friend, Jim, describes "fixies" as follows[14]:

> So, what is a "fixie" you ask? A fixie is the ultimate bicycle, ultimate in its simplicity. It has one gear, it comes with no brakes, and you cannot coast. You must always have your legs in motion for the bicycle to move. Pedal forward, and the bike goes forward, pedal backward and the bike goes backward. Sensible (that's questionable) people put a front brake on it. A rear brake really doesn't do much, since you can create the same type of drag as a rear brake by trying to push the pedals in reverse. If you go to downtown D.C. you will see a lot of bicycle messengers riding fixies and most of them ride with no brakes.

> Okay, that answered, the next most-frequently asked question is WHY?

> The gearing of a fixie, which normally is a 3 to 1 ratio (chain ring to cog), is very conducive to spinning. It helps you keep an even cadence and it helps you to turn the cranks in a round manner, as opposed to an up-down motion that can occur on a regular bike. Riding a fixie on hills also makes you stronger. Powering up a huge hill can be ugly (it sure was the first time I did it), but once you get used to it, your cadence improves and you can climb it with ease (Okay, maybe not with ease, but a lot easier than when you first started). This translates into much better climbing on your regular bike. You can hold a cadence longer, you can keep the legs spinning longer, and you can climb better.

Nine of us left for the PedalShop ride. The temperature had been in the 90s all week and that day was no exception. The other eight were normally mountain bikers, but that day they were riding road bikes, which gave them 16 to 20 different gear options to play with; I only had one gear.

Until this particular ride, I had ridden my fixed gear bike for only one hour at a time, which was the length of my commute from home to work, so I was a little apprehensive about being able to keep up with the group, especially on an unfamiliar route and hilly terrain. Furthermore, I had already ridden three hours on my road bike that morning.

The initial pace was moderate as we headed out on paved roads. I rode comfortably. At one point, we crossed a road and were suddenly riding on dirt. Dust was kicked up everywhere into our faces as the group quickly thinned out. I was a little nervous about my bike handling skills since I usually ride on paved roads and the other riders were used to mountain biking.

The descents were fun even though my legs were on the verge of spinning out of control (remember, I couldn't coast on my fixed gear bike); I hoped that the fast leg turnover training would improve my cycling efficiency. The jury is still out on that urban training legend though.

I didn't crash at all on the ride but I had a few close calls on big descents with turns where my wheels seemed to slide out from under me as I made the turn; yet somehow I kept my balance and didn't fall.

Okay, I admit it. I had to walk up one brief section of a big climb. This was the first time I ever had to get off my bike to get up a hill. I had no choice in the matter. The road was steep and narrow and I couldn't crisscross back and forth effectively in order to lessen the grade. I swallowed my pride and hopped off my bike. Still, I was not the last one up the hill.

***

Not until the week before Roth did my body start to feel "right" again. The muscles in my right glute area were still tight, but otherwise I felt good. I had three massages and two chiropractic adjustments within a period of two weeks to work out the nagging tight spots and put my body in optimal alignment for optimal performance.

Just as important as the physical feelings, were my mental feelings. My motivation climbed and my self confidence returned. I was ready to commit to a hard day of racing in order to achieve a personal best. I was ready to suffer and pay the price for finishing well under nine hours. Most importantly, I now believed that I could do well at Roth.

Quelle Challenge – Roth

In hindsight, Laura and I should have arrived in Roth at least one week before the race, not three days before as planned or two days before as actually happened. Because of storms in the northeast United States when we left Virginia, our flight was repeatedly delayed before finally being cancelled at 9:00 p.m. that night.

After being assured that our checked luggage would arrive with us on our rescheduled flight the following day, we caught a taxi back home without our luggage. Leaving Thursday (a day later than planned) we finally arrived in Munich on Friday morning. Our luggage didn't arrive with us, nor was it waiting for us from an earlier flight. This was Friday. The race was on Sunday morning.

"Welcome to Roth." said the sign that greeted us as we approached the door of our host family, Franz, Annette and Annika Spiegl, who warmly welcomed us into their home as their home stay guests for a week.

Staying with a host family was both a rewarding and enriching experience. The Spiegls opened their house to us as if we were lifelong friends. From them, we learned about the local region, the culture, the food and, of course, the excellent Weiss (wheat) beer and Frankish wine. Annette even arranged for a back-up bike for me from a local bike shop in case mine didn't arrive in time while Franz drove Laura and I around the bike course.

On Saturday, I showed up at the bike shop to be fitted for my backup bike. I dreaded the thought of having to purchase a full set of triathlon gear: tri shorts, goggles, wetsuit, bike jersey, bike shoes, bike helmet and running shoes but I wasn't about to miss the race after my training and travel. Fortunately, it never went that far. My bike and the rest of our luggage were delivered to the Spiegl's house on Saturday evening. I quickly re-assembled the bike, test rode it for about two minutes and then threw it in the car to take to the swim-to-bike transition area for bike check in—about two hours past the deadline for check in. I hoped that everything was tightened and adjusted correctly.

Lunch and dinner the day before the race was pasta with a light red sauce made by Annette, bread, fruit and a Weiss beer. I was reluctant to go to bed on Saturday night. Procrastinating sleep until the last reasonable minute was not a smart idea as my body and my bodily functions were already out of whack from the six-hour time zone change.

The Race

The 2.4 mile-swim took place in the Main-Donau Canal, which is a transportation channel for boats and barges connecting the Main and Donau Rivers across a series of locks between the rivers. The canal is straight and narrow, roughly 50 meters across, making it an ideal layout for a fast and easily navigated swim.

I swam in the first wave of 300 athletes at 6:30 a.m. along with race favorites and well-known triathletes Chris McCormack, Lothar Leder, Luke Bell, Nicole Leder and Belinda Granger to name only a few of the superbly talented field.

While treading water at the start I glanced up at the bridge to see solid masses of people across the entire bridge span. There were easily another thousand spectators lining the sides of the canals with several small zeppelins, hot air balloons and helicopters overhead.

The gun went off and we were on our way!

I managed to find a small pack of swimmers about half a mile into the swim who I could draft behind for much of the swim. I felt comfortable and relaxed the entire time. I was a little warm in my full wetsuit, so I let in water by my neck mid stroke every few minutes but this didn't seem to cost me any time. I exited the swim in a little over 55 minutes, a new PR for me by a minute.

After a quick transition, I headed out on the bike course for the first of the two loops. I mistakenly thought that this would be an "easy" bike course—by no means was it the hardest bike course I had ever done—but my bike computer measured close to 5,000 feet of vertical climbing when it was all said and done.

The bike course was still ideal for my style of riding and training, as it was a little bit of everything broken up by small towns with mobs of wild, noisy and crazy spectators, many of whom had set up tables alongside the road to cheer and drink beer. The crowds were so thick climbing up through the town of

Hipolstein that we could only ride single file with the crowds directly ahead, only parting at the last minute to let us through. The noise was deafening but motivating as it conveyed the sheer energy of all the people.

"Hop! Hop! Hop!"

"Super! Super!" The Germans pronounce their "s" like a "z" so that it sounded like "Zuper! Zuper!"

My experience at this race, as well as at Ironman Austria in 2000, was that the European cycling talent bench is quite deep compared to the U.S. cycling bench. Surprisingly, my swim turned out to be my best overall split by position relative to the other athletes, not my bike. That is not what I expected given my swim times at the two races I did earlier in the year.

I wanted to ride close to a time of 4:45 but finished in 5:03. My legs just weren't there. I think the combination of the physical and mental challenges leading up to the race plus cramping, vomiting during the race (to be expected) and exhaustion from jet lag held me back. I also made an unexpected stop in the bushes to relieve my digestive system.

I started the run right at the six-hour mark. Hmm, I thought to myself, I "could" break nine hours if I "could" run a sub three-hour marathon. I did some quick math in my head to convert minutes per mile to minutes per kilometer.

As an aside, I'm still undecided on whether I prefer running 26.2 miles or 42 kilometers as the kilometers go by faster but there are more of them. Six of one, half dozen of the other, I suppose.

Most of the run course was along the Main-Donau Canal, where we had swam, on a hard-packed dirt trail. The course was mostly flat with a few gradual hills. Definitely a fast course as winner Chris McCormack and the other leading finishers showed with their world-class times.

My initial pace was on target, but I quickly realized that a sub three-hour marathon wouldn't happen for me for all the reasons mentioned above for the bike plus the temperature was unseasonably hot in the 80s.

Again, the crowds were amazing. I saw Laura, the Spiegls and my mom—who traveled from California to visit German friends—numerous times as they popped up at various points along the course. Noise and energy emanated from the crowds. "Go David!" I heard many times with a German accent as they read my name off of my race number.

I felt like a rock star coming into a sold out stadium as I ran into the stands that were filled with thousands of screaming spectators. I ran around the track, pumped my hands in the air and crossed the finish line in 9:36.

My run was a little slow for me (3:33), but all things considered, I couldn't really complain. I also managed not to destroy all my toenails for once (I only lost one nail versus the usual five to six nails), so that was an accomplishment by itself.

The Speigls, Laura and I came back to the finish line for a fireworks display later that night. The stadium was still packed as we squeezed in with everyone else. This time, I entered the stadium with a beer, not a race number. I have a vibrant memory of John Denver's "Country Roads" playing in the background as thousands of happy Germans sang along with their German accents. The memory was priceless.

I did the race because I wanted to experience the magic of Roth. I was not disappointed at all.

Seeking Balance

"Moderation in all things, including moderation."
- *Mark Twain, American Author*

When I turned 30, one of my co-workers, who had also recently turned 30, said to me, "Doesn't it really suck turning 30? I mean that I'm starting to feel old. Things start to hurt. It's harder to stay in shape."

I smiled and said, "I have no idea what you're talking about."

One of the greatest challenges as an active triathlete that I still struggle with is how to maintain balance in my life. I work a full-time job that requires me to travel. I recently adopted another dog, so now I have two that need to be walked at least three times a day and I'm also a homeowner. These are just the routine responsibilities without considering other commitments like my girlfriend, other friends, family or other hobbies. If I add in 15 plus hours a week of endurance training, my time suddenly becomes a very scarce commodity. Furthermore, as my level of activity increases, I need more sleep to recover from the increased training. Sleep tends to be the first thing that suffers as time shrinks. It's a Catch-22. I exercise more therefore I need more sleep, but because I'm exercising more, I have less time to sleep.

Balance is a nebulous and relative term. My definition of balance is unique to me and there is no point in trying to compare my lifestyle to someone else's. To me, I feel balanced when at a minimum:

1.   I have good health.
2.   I live an active lifestyle.
3.   I maintain strong personal relationships with others.

Although the path I've taken is unique to me, I've learned many things along the way that can be useful to anyone wishing to pursue a demanding training schedule while working full time. First and foremost, is to realize that although it may seem impossible, with careful planning and time management, anything is achievable. For me, simplicity and flexibility are the keystones to my training. If I remain flexible and keep my training schedule simple, I'm less likely to become stressed when events out of my control disrupt my training schedule (and they always do!).

I've made a conscious decision not to make my job my top priority. My job is very important, as it is the means by which I live and can afford to participate in the activities that I truly enjoy, but I'm not willing to sacrifice my lifestyle and my attempt at a balanced lifestyle in order to climb the corporate ladder. To me, the extra money and prestige is not worth the cost. I realize this isn't the case for many people. Others have families and financial responsibilities that do not offer them this luxury. No matter what your situation, the lessons I've learned from incorporating training into everyday activities, like biking to work, making time for a workout at lunch, or seeking opportunities to maximize travel time rather than let it negatively impact my training schedule can be applied to nearly anyone. Embrace your situation and the free time you do have and make every minute count.

Over the years, I have met many like-minded friends who share my passion for triathlon. Finding these people at work and through local clubs, among other places, has given me a support group that both motivated me and kept me honest with my training. It's much easier to wake up at 5:00 a.m. to go biking knowing that a friend is waiting.

Maintaining healthy, long-term relationships with members of the opposite sex has been a challenge for me as well. I have struggled through two failed relationships that resulted in resentment. I made the decisions I made at the time because they seemed like the right ones for me. In hindsight, some of the decisions were selfish. I put my own interests ahead of other people. Maybe this was my unconscious way of telling my significant others that we were just not meant to be together.

Based on my lifestyle and past experiences, I guess that leaves me two options for finding a lifetime partner. I can find someone who either shares my interests or will not resent how I spend my time and my money or I can find someone for whom I will give up my active lifestyle. So far, the second option doesn't seem feasible for me. I love my lifestyle. It helps define who I am and I think I can find someone who shares my interests without begrudging me the time. "The third time's the charm," I tell myself as I am in the early stages of my third long-term relationship.

Perhaps, above all, the most important thing for me is to take time off from training. Time away from the sport provides perspective on myself, my relationships and even on my training. Without a step back the sport becomes the be-all end-all, and everything else tends to fall into the background. The lesson, which I am still striving to achieve, is to fit triathlon comfortably into my life, rather than fitting life into triathlon.

About the Author

Since 1995, David has competed in over 50 triathlons including 19 Iron distance races (2.4-mile swim, 112-mile bike, 26.2-mile run). He has achieved a personal best time of less than nine hours at the Iron distance and placed in the top 10 overall 10 times including four overall wins at the Iron-distance and two at the International distance. He is also a five-time USA Triathlon All-American.

David has completed the following Iron distance races in chronological order:

Race	Year	Iron Distance	Location	Time	Overall Place
19	2005	Blue Devil	Durham, NC	10:07	2nd
18	2005	Quelle Challenge	Roth, Germany	9:36	83rd
17	**2004**	**Blue Devil**	**Durham, NC**	**9:34**	**1st**
16	2004	Vineman	Santa Rosa, CA	9:28	2nd
15	2004	Ironman, USA	Lake Placid, NY	9:49	31st
14	2003	Great Floridian	Clermont, FL	10:30	6th
13	**2003**	**Blue Devil**	**Durham, NC**	**9:17**	**1st**
12	2003	Ironman Coeur d'Alene	Coeur d'Alene, ID	9:54	17th
11	2002	Ironman Hawaii	Kona, HI	10:29	395th
10	**2002**	**Blue Devil**	**Durham, NC**	**8:57**	**1st**
9	2001	Mohican Pineman	Perrysville, OH	10:34	2nd
8	**2001**	**Vineman**	**Santa Rosa, CA**	**9:43**	**1st**
7	2000	Great Floridian	Clermont, FL	9:49	7th
6	2000	Ironman Austria	Klagenfurt, Austria	9:16	62nd
5	1999	Ironman USA	Lake Placid, NY	10:19	73rd
4	1998	Great Floridian	Clermont, FL	9:45	3rd
3	1998	Vineman	Santa Rosa, CA	9:29	5th
2	1997	Great Floridian	Clermont, CA	10:43	21st
1	1997	Ironman Canada	Penticton, Canada	10:14	169th

David is a founder of the Reston Area Triathletes (RATS), a non-profit triathlon club whose purpose is to help Northern Virginia endurance athletes link up in order to train together and learn from each other. Since starting in February 2001, RATS has an active online discussion board (500+ members), organized training sessions and social events. Website: www.trirats.net.

David is also one of the race organizers for the Reston Triathlon, an annual event in Reston, Virginia, which attracts more than 500 local triathletes. The race website is, www.restontriathlon.org.

As the founder of EnduranceWorks, LLC, David produces the Luray Triathlon in Luray, Virginia and the General Smallwood Triathlon in Indian Head, Maryland. Both venues feature both Sprint and International distance races.

Endnotes

[1] United States Naval Academy, www.usna.edu; INTERNET.

[2] National Cancer Institute, www.cancer.gov; INTERNET.

[3] Sally Jenkins, "Extra Ordinary in Ways Unseen," Washington Post, 28 July 2003, sec. D, 11.

[4] Rob Sleamaker and Roy Browning, SERIOUS Training for Endurance Athletes (Champaign, IL: Human Kinetics, 1996).

[5] World Health Organization, "WHO definition of Health" [cited 31 July 2004]; available from www.who.int; INTERNET.

[6] Diane Dahm, M.D. and Jay Smith, M.D., eds. Mayo Clinic: Fitness for Everybody, (Rochester, MN: Kensington Publishing Corporation, 2005), 346.

[7] Ironman Austria, www.ironmanaustria.at; INTERNET.

[8] Capital One, www.capitalone.com; INTERNET.

[9] Capital One, www.capitalone.com; INTERNET.

[10] Aaron Schwartzbard, "Re: Triathlon / Bike Leg HR" [cited 9 February 2005]; available from http://sports.groups.yahoo.com/group/trirats/message/8749; INTERNET.

[11] Phil Maffetone, Training for Endurance, (Stamford, New York: David Barmore Productions, 2000), 17.

[12] Aaron Schwartzbard, "Re: [Tri RATS] Re: GREAT article on Anaerobic training by Brad Kearns" [cited 11 April 2003]; available from http://sports.groups. yahoo.com/group/trirats/message/2978; INTERNET.

[13] Michael Guzek, "Race Report: Duke Blue Devil" [cited 16 October 2004]; available from www.trirats.net; INTERNET.

[14] Jim Desrosiers, "FIXIE?? For a Century??" [cited 29 August 2005]; available from http://sports.groups.yahoo.com/group/trirats/message/10846; INTERNET.